Blueprint For Wealth Building

Starting from zero

A practical guide to wealth building step by step

Obinna Okeke

ISBN:9798270903701

Dedication

To everyone who has ever started from zero

may this blueprint remind you that your beginning

does not define your ending.

Acknowledgments

This book would not exist without the people who believed in me, challenged me, and reminded me why this work matters.

To my family thank you for your unwavering love, patience, and encouragement. You are the foundation of everything I build.

To my mentors and friends your wisdom, feedback, and honest conversations shaped these pages more than you know.

To my readers you are the reason I write. Every story of resilience, every step you take toward building wealth and legacy, fuels my passion to keep creating.

And finally, to the countless voices of authors, thinkers, and dreamers whose work I've studied and drawn from this book is part of a larger conversation, and I am grateful to stand on your shoulders.

Preface

Wealth is often spoken about as if it belongs to a chosen few the lucky, the privileged, the already-established. But the truth I've learned, both through my own journey and through the stories of countless people I've met, is far simpler: wealth is a skill, not a birthright, and skills can be learned, sharpened, and passed on.

I wrote this book for the person standing at the very beginning. The person with no savings, no safety net, no connections, and no clear map. The person who has been told directly or indirectly that wealth is "not for people like you." If that's you, I want you to know something from the start: you are not behind. You are not late. You are not disqualified. You are simply at the beginning of a journey that millions have walked before you and millions will walk after you.

This book is not built on theory. It is built on lived experience, practical frameworks, and the real challenges people face when they are starting from zero. There is no jargon here, no fluff, and no unrealistic promises. What you will find are clear steps, honest truths, and strategies that work in the real world. You will not find overnight success, but you will find momentum. You will find clarity. And you will find a blueprint that grows with you whether you're trying to escape debt, build your first income stream, or create long-term generational wealth.

My hope is that as you read these pages, you feel seen, supported, and empowered. Not because I have all the answers, but because I know what it feels like to start with nothing and still choose to build something meaningful. If you commit to the process, this book will meet you where you are and take you where you want to go.

Let's begin.

Obinna Okeke

Table of Contents

Introduction:

Reframing Wealth, Rewriting the Journey

Wealth. The word alone carries weight. For some, it stirs exciting visions of freedom, choice, and abundance. For others, it triggers unease memories of scarcity, debt, or the quiet shame of never feeling "enough." Wherever you stand, this book is an invitation to step into a new relationship with wealth: one that is practical, deeply human, and built step by step.

This is not a book of shortcuts. It will not promise you overnight riches or a secret formula hidden from the world. Instead, it offers something far more enduring: a framework for building wealth that lasts, wealth that aligns with your values, and wealth that feels like home.

As Robert Kiyosaki wrote in Rich Dad Poor Dad, "It's not how much money you make. It's how much money you keep, how hard it works for you, and how many generations you keep it for." That single sentence captures the essence of what we'll explore together. Wealth is not about speed; it's about structure. It's not about appearances; it's about endurance. And it's not about accumulation alone; it's about stewardship how you manage, grow, and pass on what you've built.

Wealth Beyond Numbers

Too often, wealth is reduced to numbers: income, assets, net worth. But numbers alone don't tell the full story. A person can earn six figures and still live in constant anxiety, while another with modest means feels secure, free, and fulfilled. Why? Because wealth is multidimensional. It includes financial stability, yes, but also emotional clarity, time freedom, and the ability to make decisions without fear.

Napoleon Hill, in his timeless classic Think and Grow Rich, put it this way: "Whatever the mind can conceive and believe, it can achieve." Hill wasn't simply talking about positive thinking. He was pointing to the reality that wealth begins in the mind shaped by beliefs, habits, and the stories we tell ourselves. If your story is one of scarcity, you will live within its limits. If your story is one of possibility, you will build within its horizons.

This book is about changing that story. It's about equipping you with the tools to not only manage money but to reshape the way you think and feel about it. Because when the story changes, the outcome changes.

Every financial decision you make is rooted in a narrative. Some of us grew up with stories of scarcity: "Money doesn't grow on trees." Others inherited silent scripts: "We don't talk about money in this family." Still others absorbed cultural myths: "Success means driving the right car, wearing the right clothes, living in the right postcode." These stories shape how we earn, spend, save, and invest often without us even realizing it.

Morgan Housel, in The Psychology of Money, captures this truth with piercing clarity: "Your personal experiences with money make up maybe 0.00000001% of what's happened in the world, but maybe 80% of how you think it works." In other words, our financial worldview is not objective, it's personal, emotional, and deeply biased. And unless we examine those stories, they will quietly dictate our financial lives.

That is why this book weaves storytelling into every chapter. You will encounter metaphors of building foundations, bricks, storms, and homes. You will read about people who started with nothing and built something lasting, not because they had extraordinary luck, but because they rewrote their financial story. And you will be invited to reflect on your own story, to see where it has served you and where it has held you back.

Wealth building is not a sprint. It is a journey, one that requires patience, discipline, and resilience. Along the way, you will face setbacks with unexpected expenses, market downturns, moments of doubt. But those setbacks are not failures; they are part of the process. Just as a builder expects storms while constructing a house, you must expect challenges while constructing wealth.

Kiyosaki reminds us: "The rich don't work for money. They make money work for them." This principle will echo through the chapters ahead. The goal is not to chase money endlessly, but to design systems where money begins to serve you through investments, assets, and strategies that grow even while you sleep.

But before we get there, we must start with the ground beneath our feet. We must clear away debt, shame, and confusion. We must lay a foundation for budgeting and clarity. Only then can we build upward, brick by brick, toward financial freedom.

What This Book Offers

This book is structured to guide you step by step. Each chapter builds upon the last, moving from mindset to mechanics, from clearing the ground to expanding the structure. Along the way, you will learn how to:

- Identify and dismantle limiting beliefs around money
- Build a financial foundation that supports long-term growth
- Create systems for earning, saving, investing, and protecting wealth
- Understand the emotional and psychological patterns that shape financial behavior
- Use storytelling your own and others to reframe your financial identity

This is not a formal textbook, but it is rigorous. It is not academic, but it is deeply informed. You will find frameworks, case studies, reflection prompts, and practical tools. But you will also find metaphors, emotional insight, and a tone that respects your intelligence without talking down to you.

You Are Not Behind

Perhaps the most important message of this introduction is this: you are not behind. Wherever you are starting from whether in debt, in doubt, or in transition, you are not broken. You are simply beginning. And beginnings are powerful.

Napoleon Hill's words echo here again: "Success comes to those who become success conscious." Becoming conscious of your financial life, your habits, your beliefs, your systems is the first step toward transformation. This book will help you take that step, and then the next, and the next.

Think of this book as a companion, not a lecture. It will walk with you, not talk down to you. It will challenge you but also encourage you. It will give you tools, but also stories. And it will remind you, again and again, that wealth is not just about money, it is about meaning.

As we begin, remember Housel's warning: "Spending money to show people how much money you have is the fastest way to have less money." Let that be a guiding principle. Wealth is not performance. It is not about impressing others. It is about building a life of freedom, integrity, and impact.

So let us begin. Together, we will clear the ground, lay the foundation, and build a structure that can withstand storms and stand the test of time. Step by step, brick by brick, story by story you will build wealth that lasts.

Part One: Laying the Foundations

Chapter 1: Shaping Your Wealth Mindset

Every building begins with a foundation. Before bricks are laid or walls are raised, the ground must be prepared. Wealth is no different. Before you can build financial systems, accumulate assets, or design strategies, you must first shape the mindset that will sustain them. Without this, even the most sophisticated financial plan will eventually collapse under the weight of old habits and limiting beliefs.

The Invisible Blueprint

Your financial life is built on an invisible blueprint: your mindset. It is the sum of your beliefs, assumptions, and stories about money. Some of these beliefs empower you "I can learn to manage money wisely." Others quietly sabotage you 'll never be good with money."

Napoleon Hill, in Think and Grow Rich, captured this truth nearly a century ago: "Whatever the mind can conceive and believe, it can achieve." Hill wasn't speaking about wishful thinking. He was pointing to the reality that wealth begins in the mind. If you believe wealth is unattainable, you will unconsciously act in ways that confirm that belief. If you believe wealth is possible, you will begin to notice opportunities, take risks, and persist through setbacks.

Your mindset is the soil in which your financial seeds are planted. Poor soil yields weak growth. Rich soil yields abundance.

Stories We Inherit

Our beliefs about money rarely begin with us. They are inherited passed down through family, culture, and experience. Perhaps you grew up hearing, "Money doesn't grow on trees," or "Rich people are greedy." These phrases may seem harmless, but they shape the way you relate to money as an adult.

Morgan Housel, in The Psychology of Money, explains: "Your personal experiences with money make up maybe 0.00000001% of what's happened in the world, but maybe 80% of how you think it works." This means your financial worldview is not objective, it is deeply personal, shaped by a handful of experiences that may not reflect reality.

If your parents struggle with debt, you may carry a fear of credit. If you grew up in scarcity, you may overspend the moment money arrives, afraid it will disappear. These stories are powerful, but they are not permanent. They can be rewritten.

Scarcity vs. Abundance

One of the most important mindsets shifts in wealth building is moving from scarcity to abundance. Scarcity says, "There's never enough." Abundance says, "There are opportunities to create more." Scarcity hoards. Abundance invests. Scarcity fears loss. Abundance embraces growth.

Robert Kiyosaki, in Rich Dad Poor Dad, contrasts these two mindsets vividly: "The poor and the middle-class work for money. The rich have money work for them." Scarcity keeps you trapped in the cycle of working harder for every pound. Abundance teaches you to build systems where money begins to generate more money through investments, assets, and creativity.

This shift is not about ignoring reality. It's about training your mind to see possibilities instead of only problems. It's about asking, "How can I make this money grow?" instead of, "How long until this money runs out?"

The Role of Self-Image

Your financial results will rarely exceed your self-image. If you see yourself as someone who "just gets by," you will unconsciously sabotage opportunities for growth. If you see yourself as someone capable of building wealth, you will act in alignment with that identity.

This is why shaping your wealth mindset is not optional, it is foundational. You cannot out-earn a poor self-image. You cannot out-invest a scarcity mindset. The inner work must come first.

1.1 Practical Steps to Shape Your Wealth Mindset

1. Identify Your Money Story

Write down the earliest messages you remember about money. Were they empowering or limiting? How do they still influence you today?

2. Challenge Limiting Beliefs

When you catch yourself thinking, "I'll never be wealthy," ask: Is this belief based on fact, or on a story I inherited?

3. Reframe Scarcity into Abundance

Instead of saying, "I can't afford this," try, "How can I afford this?" This small shift opens the door to creativity.

4. Visualize Your Financial Identity

Picture yourself five years from now, financially secure and confident. What habits did that version of you adopt? Begin practicing them now.

5. Surround Yourself with Wealth-Conscious Voices

Read books, listen to podcasts, and engage with people who think abundantly. As Hill wrote, "Success comes to those who become success conscious."

1.2 A Story to Remember

Consider the story of two friends who both earned the same salary. One lived paycheck to paycheck, always anxious, always chasing the next raise. The other began with the same income but shifted her mindset. She saw money not as something to spend, but as something to grow. She budgeted, invested, and learned. Ten years later, one was still trapped in scarcity. The other had built a foundation of wealth. The difference wasn't intelligence or luck. It was mindset. Before we move into the mechanics of budgeting, saving, and investing, pause here. Reflect on your own mindset. What stories have you inherited? What beliefs are shaping your financial life? And most importantly what new story will you choose to write?

Because wealth is not built by accident. It is built by design. And the design begins in the mind.

Transforming beliefs about money

Money is never just about arithmetic. Long before it appears in our wallets or bank accounts, it takes root in our minds. Each of us carries a set of convictions, some inherited, some absorbed, some forged in hardship that quietly dictate how we earn, spend, save, and invest. These convictions are not neutral; they are the invisible architecture of our financial lives. To build lasting wealth, we must first confront and transform the beliefs that shape our relationship with money.

Phineas Taylor Barnum once observed that "Money is a terrible master but an excellent servant." That single line captures the essence of the struggle many people face. When money rules us, it drives our choices, our time, and even our sense of worth. We chase it, fear it, and sometimes resent it. But when we reverse the relationship when money becomes the servant it buys us freedom, time, and peace of mind. The first step in transformation, then, is to ask honestly: am I serving money, or is money serving me?

For many, the answer is tangled in scarcity. Samuel Langhorne Clemens better known as Mark Twain remarked with his characteristic bite that "The lack of money is the root of all evil." Scarcity breeds desperation. It pushes people into survival mode, where long-term thinking disappears and fear dictates every decision. If you grew up hearing that there was "never enough, you may still carry that script, even if your circumstances have changed. Belief itself becomes a trap. Transforming it requires a new perspective: money is not the villain, nor is it the savior. It is a neutral tool until directed by the hand that holds it.

This is where education enters the picture. Not the kind confined to classrooms, but the kind that reshapes identity. Emanuel James Rohn better known as Jim Rohn once said, "Formal education will make you a living; self-education will make you a fortune." Wealth requires a different kind of learning self-driven, curious, and relentless. It is the willingness to read, to experiment, to fail, and to try again. Transforming your beliefs about money means embracing the role of a lifelong student, one who understands that financial literacy is not a subject studied once, but a discipline practiced daily.

Yet knowledge alone is not enough. Many people know what they "should" do with money but feel paralyzed by guilt or shame. Susan Lynn Orman known worldwide as Suze Orman put it plainly: "You can't fix a financial problem with money. You fix it with your head and your heart." Shame whispers, "I don't deserve wealth." Guilt insists, "I'll always be bad with money." These emotions harden into beliefs, and beliefs harden into barriers. Transformation begins when you give yourself permission to let go of shame. Mistakes are not life sentences; they are lessons. Wealth is not about perfection it is about progress.

Progress, however, requires ownership. David Lawrence Ramsey III known simply as Dave Ramsey—declared: "You must gain control over your money, or the lack of it will forever control you." Ownership is the soil in which new beliefs grow. It is the moment you stop blaming circumstances, upbringing, or luck, and instead take responsibility for your financial choices. Ownership transforms excuses into action. It shifts the question from "Why me?" to "What can I do next?"

To transform beliefs about money is to rewrite the script you live by. Instead of "Money is scarce," you begin to say, "Money is a tool I can grow." Instead of "I'm bad with money," you affirm, "I am learning to master money." Instead of "Wealth is for others," you claim, "Wealth is possible for me." These new stories are not fantasies; they are blueprints. And when you live by them, your behavior shifts slowly at first, then dramatically.

Phineas Taylor Barnum warned us not to let money be our master. Samuel Langhorne Clemens reminded us that scarcity, not money itself, breeds evil. Emanuel James Rohn urged us to keep learning. Susan Lynn Orman called us to heal our relationship with money. David Lawrence Ramsey III demanded ownership. Together, their voices form a chorus: wealth is not just about numbers—it is about beliefs. And beliefs can be transformed.

When you change the way you think about money, you change the way you use it. And when you change the way you use it, you change your life.

1.3 Comparing Old and New Perspectives on Money

For generations, money has been surrounded by myths, fears, and half-truths. Many of us inherited beliefs that were never questioned, passed down like family heirlooms. These "old perspectives" often came from times of scarcity, where survival was the priority. Today, however, we live in a world of expanded opportunity, where access to knowledge, tools, and global markets has transformed what is possible. To build wealth, we must examine these contrasting perspectives and choose which story we want to live by.

Old Perspective: Money is scarce

In the past, money was often seen as a limited resource. Families repeated phrases like "We can't afford that" or "Money doesn't grow on trees." This mindset created fear and a sense of lack, leading people to hoard rather than grow their resources.

New Perspective: Money is a tool

Today, wealth builders understand that money is not fixed, it can be created, multiplied, and directed. Through investments, entrepreneurship, and financial literacy, money becomes a tool that works for you. As Warren Buffett once said, "If you don't find a way to make money while you sleep, you will work until you die." The new perspective shifts from fear to strategy.

Old Perspective: Debt is shameful
In many households, debt was treated as a moral failing. People carried guilt and silence around financial struggles, often hiding them rather than addressing them.

New Perspective: Debt is a decision
Modern financial thinking reframes debt as a tool that can either hinder or help, depending on how it is used. Productive debt such as a mortgage on an appreciating asset or a loan for education can be leveraged for growth. The shame is not in borrowing; it is in borrowing without strategy.

Old Perspective: Wealth is for the few
Historically, wealth was seen as something reserved for elites, business magnates, or those born into privilege. Ordinary people often believed financial freedom was out of reach.

New Perspective: Wealth is accessible
With the rise of digital platforms, global markets, and democratized investing, wealth-building is no longer limited to a select few. Anyone with discipline, education, and persistence can create financial security. As financial educator Chris Hogan puts it, "You don't accidentally get wealthy. You must decide to do it on purpose."

Old Perspective: Talking about money is taboo
In many cultures, money was a private matter, not to be discussed openly. This silence perpetuated ignorance and repeated cycles of financial struggle.

New Perspective: Financial literacy is empowerment
Today, conversations about money are essential. Books, podcasts, and communities encourage transparency and education. The more we talk about money, the more we normalize learning, sharing, and growing together.

The Shift That Matters
The difference between old and new perspectives is not just intellectual, it is transformational. Old beliefs were rooted in fear, silence, and limitation. New beliefs are grounded in empowerment, education, and possibility.
Transforming your financial life begins with this comparison. Ask yourself: Which perspective am I living by? Which one will I choose moving forward?
Because wealth is not only about numbers it is about the lens through which you see them. Change the lens, and the picture of your financial future changes with it.

1.4 An Inspiring Transformation Story: From Survival to Significance

When Daniel looked at his life five years ago, he saw a cycle he couldn't seem to escape. Every month ended the same way: bills stacked high, credit cards maxed out, and a gnawing sense of failure. He worked hard, but his efforts never seemed to translate into stability. "I thought money was something that happened to other people," he later admitted. "I believed I was destined to struggle."
His story is not unusual. Many people inherit beliefs about money that quietly dictate their choices. For Daniel, the belief was simple: I'll never get ahead. That belief shaped his actions avoiding budgets, ignoring debt, and numbing his stress with impulse spending. But transformation often begins in the smallest of shifts, and for Daniel, it started with a single question: What if I could learn to think differently about money?
The turning point came when he stumbled across a community workshop on financial literacy. At first, he was sceptical. He had always assumed that wealth was reserved for people with higher salaries or privileged

backgrounds. But the facilitator's words struck him: "Wealth isn't about how much you earn. It's about how you manage what you have, and the story you tell yourself about it." That idea unsettled him and then it ignited him.

Daniel began by confronting his old beliefs. He wrote down every phrase he remembered from childhood: Money doesn't grow on trees. We can't afford that. People like us don't get rich. Seeing those words on paper was like holding up a mirror. They weren't facts; they were inherited scripts. And scripts, he realised, could be rewritten.

He started small. Instead of saying, "I can't afford this," he asked, "How can I afford this?" That subtle shift opened his mind to creative solutions. He built a simple budget, tracked his spending, and set aside even the smallest amounts for savings. At first, progress was slow. But each month he saw a little more breathing room, and with it, a little more confidence.

The real transformation, however, wasn't just financial, it was emotional. Daniel stopped seeing himself as a victim of circumstance and began to see himself as a steward for his resources. He devoured books, listened to podcasts, and surrounded himself with people who thought abundantly. He learned that mistakes weren't proof of failure but steppingstones toward wisdom. Within three years, he had paid off his credit cards, built an emergency fund, and even started investing. More importantly, he had rewritten his identity: from someone who "could never get ahead" to someone who was building a future with intention.

Today, Daniel shares his story with others who feel trapped in the same cycle. "It's not about perfection," he tells them. "It's about progress. If you can change your beliefs, you can change your life."

His journey is proof that transformation doesn't begin with a windfall or a miracle. It begins with a shift in perspective, a willingness to challenge old stories, and the courage to write new ones.

Daniel's story reminds us all: wealth is not just about numbers it is about belief. And belief, once transformed, can change everything.

1.5 Effective steps to develop a growth-focused mindset

1. Recognize Fixed Thinking When It Appears

The first step is awareness. A growth mindset begins by noticing when you slip into fixed beliefs like "I'm just not good at this" or "I'll never change." Catching these thoughts in the moment allows you to challenge them before they harden into self-limiting truths.

When Daniel was promoted to team leader at his company, excitement quickly gave way to self-doubt. In his first week, he was asked to present a new strategy to senior management. As he stared at the blank PowerPoint slide, a familiar voice crept in: "I'm just not good at public speaking. I'll embarrass myself. Maybe I'm not cut out for leadership after all."

This was fixed thinking at work, an old belief resurfacing, telling him his abilities were set in stone. In the past, Daniel would have accepted this thought as truth and avoided the challenge. But this time, he paused. He remembered a mentor once telling him, "Notice the story you're telling yourself. Is it fact, or is it fear?"

By catching the thought in the moment, Daniel created space to challenge it. He asked himself: "Is it true that I'll never be good at presenting? Or is it that I haven't practiced enough yet?" That single shift from "never" to "not yet" changed everything.

Instead of retreating, Daniel sought help. He practiced with a colleague, watched videos on effective communication, and rehearsed until he felt more confident. On presentation day, he wasn't flawless, but he was clear, composed, and authentic. His manager praised his effort, and Daniel walked away with a new belief: "I can grow into this role."

The key wasn't instant mastery it was awareness. By recognizing the fixed thought as it appeared, Daniel prevented it from hardening into a self-limiting truth. He replaced it with a growth-focused perspective that opened the door to progress.

2. Reframe Challenges as Opportunities

Instead of seeing obstacles as proof of inadequacy, we view them as training grounds. Ask: "What can this teach me?" or "How will this stretch me?" Every setback becomes a steppingstone when you choose to see it as part of the process.

When Lila launched her first bakery, she poured her savings and heart into the business. But within six months, sales were slow, bills piled up, and she faced the painful reality of closing doors. At first, she saw it as proof of failure: "Maybe I'm just not cut out for business."

One evening, while reflecting, she asked herself a different question: "What can this teach me?" That shift reframed the entire experience. Instead of labelling herself inadequately, she began to see the bakery as a training ground.

She realized she had chosen a poor location with little foot traffic, relied too heavily on word-mouth, and hadn't built an online presence. These weren't signs she was incapable they were lessons in strategy.

Armed with this insight, Lila started again, this time with a smaller food truck. She applied everything she had learned: better marketing, smarter budgeting, and a stronger connection with her customers. Within a year, her food truck was thriving, and she was saving toward opening a second one.

The failure hadn't ended her journey, it had stretched her, sharpened her, and prepared her for greater success.

3. **Embrace the Power of "Yet"**

Adding the word "yet" to your self-talk transforms defeat into possibility. "I can't do this" becomes "I can't do this yet." This small linguistic shift keeps the door open for growth and signals to your brain that learning is ongoing.

When Olivia was in secondary school, mathematics felt like an enemy she could never conquer. Every test ended with red marks; every homework assignment left her in tears. She began to tell herself, "I just can't do maths. I'm not a numbers person." That phrase became her shield and her prison.

One afternoon, after another disappointing grade, her teacher sat beside her and quietly added a single word to her sentence: "You can't do maths yet." Olivia laughed at first, but the word lingered. Yet. It suggested possibility. It hinted that her struggle wasn't permanent, only unfinished.

The next time she faced a difficult problem, instead of shutting her book in frustration, she whispered to herself, "I don't understand this yet." That small shift softened herself-criticism and gave her permission to try again. She began staying after class for extra help, watching tutorials online, and practicing a little each day.

Months later, Olivia passed her exam not with perfect marks, but with a sense of triumph. More importantly, she carried a new mindset into other areas of life. When she struggled to learn coding in university, she reminded herself, "I don't get this yet." When she stumbled in her first job interview, she thought, "I haven't mastered this yet."

The word "yet" became her anchor. It transformed defeat into possibility, failure into process, and self-doubt into resilience.

Olivia's story reminds us that growth is rarely instant. Sometimes, the only difference between giving up and pressing forward is a single word that keeps the door open.

4. Seek Feedback, Not Validation

A growth-focused mindset thrives on constructive feedback. Instead of asking, "Did I do well?" ask, "How can I improve?" Feedback becomes fuel for refinement rather than a verdict on your worth.

When Alex landed his first role as a junior graphic designer, he was eager to impress. After finishing his first big project, a logo for a new client he nervously showed it to his manager. His voice trembled as he asked, "Did I do well?" What he really wanted was reassurance, a pat on the back to quiet his self-doubt.

His manager paused, then gently replied, "The question isn't whether you did well. The question is: how can this be even better?"

At first, Alex felt stung. He had poured hours into the design, and part of him wanted validation, not critique. But instead of retreating, he leaned in. He asked, "Okay, what would you change?"

That shift opened the door to growth. His manager pointed out that the font choice didn't align with the brand's tone and that the color palette could be simplified for stronger recognition. Alex went back, revised the design, and presented a cleaner, sharper version. The client loved it.

More importantly, Alex learned a lesson: feedback wasn't a judgment of his worth, it was a tool for refinement. Over time, he began to actively seek it out. Instead of asking colleagues, "Do you like this?" he asked, "What's one thing I could improve?"

This mindset transformed his career. Within two years, Alex was leading projects, not because he was flawless, but because he was teachable.

The story shows that validation soothes the ego, but feedback strengthens the skill. A growth-focused mindset thrives not on applause, but on the courage to ask, "How can I improve?"

5. Celebrate Effort as Much as Results

Carol Dweck, the psychologist who pioneered growth mindset research, emphasizes rewarding effort, strategies, and persistence not just outcomes. By valuing the process, you train yourself to see growth as continuous, not conditional on immediate success.

When Ethan joined his school's track team, he was far from the fastest runner. In fact, during his first race, he finished last well behind his teammates. As he crossed the finish line, his head hung low, convinced he had failed.

But his coach saw something different. Instead of focusing on Ethan's placement, he praised his persistence: "You didn't quit. You pushed through every lap. That's what champions are made of." The words surprised Ethan. He had expected disappointment, but instead, his effort was celebrated.

Encouraged, Ethan began to train harder. He set small goals shaving seconds off his time, improving his breathing, strengthening his stride. Each practice became less about winning and more about progress. His teammates noticed too; they began cheering not just for victories but for personal improvements.

By the end of the season, Ethan wasn't the fastest, but he had cut his race time by nearly a minute. More importantly, he had learned to value persistence over perfection. The celebration of his effort gave him the confidence to keep growing, both on and off the track.

Carol Dweck's research shows that when we reward effort, strategies, and persistence, we reinforce the behaviors that lead to long-term success. Ethan's story proves that results are important, but the process the sweat, practice, the resilience is what truly builds character.

Celebrating effort transforms growth into a continuous journey, not a one-time achievement.

6. Surround Yourself with Growth-Minded Voices

The people you listen to shape your perspective. Spend time with those who encourage learning, resilience, and experimentation. Books, podcasts, mentors, and communities can all reinforce the belief that growth is possible.

When David graduated from university, he was full of ambition but unsure of his direction. Most of his friends spent evenings complaining about their jobs, scrolling endlessly on their phones, and joking that "life after school is just survival." Slowly, David noticed their words shaping his own thoughts. He began to believe that growth was unrealistic, that success was reserved for the lucky few.

One day, he attended a local networking event where he met a small group of entrepreneurs. Their energy was different. Instead of complaining, they swapped book recommendations, shared lessons from failures, and encouraged each other's experiments. David fell out of place at first, but something inside him stirred.

He started joining their weekly meetups. They introduced him to podcasts on resilience, books like Mindset by Carol Dweck, and mentors who challenged him to think bigger. When David hesitated to launch his side project, one of them said, "Don't wait until it's perfect start, and let the process teach you."

Surrounded by these voices, David's perspective shifted. He stopped asking, "What if I fail?" and began asking, "What will I learn?" Within a year, his side project grew into a small business.

David's story shows that the voices around us either limit us or lift us. Growth-minded people don't just inspire they normalize resilience, experimentation, and progress. By choosing your circle wisely, you choose the mindset that will shape your future.

7. Turn Setbacks into Stories of Progress

Instead of hiding failures, reframe them as part of your narrative. Ask: "What did this experience add to my journey?" By integrating setbacks into your story, you transform them from sources of shame into sources of wisdom.

When Clara launched her first photography business, she imagined instant success clients lining up, her work featured in magazines, and financial freedom within a year. Reality was harsher. Bookings were scarce, her marketing fell flat, and after twelve months she was forced to close the studio, she had poured her savings into.

At first, Clara carried the weight of shame. She avoided conversations about her business, convinced that failure defined her. But one evening, while journaling, she asked herself a different question: "What did this experience add to my journey?"

The answer surprised her. She realized she had learned how to manage clients, negotiate contracts, and master editing software. She had discovered the importance of branding and the pitfalls of poor financial planning. These weren't signs of defeat, they were lessons.

Clara began to share her story openly, not as a tale of failure, but as a chapter of growth. When she later applied for a marketing role, she highlighted her entrepreneurial experience, explaining how the setbacks had sharpened her problem-solving skills. The interviewer was impressed not by perfection, but by resilience. She got the job.

Clara's story shows that setbacks don't have to be hidden in shame. When reframed, they become powerful narratives of progress. Each stumble adds wisdom, each closed-door points to another path. By integrating failures into your story, you transform them into steppingstones that carry you forward.

8. Practice Daily Reflection

Growth is not automatic it requires intentional reflection. Journaling, meditation, or even five minutes of quiet thought at the end of the day helps you notice patterns, celebrate small wins, and identify areas for improvement.

I call it "The Five-Minute Habit"

When Samuel started his first corporate job, his days blurred together. Meetings, deadlines, and endless emails left him exhausted. At night, he collapsed into bed, only to wake up and repeat the cycle. Weeks passed, and though he was working hard, he felt stuck like he was running but not moving forward.

One evening, a mentor suggested a simple practice: "Take five minutes before bed to reflect. Write down what went well, what didn't, and what you learned." Samuel was skeptical. How could five minutes change anything? But he decided to try.

That night, he scribbled in a notebook:

- Win: Spoke up in a meeting, even though I was nervous.
- Struggle: Missed a deadline because I underestimated the time needed.
- Lesson: Break big tasks into smaller steps.

The next day, he applied for the lesson. Slowly, the habit grew. His journal became a mirror, showing him patterns he hadn't noticed like how procrastination crept in when he skipped breakfast, or how his best ideas came after morning walks.

Over time, Samuel began to celebrate small wins he would have otherwise ignored: finishing a report early, handling a tough conversation with grace, or simply staying calm under pressure. Reflection turned his chaotic days into a story of progress.

Samuel's journey shows that growth isn't automatic, it's intentional. By pausing to reflect, even briefly, we transform daily experiences into steppingstones for improvement.

9. Adopt a Long-Term Lens

A growth-focused mindset is patient. It understands that mastery is built over years, not days. By zooming out and focusing on the bigger picture, you reduce the pressure of immediate perfection and embrace steady progress.

When Priya decided to learn the violin at age 30, many of her friends raised their eyebrows. "Isn't it too late to start?" they asked. At first, she wondered if they were right. Her early lessons were clumsy, her fingers stiff, and the sounds she produced were far from music. After weeks of slow progress, she caught herself thinking, "Maybe I'll never get good at this."

But then she remembered something her teacher said: "Think of this as a marathon, not a sprint. Every practice session is a brick in the foundation of your future skill."

Priya began to zoom out. Instead of judging herself by daily results, she looked at her growth over months. She tries small improvements her bowing became smoother, her ear more attuned, her confidence stronger. By the end of her first year, she could play simple songs with joy. By year three, she was performing at community events.

The long-term lens freed her from the pressure of immediate perfection. She no longer asked, "Am I good yet?" but instead, "Am I better than yesterday?"

Priya's journey shows that mastery is built brick by brick, year by year. A growth-focused mindset is patient because it knows that steady progress compounds. When you zoom out, setbacks shrink, persistence shines, and the bigger picture keeps you moving forward.

10. Anchor Growth in Purpose

Finally, connect your growth to something larger than yourself. Whether it's building a career, raising a family, writing a book, or leaving a legacy, purpose gives growth meaning. It transforms effort from a chore into a calling.

When Elena decided to return to university in her forties, many of her colleagues questioned her choice. "Why put yourself through the stress of exams at this age?" they asked. At first, Elena wondered the same. Balancing work, family, and late-night study sessions was exhausting. There were moments she wanted to quit, especially when assignments piled up and her energy ran low.

But Elena wasn't pursuing a degree just for herself. Her purpose was clear: she wanted to become a counsellor to support young people in her community who struggled with mental health challenges. She had seen too many teenagers fall through the cracks, and she believed her training could make a difference.

Whenever she felt overwhelmed, Elena reminded herself of that purpose. Each textbook wasn't just theory it was a tool she would one day use to help someone feel less alone. Each late night wasn't just sacrifice it was an investment in lives she hoped to touch.

By anchoring her growth in something larger than herself, Elena transformed her effort from a burden into a calling. The long hours became meaningful, the setbacks became tolerable, and the journey itself became fulfilling.

Her story shows that growth without purpose can feel hollow, but growth tied to a deeper mission becomes unstoppable. Purpose is the compass that turns discipline into devotion and effort into legacy.

1.6 Reflection

A growth-focused mindset is not about blind optimism. It is about resilience, curiosity, and the courage to keep learning. By shifting your language, reframing your challenges, and anchoring your journey in purpose, you create a mindset that not only survives difficulty but thrives because of it.

Wealth begins in the mind long before it appears in the bank. It's not just about earning more, it's about thinking differently. A wealthy mindset is the quiet force behind every smart decision, every moment of discipline, and every leap of faith. It's the belief that your financial future is not dictated by your past, your circumstances, or your limitations but by your vision, your habits, and your willingness to grow.

As you close this chapter, pause and ask yourself: What do I truly believe about money? Do you see it as a tool for freedom, or a source of stress? Do you feel empowered to build wealth, or conditioned to chase survival? These beliefs shape your behavior more than any budget ever will.

The truth is, your mindset is either your greatest asset or your biggest liability. If you believe wealth is possible, you'll seek opportunities. If you believe it's out of reach, you'll sabotage progress. That's why shaping your mindset isn't optional, it's foundational.

Start small. Practice gratitude for what you already have. Celebrate every financial win, no matter how minor. Surround yourself with people who think expansively. Read stories of transformation. Reframe setbacks as tuition for growth. And most importantly, speak to yourself with the language of possibility: I am capable. I am learning. I am building.

This isn't about toxic positivity it's about strategic optimism. It's about choosing a lens that helps you see solutions instead of roadblocks. Because when your mindset shifts, your actions follow. And when your actions align with your vision, wealth becomes inevitable.

So before you dive into the mechanics of goal setting, investing, or income streams, take this moment to commit to a new way of thinking. You are not just managing money you are shaping a legacy. You are not just chasing wealth you are becoming the kind of person who attracts it.

Let this be your declaration: I will think like a builder, act like a strategist, and grow like a visionary. The journey ahead will challenge you, stretch you, and reward you. But it starts here with belief, intention, and the mindset of someone who knows that wealth is not a wish. It's a decision.

Chapter 2: Defining Your Financial Goals

2.1 Introduction: Wealth Is Never Accidental

"Wealth is never accidental it's the result of clarity, discipline, and direction." This philosophy sits at the core of every personal, corporate, and even national success story. Whether building a protective financial cushion for your family, pursuing independence, or leaving a lasting legacy, the path to true wealth begins not with random wins or strokes of luck, but with vision and intentionality. Echoing Stephen Covey's enduring wisdom "Begin with the end in mind" we realize lasting financial achievement always starts with a clearly defined destination.

Without specific goals, you risk drifting, your daily money choices overshadowed by short-term impulses or the agendas of others. But with purpose and defined targets, each decision becomes a building block toward your unique vision for life. Let's embark on a journey of self-discovery and practical strategy, transforming vague hopes into actionable financial goals that steadily make your dreams a reality.

Foundations of Wealth: Clarity, Discipline, and Direction

At the crossroads of every thriving financial journey stand three powerful pillars: clarity, discipline, and direction.

• Clarity is the ability to see and articulate precisely what you want your money to achieve whether it's independence, security, experiences, or impact.

• Discipline is the commitment to consistent action budgeting, saving, and investing even when the emotional pull of instant gratification beckons.

• Direction ensures each daily money choice points you toward your desired future, rather than leaving you adrift in a sea of financial randomness.

These pillars are not abstract ideals; they're practical mindsets and habits. For example, clarity might start with a written vision statement for your financial life. Discipline is practiced through routines like automating savings or tracking spending. Direction is sustained through regular check-ins to ensure your actions genuinely align with your long-term vision.

By consciously developing these traits, you build a foundation not just for wealth accumulation, but also for a more empowered, less stressful, and ultimately more fulfilling life.

Stephen Covey's Wisdom: "Begin with the End in Mind" in Finance

"Begin with the end in mind" Covey's second habit frames wealth-building as a journey guided by a clear destination. If your financial life were a road trip, would you simply "drive," hoping to land somewhere nice, or would you choose your destination and chart the route?

In practice, this means:

• Visualizing your future: What does your "wealthy life" look and feel like? Is it about freedom to travel, security for your family, creative or career pursuits, giving to charity, or leaving a legacy?

• Reverse engineering the path: What major steps and resources would you need? (Consider home ownership, retirement, debt freedom, sufficient insurance, or education funds, as fitting your vision.)

• Making every decision count: With your "end" in mind, saving a specific amount each month isn't a deprivation it's a daily step toward your unique version of success.

Case Example:

Consider "Olivia," a graphic designer who envisioned traveling the world with her family in ten years. Instead of a vague "save money" goal, Olivia and her partner mapped out what such adventures would cost, identified the savings and investment vehicles needed, and charted intermediate milestones for each year. Having her "end in mind" turned daily budgeting, studying investment options, and skipping short-term luxuries into empowering steps toward a life-changing experience.

Why Goals Matter
Imagine two friends, both earning the same salary. One spends freely, hoping that "someday" things will fall into place. The other sets a clear goal: to save £20,000 in three years for a property deposit. Three years later, one is still living paycheck to paycheck, while the other is holding the keys to their first home.
The difference isn't intelligence or luck it's clarity. Goals transform vague desires into measurable outcomes. They give you a reason to say no to distractions and yes to discipline. Napoleon Hill, in Think and Grow Rich, called this "definiteness of purpose." Without it, even the hardest work can feel aimless.

The SMART Goals Framework
The SMART method is one of the most practical tools for turning dreams into reality. Let's break it down:
• Specific – Define exactly what you want.
• Measurable – Attach numbers so you can track progress.
• Achievable – Set goals that stretch you but remain realistic.
• Relevant – Align goals with your values and long-term vision.
• Time-bound – Give each goal a deadline.

Example:
• Vague: "I want to save more money."
• SMART: "I will save £10,000 in 18 months by setting aside £555 each month for a property deposit."
Notice how the second goal creates a roadmap. You know the target, the timeline, and the steps.

Case Study: Aisha's Entrepreneurial Journey
Aisha was a 27-year-old entrepreneur who launched a small online clothing brand. At first, her goal was simply to "make money." She worked long hours, posted on social media, and reinvested profit but progress felt random.

One evening, exhausted and frustrated, she sat down and redefined her vision using SMART goals:
• Specific: Generate £50,000 in revenue.
• Measurable: Track monthly sales and customer growth.
• Achievable: Based on her current growth, this was ambitious but realistic.
• Relevant: Aligned with her dream of scaling her business.
• Time-bound: Within 12 months.
She broke the goal into milestones: £10,000 by month three, £25,000 by month six, £40,000 by month nine. Each milestone guided her decisions how much inventory to order, when to hire help, and which markets to expand into.
By the end of the year, she not only hit her target but also built a sustainable system for growth. Her story illustrates a powerful truth: when you define your goals, you give your energy direction.

2.2 Goal Setting Exercises: From Intention to Impact

Setting goals is one of the most powerful ways to shape your future. It's how you move from vague desire to deliberate action. But goal setting isn't just about writing down what you want, it's about structuring your vision in a way that makes progress inevitable. It's about aligning your ambitions with your values, your energy with your priorities, and your time with what truly matters.

In wealth-building, as in life, clarity is power. Without it, we drift. With it, we direct. This section is your invitation to pause, reflect, and define what you're really working toward not just in numbers, but in meaning.

Why Goals Matter

A goal is more than a target. It's a declaration of intent. It says, "I'm not leaving this to chance." It gives your daily choices a compass. When you know what you're aiming for, you can say no to distractions and yes to the things that move you forward.

But not all goals are created equal. Some are too vague to act on. Others are so ambitious they become overwhelming. And some, though well-crafted, fail to inspire because they don't reflect your deeper values. That's why structure matters. And so does soul.

Let's walk through a simple, powerful process to help you set goals that are clear, motivating, and achievable.

Step 1: Choose 3 to 5 Financial Goals

Start by writing down three to five financial goals that feel meaningful to you right now. These could be short-term (like building an emergency fund), medium-term (like saving for a home deposit), or long-term (like achieving financial independence).

Don't worry about making them perfect. Just get them out of your head and onto paper. The act of writing them down is the first step toward making them real.

Examples might include:

- Save £10,000 for a home deposit
- Pay off all credit card debt within 12 months
- Launch a side business that earns £500/month
- Build a £5,000 emergency fund
- Invest consistently in a pension or ISA

Choose goals that feel both exciting and important. If a goal doesn't stir something in you, it won't sustain your motivation.

Step 2: Make Each Goal SMART

Once you've listed your goals, refine each one using the SMART framework. This turns vague hopes into actionable plans.

- Specific: What exactly do you want to achieve?
- Measurable: How will you track progress?
- Achievable: Is it realistic given your current resources and commitments?
- Relevant: Does it align with your values and long-term vision?
- Time-bound: When do you want to achieve it?

For example, instead of saying "I want to save more," you might say:

"I want to save £5,000 for an emergency fund by next June by setting aside £500 each month."

This version is clear, trackable, and time sensitive. You know what success looks like, and you know how to get there.

Step 3: Review Progress Monthly

Set a recurring date each month to check in with yourself. This could be the first Sunday of the month, the last Friday, or any day that feels right. The key is consistency.

During your review, ask yourself:

- Am I on track?
- What's working well?
- What's getting in the way?
- Do I need to adjust the timeline or strategy?

This monthly check-in keeps your goals alive. It also gives you permission to adapt. Life changes so should your goals. Flexibility is not failure. It's wisdom.

Step 4: Adjust as Needed

If you fall behind, don't abandon the goal adjust it. Maybe the timeline needs to stretch. Maybe the monthly contribution needs to shrink. Maybe the goal itself needs to evolve.
Progress isn't linear. Some months will be strong. Others will be messy. What matters is that you keep showing up. That you keep choosing direction over drift.

2.3 Common Mistakes to Avoid

Even with the best intentions, many people fall into traps that quietly sabotage their progress. Here are four of the most common and how to avoid them:

1. Being too vague
Saying "I want to be rich" isn't a goal it's a wish. Define what "rich" means to you. Is it £100,000 in savings? A debt-free life? Passive income from investments? Clarity creates momentum.

2. Setting too many goals at once
Ambition is admirable, but trying to juggle ten goals at once leads to overwhelm. Focus on three to five priorities. You can always add more once momentum builds.

3. Unrealistic timelines
Wanting to double your income in three months might sound exciting, but if it's not feasible, it leads to burnout. Stretch yourself but stay grounded. A goal should challenge you, not crush you.

4. Ignoring your values
A goal that doesn't align with your deeper purpose won't sustain motivation. If you value freedom, but your goal demands rigid control, you'll resist it. Make sure your goals reflect what truly matters to you not just what looks good on paper.

A Deeper Layer: Emotional Anchoring
Numbers are important but they're not enough. Behind every financial goal is an emotional driver. Maybe you want to save because you never felt secure growing up. Maybe you want to build wealth so you can give your children the opportunities you never had. Maybe you want to retire early so you can travel, write, or serve your community.
Whatever your reasons, name them. Write them down. Revisit them often. Because when the numbers feel abstract, your "why" will keep you going.

A Simple Exercise to Anchor Your Goals
For each goal, write a short paragraph that answers the question:
"Why does this matter to me?"
For example:
"I want to build a £5,000 emergency fund because I never want to feel the panic I felt when my car broke down last year, and I had no savings. I want to feel safe, prepared, and in control."
This emotional clarity turns your goal from a task into a mission. And missions are harder to abandon.
Goal setting is not just a productivity tool it's a legacy practice. It's how you shape your future, protect your values, and build a life that reflects who you are and what you stand for.
When your goals are clear, meaningful, and reviewed regularly, they become part of your identity. They guide your decisions, shape your habits, and move you closer to the life you want to build not just for yourself, but for those who come after you.
So take the time. Write them down. Refine them. Review them. Adjust them. And most importantly, believe in them.
Because the future doesn't just happen. It's built one goal, one step, one decision at a time.

2.4 The Psychology of Goals

Clarity reduces anxiety. When you know what you're working toward, decisions become easier. Should you spend £200 on a new gadget or put it toward your savings goal? The answer is clear when your goals are defined.

Goals also fuel resilience. When setbacks come and they will your goals remind you why you started. Jim Rohn once said, "Discipline is the bridge between goals and accomplishment." That bridge is built one choice at a time.

Clarity Reduces Anxiety

Psychologists have long noted that uncertainty fuels stress. When you don't know what you're working toward, every financial decision feels like guesswork. But when you have a defined goal, you reduce that uncertainty. You know what matters and what doesn't. This mental clarity lightens the emotional load, giving you confidence that your daily actions are aligned with your bigger vision. Take the example of Amara, a young professional who constantly worried about money. She earned well but felt anxious every time she opened her bank app. Once she set a clear goal building a £5,000 emergency fund within 12 months her anxiety began to ease. Each deposit, no matter how small, reassured her that she was moving forward. The clarity of her goal replaced vague worry with measurable progress.

Goals Fuel Resilience

Setbacks are inevitable. You will face unexpected bills, market downturns, or personal challenges. Without goals, these obstacles can feel crushing. But with goals, they become temporary detours rather than dead ends.

Consider Michael, who lost his job during an economic downturn. Instead of spiraling into despair, he leaned on his long-term goal: financial independence by age 50. That goal reminded him why he had been saving and investing diligently. Even though his income paused, his vision didn't. He adjusted his timeline, cut unnecessary expenses, and used the setback as motivation to upskill. His goal gave him resilience the ability to bend without breaking.

Jim Rohn captured this truth when he said, "Discipline is the bridge between goals and accomplishment." That bridge is not built in a single day; it is laid brick by brick, choice by choice. Each time you resist an impulse purchase, each time you contribute to your savings, each time you stay focused despite setbacks, you are strengthening that bridge.

The Bigger Picture

The psychology of goals is not just about money, it's about meaning. Goals give your financial journey a narrative. They remind you that every sacrifice has a purpose, every delay has a destination. Without them, money feels like a treadmill constant motion with no progress. With them, money becomes a vehicle, carrying you toward freedom, security, and legacy.

Reflection Prompts

- What do you want money to make possible in your life?
- Which financial goals excite you the most?
- Which ones feel urgent?
- How will achieving these goals change your daily life?

Write your answers down. The act of writing transforms ideas into commitments.

2.5 Reflection

Defining your financial goals is like drawing the blueprint before building a house. Without it, you risk constructing something unstable walls that lean, foundations that crack, and rooms that don't serve their purpose. With it, every brick you lay every pound you save, every investment you make becomes part of a structure designed to last.

Think of a builder who begins without a plan. He may gather the finest materials, but without a clear design, the result is chaos. Now imagine another builder who starts with a detailed blueprint. Every nail, every beam, every brick is placed with intention. The difference is not in the resources but in the clarity of vision. Your financial life works the same way.

Wealth is not about chasing money for its own sake. Money without meaning is like a house without a foundation, it may look impressive for a while, but it cannot stand the test of time. True wealth is about alignment: aligning your resources with your values, your dreams, and your purpose. For one person, that may mean financial independence and freedom of time. For another, it may mean providing security for their family, funding education, or leaving a legacy that outlives them.

The journey begins with small, intentional steps. Write down your goals. Make them SMART Specific, Measurable, Achievable, Relevant, and Time-bound. Review them often, not as rigid rules but as guiding stars. Life will shift, circumstances will change, but your goals will serve as anchors, keeping you steady through uncertainty.

Remember, prosperity is not built in a single leap but in consistent, deliberate choices. Each time you choose to save instead of spending, to invest instead of delay, to plan instead of drift, you are laying another brick in the house of your future.

Begin today. Define your goals. Let them guide your decisions, fuel your discipline, and remind you why the journey matters. Wealth is not just about numbers—it is about building a life of stability, freedom, and purpose. And when your goals are clear, every step you take becomes a step toward lasting prosperity.

Chapter 3: Building Multiple Income Streams

3.1 Introduction: A Financial strategy.

Wealth rarely comes from a single source. Relying on one paycheck, one business, or one investment is like standing on one leg and any disruption can knock you off balance. True financial security and growth come from diversification: building multiple streams of income that flow together to create stability, resilience, and abundance.

As Warren Buffett once said, “Never depend on a single income. Make investment to create a second source.” This principle has been echoed by many financial thinkers and authors who have studied the habits of the wealthy.

Robert Kiyosaki, in his bestselling book Rich Dad Poor Dad, emphasizes that the wealthy rarely rely on a single paycheck. Instead, they build assets businesses, real estate, and investments that generate income even when they are not actively working. Kiyosaki himself transitioned from being an employee to an investor and entrepreneur, proving that multiple streams are not just theory but a lived reality.

Similarly, Thomas J. Stanley and William D. Danko, authors of The Millionaire Next Door, found in their research that self-made millionaires often had diverse income sources. Many combine professional earnings with investments, side businesses, or real estate ventures. Their achievement was not flashy wealth, but steady, resilient prosperity built over time.

Active and Passive Income

T. Harv Eker, author of Secrets of the Millionaire Mind, distinguishes between working for money and having money to work for you. Active income from your salary, freelance work, or business profits requires your time and energy. Passive income dividends, royalties, rental income flows even when you sleep. Eker’s achievement lies in showing readers how to rewire their financial mindset so they can transition from dependence on active income to building passive streams that create freedom.

Real-World Inspiration

Chris Guillebeau, in Side Hustle: From Idea to Income in 27 Days, demonstrates how ordinary people can create additional income streams without quitting their jobs. His achievement is not just writing about theory but documenting hundreds of real stories teachers, nurses, and office workers who turned hobbies into profitable ventures. His work proves that diversification is not reserved for the wealthy elite; it is accessible to anyone willing to take small, consistent steps.

Building multiple income streams is not about chasing money endlessly. It is about designing a life of stability and choice. Each stream you create is another layer of security, another step toward freedom. Begin with one, nurture it, and then add another. Over time, you’ll find yourself standing not on one fragile leg, but on a strong foundation supported by many.

The authors who have studied wealth from Kiyosaki to Stanley, from Eker to Guillebeau achieved success not only in their own financial lives but in empowering millions of readers to rethink money. Their collective wisdom reinforces this truth: multiple streams of income are not optional; they are essential for lasting prosperity.

3.2 Income Management

1. Boosting Earnings Through Diversification

Imagine a river fed by many tributaries. If one dries up, the river still flows. Your income should work the same way. Diversification doesn't just increase earnings, it reduces risk.

- Employment + Side Hustle: A teacher who tutors online in the evenings.
- Business + Investments: An entrepreneur who reinvests profits into rental properties.
- Creative Work + Royalties: A writer who earns from book sales while freelancing.

Diversification allows you to weather storms. If one stream slows, others sustain you. It also accelerates wealth building by creating multiple inflows that can be directed toward savings, investments, or debt repayment.

Maria's Three Streams

Maria was a high-schoolteacher who loved her job but often worried about money. Her salary covered the basics, but when her car broke down or unexpected bills arrived, she felt the strain. For years, she told herself, "At least I have a stable paycheck." But when her school district announced budget cuts, she realized how fragile that stability really was.

Instead of panicking, Maria decided to diversify. She began tutoring students online in the evenings. At first, it was just two hours a week, but soon word spread, and she had a steady roster of clients. That side hustle became her first tributary.

With the extra income, Maria started saving and eventually invested in a small rental property. It wasn't glamorous, but the monthly rent covered the mortgage and left her with a modest profit. That became her second tributary.

Finally, Maria leaned into her passion for writing. She self-published a short guide for parents on helping teenagers' study effectively. Sales trickled in at first, but over time, the royalties grew into a reliable stream. That was her third tributary.

When the school district eventually reduced her hours, Maria didn't panic. Her other streams kept her afloat. More than the money, she felt empowered no longer dependent on a single paycheck.

Maria's story shows that diversification isn't about greed; it's about resilience. Like a river fed by many tributaries, her financial life kept flowing even when one stream slowed.

2. Active vs. Passive Income Explained

Not all income is created equal. Understanding the difference between active and passive income is crucial.

- Active Income requires your time and effort. Examples: salaries, consulting, freelancing. If you stop working, the income stops.
- Passive Income continues to flow with minimal ongoing effort once established. Examples: dividends, rental income, royalties, digital products.

Think of active income as planting seeds and passive income as harvesting fruit from trees you've already grown. Both are essential. Active income builds momentum, while passive income builds freedom.

Daniel worked as a software engineer, earning a comfortable salary. Every month, his active income arrived like clockwork steady, predictable, but entirely dependent on his time. If he stopped coding, the paycheck stopped too. For years, he believed this was the only way to earn.

One winter, Daniel fell ill and had to take several weeks off. His sick pay covered part of his salary, but the gap left him anxious. Lying in bed, he realized how fragile his financial security was. That's when he began exploring passive income.

He started small, writing a simple e-book about coding best practices. At first, sales were slow, but over time, the book began generating royalties. Encouraged, Daniel invested in dividend-paying stocks. Soon, quarterly dividends trickled into his account money earned without extra hours at his desk.

The contrast was eye-opening. His active income still paid the bills, but his passive income gave him breathing room. When unexpected expenses arose, he didn't panic. When he dreamed of taking a sabbatical, he knew he had streams that would keep flowing.

Daniel's story shows the difference clearly: active income trades time for money, while passive income builds freedom. Both are valuable, but together they create resilience. Active income is the engine that gets you moving; passive income is the fuel that keeps you going even when you pause.

3. Personal Story: Journey to Multiple Streams

When I first entered the workforce, I believed a single paycheck was enough. But one unexpected layoff shattered that illusion. Overnight, my "secure" income vanished, and I realized how fragile my financial foundation was.

That moment became a turning point. I started small freelancing in the evenings, offering writing services. The extra income wasn't huge at first, but it gave me breathing room. Next, I invested in dividend-paying stocks and created a modest stream of passive income. Later, I launched a digital course, which began generating sales even while I slept.

Each stream was like adding another leg to the table of my financial life. Today, if one stream slows, others keep me steady. More importantly, I no longer live in fear of a single point of failure. My journey taught me that multiple streams aren't just about money, they're about peace of mind, freedom, and resilience.

3.3. Key Takeaways: Building Income with Intention

As you explore the world of multiple income streams, it's easy to feel overwhelmed by options, strategies, and success stories. But beneath the complexity lies a simple truth: wealth is built through consistency, clarity, and alignment. These five key takeaways are your compass guiding you not just toward financial growth, but toward a life that feels secure, energizing, and purpose driven.

1. Diversification Is Protection

Relying on a single paycheck or one business is like walking a tightrope without a safety net. If that income source falters due to layoffs, illness, market shifts, or burnout your entire financial stability is at risk. Diversification spreads that risk. It's not just about having more money it's about having more resilience. Whether it's a side hustle, rental income, dividends, or royalties, each stream adds a layer of protection. If one slows down, the others keep you afloat. Diversification is how you move from fragile to fortified.

2. Active Income Builds Momentum; Passive Income Builds Freedom

Active income like freelancing, consulting, or running a business requires your time and energy. It's powerful for building momentum, learning skills, and generating cash flow quickly. Passive income like investments, rental properties, or digital products requires upfront effort but eventually earns while you sleep.

Both are necessary. Active income gets you moving. Passive income keeps you moving even when you're resting, traveling, or spending time with loved ones. The goal isn't to choose one, it's to balance both, so your income reflects both effort and ease.

3. Start Small

You don't need a massive budget or a perfect plan to begin. Some of the most successful income streams started as modest side hustles a weekend gig, a single product, a few shares in a dividend-paying stock. What matters is starting.

Small steps compound. A £100 investment today can grow into thousands. A few hours a week on a side project can evolve into a full-time business. Starting small removes the pressure and builds confidence. It's how you learn, adapt, and gain momentum without risking everything.

4. Think Long Term

Building multiple income streams isn't a sprint, it's a marathon. It takes time, patience, and persistence. You might not see results in the first month, or even the first year. But each step is each sale, each investment, each connection compounds.

Think in decades, not days. Ask yourself: What kind of life do I want to live five, ten, twenty years from now? Then build streams that support that vision. Long-term thinking turns short-term effort into lasting impact.

5. Align Streams with Your Strengths and Passions

The best income streams aren't just profitable, they're sustainable. And sustainability comes from alignment. When your income reflects your strengths, passions, and values, it energizes you. You're more likely to stick with it, improve it, and grow it.

If you love writing, consider digital publishing. If you're great with people, explore coaching or consulting. If you're analytical, look into investing or data-driven businesses. Your income should feel like an extension of who you are not a drain on your spirit.

3.4 Reflection

Building multiple income streams is not about chasing money endlessly, it's about designing a life of stability, freedom, and choice. Each stream you create is another layer of security, another step toward independence. Begin with one, nurture it, and then add another. Over time, you'll find yourself standing not on one fragile leg, but on a strong foundation supported by many.

Napoleon Hill, in his timeless classic Think and Grow Rich, argued that definiteness of purpose is the starting point of all achievement. His research into the habits of successful people revealed that wealth was rarely the result of chance it was the product of intentional design. Multiple income streams reflect that principle: they are not random pursuits, but deliberate strategies aligned with a clear vision.

David Bach, author of The Automatic Millionaire, demonstrated how ordinary individuals could build wealth by automating their savings and investments. His achievement lies in showing that financial growth doesn't require extraordinary talent it requires systems. When you create multiple income streams, you are essentially building systems that work for you, even when you're not actively paying attention.

Grant Cardone, in the 10X Rule, pushes readers to expand their thinking and scale their efforts. He insists that extraordinary results demand extraordinary action. His philosophy reminds us that one stream of income is rarely enough to achieve big goals. Diversification is not just a financial tactic, it's a mindset of expansion, resilience, and abundance.

Barbara Huson (formerly Stanny), in Secrets of Six-Figure Women, highlighted how women who broke income barriers often did so by cultivating multiple avenues of earning consulting, speaking, writing, and investing. Her achievement was not only documenting these stories but proving that diversification is a path to empowerment, especially for those who have historically been excluded from wealth-building conversations.

Chris Guillebeau, author of the $100 Startup and Side Hustle, has shown through hundreds of case studies that anyone can create additional streams of income without massive capital. His achievement lies in democratizing entrepreneurship proving that you don't need to quit your job or raise millions in funding to diversify your income. You can start small; with skills and passions you already have.

Together, these voices affirm a timeless truth: wealth is not an accident. It is the result of clarity, discipline, and diversification. Each author, in their own way, has shown that multiple streams of income are not reserved for the elite and they are accessible to anyone willing to take consistent, intentional steps.

So begin today. Write down your vision. Identify one new stream you can start whether it's a side hustle, an investment, or a creative project. Nurture it, and when it grows, add another. Over time, you'll discover that wealth is not about chasing money, it's about aligning your resources with your values, your dreams, and your purpose. That is the true foundation of lasting prosperity.

Chapter 4: Creating a Practical Budget

4.1 Introduction: Budgeting builds resilience

A budget is not a cage, it's a compass. It doesn't restrict your freedom; it directs it. Without a budget, money slips through your fingers unnoticed. With one, every pound has a purpose, and every decision moves you closer to your financial goals.

Think of a budget as the architect's blueprint before a house is built. Without it, you may gather bricks, wood, and cement, but the structure will be unstable. In the same way, you can earn money, spend it, and even save sporadically, but without a budget, your financial life lacks structure. A budget provides clarity, showing you not only where your money is going but also where it should be going.

Many people resist budgeting because they see it as restrictive, a constant reminder of what they cannot do. But the truth is the opposite. The budget is liberating. It allows you to spend with confidence, knowing that your essentials are covered, your goals are funded, and your lifestyle choices are intentional. As Dave Ramsey, author of The Total Money Makeover, often says: "A budget is telling your money where to go instead of wondering where it went."

The psychology of budgeting is powerful. When you assign every pound a role, you reduce anxiety and increase control. Suddenly, financial decisions become easier. Should you splurge on a new gadget or put that money toward your savings goal? The answer is clear when your budget is clear.

Budgeting also builds resilience. Life will throw unexpected expenses your way a car repair, a medical bill, or a sudden job change. Without a budget, these moments feel like crises. With one, they become manageable setbacks. John C. Maxwell, in Today Matters, reminds us that daily disciplines shape long-term success. Budgeting is one of those disciplines: small, consistent choices that compound into financial stability.

This chapter will guide you through practical tools to make budgeting simple and sustainable. You'll see templates that fit everyday life, stories of real people who turned setbacks into breakthroughs, and monthly tracking tables you can adapt to your own situation. Whether you're just starting out or refining your financial strategy, the goal is the same: to give you a clear, practical system that aligns your spending with your values and your vision.

Budgeting is not about perfection it's about progress. It's not about restriction it's about direction. And once you embrace it, you'll discover that a budget is not a burden but a bridge: a bridge between where you are today and the financial future you want to build.

4.2 Simple Templates for Everyday Use

Budgeting doesn't have to be complicated. In fact, the simpler the system, the more likely you are to stick with it. A budget should feel like a tool you can use every day not a spreadsheet so complex it gathers digital dust. Below are three tried-and-tested templates that ordinary people have used to transform their finances.

One of the biggest myths about money management is that it requires complex spreadsheets, financial jargon, or hours of number crunching. The truth is that most people don't need a finance degree, they need a system that's simple, flexible, and easy to apply in real life. A budget should feel like a tool you can use every day not a burden that adds more stress.

That's why this chapter introduces three practical budgeting templates that have helped countless individuals take control of their finances. These aren't abstract theories they're real-world systems that work because they're grounded in clarity and consistency. Let's begin with one of the most popular and effective: the 50/30/20 Rule.

The 50/30/20 Rule

The 50/30/20 Rule is a straightforward budgeting framework that divides your after-tax income into three main categories:

• 50% Needs

These are your essentials, the non-negotiables that keep your life running. Think of rent or mortgage, utilities, groceries, transportation, insurance, and minimum loan payments. If you stopped paying for these, your basic stability would be at risk.

• 30% Wants

This is where lifestyle lives. Dining out, streaming services, travel, hobbies, shopping, and entertainment all fall into this category. These aren't essential for survival, but they add joy, comfort, and personality to your life.

• 20% Savings and Debt Repayment

This is your wealth-building zone. It includes contributions to your emergency fund, retirement accounts, investments, and any extra payments toward debt. This category is what moves you forward financially, it's where your future lives.

Why It Works

The beauty of the 50/30/20 Rule lies in its simplicity. You don't need to track every single transaction. Instead, you focus on the big picture: are you living within your means, enjoying life, and still building for the future? It's also flexible. If you're in a season where your needs take up more than 50%, you can adjust temporarily. If you're aggressively paying off debt, you might shift more into the 20% category. The rule gives you structure without rigidity.

Real-Life Example

Let's say your monthly take-home pay is £2,000:

• £1,000 goes to needs

• £600 goes to wants

• £400 goes to savings and debt repayment

Even if your income is lower or higher, the proportions help you stay balanced. And if you're starting from zero, this rule gives you a clear, empowering path forward—one that doesn't overwhelm but invites progress. In the next sections, we'll explore two more templates—Zero-Based Budgeting and the Envelope System—each offering a different approach depending on your personality, goals, and financial habits. But if you're looking for a place to start, the 50/30/20 Rule is a powerful first step.

Zero-Based Budgeting: Giving Every Pound a Purpose

If the 50/30/20 Rule is about simplicity, Zero-Based Budgeting is about precision. It's a method that asks you to be intentional with every pound you earn assigning it a job, a destination, and a reason to exist in your financial life.

The core idea is simple:

4.3 Your income minus your expenses should equal zero.

That doesn't mean you spend everything. It means you plan for everything. Every pound is accounted for whether it's going toward rent, groceries, savings, debt repayment, or even fun money. Nothing is left floating. Nothing is wasted.

How It Works At the start of each month (or pay period), you write down your total income. Then, you list every expense you expect including fixed costs, variable costs, savings goals, and debt payments. You keep adjusting until your income minus expenses equals zero.

Here's a simplified example:

Let's say your monthly income is £2,000. You might allocate it like this:
• Rent: £800
• Utilities: £150
• Groceries: £250
• Transportation: £100
• Debt repayment: £200
• Emergency fund: £100
• Entertainment: £100
• Giving: £50
• Personal care: £50
• Miscellaneous: £100
Total: £2,000
Every pound has a purpose. Nothing is left unassigned.
Why It Works
Zero-Based Budgeting is powerful because it forces clarity. You're not guessing where your money went you're telling it where to go. It helps you:
• Avoid overspending by making sure you don't spend more than you earn.
• Prioritize goals like saving, investing, or paying off debt.
• Spot leaks in your spending that you might otherwise miss.
• Feel in control, even if your income is modest or irregular.
This method is especially helpful for people who feel like money "disappears" each month. It brings structure to chaos and turns vague intentions into concrete plans.

Real-Life Benefits
Many people who switch to Zero-Based Budgeting report feel more confident, less stressed, and more empowered. It's not just about numbers, it's about mindset. You stop reacting to your finances and start leading them.
If you're starting from zero, this method can be a game-changer. It teaches discipline, builds awareness, and helps you make progress even if your income is limited. You'll begin to see money as a tool, not a mystery.

Tips for Getting Started
• Use a notebook, spreadsheet, or budgeting app whatever feels natural.
• Review your budget weekly to stay on track.
• Be honest about your spending habits.
• Adjust as needed life changes, and your budget should too.
Zero-Based Budgeting isn't rigid, it's responsive. It meets you where you are and helps you move forward with purpose. When every pound has a job, your money starts working for you not the other way around.

4.4 The Envelope Method

This classic system, once done with physical envelopes, now thrives in digital apps. You divide your money into categories groceries, transport, leisure and once the envelope is empty, spending stops.
Example: A couple, David and Aisha, struggled with overspending on groceries. They set aside £300 in a "groceries" envelope. By week three, they had only £40 left, which forced them to meal-plan creatively. Not only did they stay within budget, but they also reduced food waste.

The Envelope Method: Spending with Intention
Before budgeting apps and digital dashboards, people managed their money with paper envelopes. Each envelope represented a spending category groceries, transport, entertainment, clothing and cash was physically placed inside. Once the envelope was empty, spending stopped. It was simple, visual, and effective.

Today, the Envelope Method has evolved. While some still use physical envelopes, many now rely on digital tools that replicate the same principle. Whether you're using cash or an app, the core idea remains: assign your money to specific categories and stick to those limits.

How It Works
At the start of each month (or pay period), you decide how much money to allocate to each category. You might have envelopes for:
• Groceries
• Transportation
• Dining out
• Entertainment
• Clothing
• Personal care
• Giving
• Miscellaneous

Each envelope gets a set amount based on your income and priorities. As you spend, you subtract from that envelope's balance. When it's empty, you stop spending time in that category until the next cycle.
This method creates built-in accountability. You're not just tracking expenses you're actively managing them. It helps prevent impulse purchases and encourages thoughtful decision-making.
Real-Life Example: David and Aisha, a young couple living in London, struggled with overspending on groceries. They'd often shop without a plan, buy in bulk, and end up wasting food. Their monthly grocery bill was unpredictable and often exceeded £400.
They decided to try the Envelope Method. They set aside £300 in a "groceries" envelope digitally tracked through a budgeting app. By week three, they had only £40 left. Instead of panicking, they got creative. They planned meals around what they already had, skipped unnecessary purchases, and even discovered new recipes using leftover ingredients.
Not only did they stay within budget, but they also reduced food waste and felt more in control. The envelope didn't just limit their spending it empowered their choices.

Why It Works
• Visual clarity: Whether physical or digital, seeing your envelope balance helps you stay mindful.
• Immediate feedback: You know exactly how much is left in each category.
• Behavioral reinforcement: It trains you to pause before spending and ask, "Is this in the envelope?"
• Customizable: You can create envelopes for any category that matters to your travel, kids, subscriptions, even date nights.

Tips for Success
• Start with 4–6 key categories to avoid overwhelm.
• Use budgeting apps like good budget, YNAB, or even simple spreadsheets.
• Review your envelopes weekly to stay on track.
• Be flexible if one envelope runs low, you can reallocate from another (with intention).
• Celebrate small wins staying within budget is progress worth acknowledging.

The Envelope Method is more than a budgeting tool it's a mindset shift. It teaches you to spend with intention, plan with purpose, and live within your means without feeling deprived. Whether you're starting from zero or refining your financial habits, this method offers structure, clarity, and control.

4.5 Why These Templates Work

Each of these methods shares a common principle: clarity. They help you see where your money is going and

make trade-offs visible. Instead of vague guilt about "spending too much," you know exactly which category is being stretched.
The key is not to find the "perfect" template but the one you'll actually use. Some people thrive on the flexibility of the 50/30/20 rule. Others prefer the discipline of zero-based budgeting. And for those who need a tactile reminder, the envelope method is powerful.
Note:
Budgeting is not about restriction, it's about direction. Whether you choose percentages, zero-based planning, or envelopes, the goal is the same: to give every pound a purpose. Once you do, you'll discover that budgeting isn't a burden, it's a tool for freedom
Stories of Budgeting Setbacks and Breakthroughs
Emma's Setback:
Emma earned a good salary but never tracked her spending. She often wondered, "Where did my money go?" When an unexpected medical bill arrived, she had no savings to cover it. The setback forced her to confront her habits. She started using the 50/30/20 rule, and within six months, she had built a £2,000 emergency fund.
David's Breakthrough:
David was drowning in credit card debt. He felt budgeting was too restrictive, but he tried the zero-based method. By assigning every pound a purpose, he discovered he was overspending on subscriptions and eating out. Redirecting that money, he paid off £5,000 of debt in 18 months. His breakthrough wasn't just financial, it was emotional. He felt in control for the first time in years.

These stories remind us that budgeting is not about perfection. It's about progress.

4.6 Reflection:

As John C. Maxwell once said: "You will never change your life until you change something you do daily." Budgeting is that daily discipline. It transforms vague intentions into measurable progress.
Remember: a budget is not about restriction, it's about direction. It's the bridge between your financial goals and your daily choices. Start simple, stay consistent, and let your budget become the compass that guides you toward freedom.
Think of it this way: every pound you earn is like a worker waiting for instructions. Without a budget, those workers wander aimlessly, some wasted, some misused. With a budget, each one is assigned a task some build your safety net, some pay down debt, some invest in your future, and yes, some are allowed to bring joy through leisure and experiences. The difference is intentionality.
Consider the person who earns well but never tracks spending. At the end of each month, they feel drained, wondering where the money went. Contrast that with someone who earns the same amount but follows a simple plan. They know exactly how much went to essentials, how much was saved, and how much was enjoyed. The second person doesn't necessarily earn more, but they live with more peace, clarity, and control.
Budgeting also creates resilience. Life will always bring surprises, an unexpected bill, sudden repair, or a change in income. Without a plan, these moments feel like crises. With a plan, they become manageable detours. A budget doesn't eliminate challenges, but it equips you to face them with confidence.
Ultimately, budgeting is not about numbers, it's about values. It's about aligning your money with what matters most: security, freedom, family, growth, or legacy. When you see your budget as a reflection of your priorities, it stops being a chore and becomes a tool of empowerment.
So begin today. Write it down. Track it. Adjust it. Let your budget be the quiet daily habit that shapes your tomorrow. Over time, you'll discover that freedom is not found in spending without limits, but in spending with purpose.

Chapter 5: Managing Debt Wisely

5.1 Introduction: Offloading Your Backpack

Debt can feel like carrying a heavy backpack filled with stones. At first, the weight seems manageable you sling it over your shoulders and keep walking. A credit card here, a small loan there, maybe a car payment. You tell yourself, "I can handle this." But as time passes, the stones multiply. Interest adds another rock, late fees slip in like pebbles, and soon the backpack digs into your shoulders. Every step forward feels harder than the last.
For some, debt feels less like a backpack and more like quicksand. At first, you're standing upright, confident you can get out. But the longer you ignore it, the deeper you sink. Each minimum payment feels like a small tug upward, but the sand keeps pulling you down. The harder you struggle without a plan, the more exhausting it becomes.

This is the hidden truth about debt: it is not just a financial issue it is an emotional one. Numbers on a page are only part of the story. Debt whispers in the quiet moments, reminding you of obligations not yet met. It can erode confidence, strain relationships, and cloud your vision of the future. Some people avoid opening bank statements out of fear. Others feel guilty spending on even small pleasures, like a coffee with a friend, because the shadow of debt looms over every choice.

Yet, debt does not have to define you. Like any heavy load, it can be unpacked, stone by stone, until the weight is gone. The key is not to ignore it because ignoring debt is like ignoring a leak in your roof. The longer you wait, the more damage it causes. The key is to face it with clarity, strategy, and persistence.

Before diving into strategies, it's important to acknowledge the emotional toll debt takes. Many people carry shame, as if owing money makes them irresponsible or unworthy. But debt is not a moral failing, it is a circumstance. Sometimes it comes from choices, yes, but often it comes from life itself: medical bills, job loss, family emergencies, or simply not being taught how to manage money.

The danger lies not in having debt but in letting it control your mindset. When you see debt as a permanent identity "I'll always be in debt" you give away your power. But when you see it as a temporary challenge, you reclaim control.

Psychologists note that progress, even small progress, reduces anxiety. Paying off a single small debt can feel like lifting a stone from your backpack. That sense of relief fuels momentum. This is why strategies like the snowball method (paying off the smallest debts first) are so effective not because they save the most money mathematically, but because they build confidence emotionally.

Debt as a Turning Point

Every debt story has a turning point. It's the moment when someone decides, "Enough is enough." For some, it's the embarrassment of a declined card at the checkout line. For others, it's the stress of avoiding phone calls from creditors. And for many, it's the quiet realization that they are working hard but not moving forward.

Imagine someone sitting at their kitchen table late at night, bills spread out in front of them. The numbers don't add up. The paycheck is already spoken for before it even arrives. They feel trapped. But then, instead of pushing the papers aside, they take a deep breath and say, "I need a plan." That moment though small is the beginning of freedom.

Debt management is not about overnight miracles. It's about consistent, intentional steps. It's about choosing to face the numbers, to make a plan, and to stick with it even when progress feels slow.

5.2 The Purpose of This Chapter

This chapter is about more than repayment plans. It's about transformation. You'll learn practical strategies like the snowball and avalanche methods tools that give structure to the repayment journey. You'll encounter real stories of people who once felt crushed by debt but found their way to freedom. And you'll explore the emotional side of debt: how to overcome the shame, rebuild confidence, and create a healthier relationship with money.

The goal is not just to help you pay off what you own. The goal is to help you see debt differently not as a life sentence, but as a challenge you can overcome. By the end of this chapter, you'll have both the tools and the mindset to manage debt wisely and move toward financial freedom.

Why Managing Debt Matters

Debt is more than a financial inconvenience. It is a thief of opportunity. Every pound spent on interest is a pound that could have gone toward savings, investments, or experiences that enrich your life. Left unmanaged, debt delays dreams: the home you want to buy, the business you want to start, the freedom to travel or retire early.

But when you manage debt wisely, you reclaim those opportunities. You free up resources to build wealth instead of servicing interest. You shift from surviving to thriving.

Picture yourself without the backpack. No stones, no weight pulling you down. Imagine opening your bank app and seeing a positive balance, not a list of debts. Imagine making choices whether to travel, invest, or give generously without the shadow of repayment hanging over you. That vision is not a fantasy. It is the future that wise debt management makes possible.

Debt may feel overwhelming, but it is not permanent. It is not who you are. It is simply where you are right now. And where you are is not where you must stay.

Managing debt wisely is not just about paying what you own it's about reclaiming your future. It's about shifting from a place of fear to a place of control, from being weighed down to walking freely. Whether your debt is large or small, old or new, the principles in this chapter will help you take the first step toward freedom and keep moving until the backpack is finally lifted.

5.3 Effective Debt Strategies: Snowball vs. Avalanche

When it comes to paying off debt, most people feel overwhelmed not by the numbers themselves but by the lack of a clear plan. Without strategy, debt feels like a tangled knot every tug only makes it tighter. But with the right method, the knot begins to loosen, and progress becomes visible. Two of the most widely used approaches are the Snowball Method and the Avalanche Method. Each has its strengths, and each appeal to a different kind of personality.

The Snowball Method: Building Momentum

The Snowball Method focuses on paying off the smallest debts first, regardless of interest rate. You make minimum payments on all debts but direct any extra money toward the smallest balance. Once that debt is cleared, you roll the freed-up payment into the next smallest debt, and so on.

The psychology behind this method is powerful. By eliminating small debts quickly, you experience early wins. Each clear balance is like a victory flag planted on the battlefield, boosting morale and proving that progress is possible.

Imagine someone juggling five debts: a £500 store card, a £1,200 credit card, a £3,000 personal loan, a £7,000 car loan, and a £15,000 student loan. Using the Snowball Method, they attack the £500 store card first. Within two months, it's gone. That sense of accomplishment fuels them to tackle the £1,200 credit card. Within a year, two debts are gone, and their confidence soars. The momentum keeps them going until the larger debts fall one by one.

The Snowball Method works best for people who need motivation and visible progress to stay consistent. It's less about mathematics and more about psychology.

The Avalanche Method takes a different approach. Instead of focusing on the smallest balance, you target the debt with the highest interest rate first. You still make minimum payments on all debts, but any extra money goes toward the costliest debt.

The advantage is clear: you save the most money in the long run. By reducing high-interest balances first, you minimize the total interest paid overtime.

Consider the same person with five debts. The store card has a 20% interest rate, the credit card 18%, the personal loan 10%, the car loan 6%, and the student loan 4%. Using the Avalanche Method, they attack the store card first, then the credit card, then the personal loan. Progress feels slower at first because the balances are larger, but over the years, they save thousands in interest compared to the Snowball approach.

The Avalanche Method works best for people motivated by logic and long-term savings. It requires patience and discipline, as the early wins may take longer to arrive.

Snowball vs. Avalanche: A Comparison

Both methods work. The "best" method is the one you'll stick with. Debt repayment is not just about numbers, it's about behavior. If quick wins keep you motivated, Snowball may be your path. If saving money is your top priority and you can stay disciplined, Avalanche may be better.

Some people combine the two methods. They start with the Snowball to build momentum, clearing a few small debts quickly. Once confidence is high, they switch to the Avalanche to save money on interest. This hybrid approach balances psychology with mathematics, offering the best of both worlds.

5.4 The Emotional Impact of Strategy

Choosing a strategy is not just about efficiency, it's about emotional alignment. Debt repayment is a long journey, and the method you choose must resonate with your personality.

- If you're someone who thrives on visible progress and needs encouragement, the Snowball will keep you engaged.
- If you're someone who values optimization and can stay focused on the bigger picture, the Avalanche will reward your patience.

The key is to avoid paralysis by analysis. Too many people spend months debating which method is "better" and never start. The truth is, both works. The real danger is inaction.

A Vision of Progress

Picture yourself six months from now. With the Snowball, you may have eliminated two or three small debts, feeling lighter and more confident. With the Avalanche, you may still be working on a larger balance, but you know you've saved hundreds in interest. In both cases, you're moving forward. The backpack is lighter, the quicksand less threatening.

Debt repayment is not about perfection, it's about persistence. Whether you choose Snowball, Avalanche, or a hybrid, the most important step is the first one.

Debt strategies are like maps. They don't walk the journey for you, but they show you the path. Snowball gives you quick victories to keep you motivated. The Avalanche saves you money and accelerates long-term freedom. Both lead to the same destination: a life no longer weighed down by debt.

The choice is yours. Pick the strategy that fits your personality, commit to it, and trust the process. Over time, the stones in your backpack will disappear, one by one, until you're walking freely toward the future you deserve.

5.5 Real-Life Debt Journey

Debt is not just numbers on a page; it's lived experience. Behind every balance sheet is a human story of stress, resilience, and eventual breakthrough. To understand how debt can be managed wisely, let's step into the journey of someone who faced overwhelming debt and found a way out.

The Beginning: Slipping Into Debt

At first, it didn't feel like debt at all. It felt like opportunity. A credit card offered "buy now, pay later." A car loan promised freedom of movement. A student loan seemed like an investment in the future. Each decision made sense in isolation. But over time, the balances grew.

The turning point came when the monthly payments began to outpace income. Minimum payments were made, but the balances barely moved. Interest piled on like invisible weight. What once felt like manageable obligations now felt like chains.

Emotionally, the toll was heavy. Anxiety crept in at night. Phone calls from creditors were ignored. Social invitations were declined because there was no money left for leisure. Debt had become more than a financial burden it was shaping identity. The thought was constant: "I'm drowning."

The Moment of Clarity

One evening, sitting at the kitchen table, the reality became unavoidable. Bills were spread out, and the numbers didn't add up. The paycheck was already spoken for before it even arrived. That night, instead of pushing the papers aside, a decision was made: "I need a plan."

This moment of clarity is common in debt journeys. It's shift from denial to determination. The debt hadn't disappeared, but the mindset had changed. And mindset is the first step toward freedom.

Choosing a Strategy

The next step was research. Two strategies stood out: the Snowball Method and the Avalanche Method.

- The Snowball promised quick wins by paying off the smallest debts first.
- The Avalanche promised long-term savings by tackling the highest interest rates.

The choice was personal. Motivation was needed more than mathematics. The Snowball Method was chosen. The smallest debt, a £600 store card was attacked first. Every spare pound went toward it. Within two months, it was gone. The sense of relief was enormous. For the first time in years, debt was eliminated. That victory created momentum.

The Climb: Setbacks and Persistence

Progress was not linear. There were setbacks. A car repair wiped out a month's progress. The holiday season brought temptation to overspend. But the plan remained. Each time, adjustments were made, cutting back on dining out, selling unused items online, finding freelance work to boost income.

The key was persistence. Even when progress slowed, the direction was forward. Each cleared debt freed up more money to attack the next one. The snowball grew larger, rolling faster.

After two years, the transformation was remarkable. Four debts were gone. The only remaining balance was a student loan, now shrinking steadily. What once felt like drowning now felt like climbing out of a pit.

The breakthrough wasn't just financial, it was emotional. Confidence returned. Anxiety lessened. Relationships improved because the constant stress of money no longer dominated conversations. Debt had once been a source of shame; now, repayment was a source of pride.

5.6 Lessons from the Journey

This story illustrates several key truths:

- Debt is emotional as much as financial. Shame and fear can paralyze, but small wins restore hope.
- Strategy matters. Whether Snowball or Avalanche, having a plan creates direction.
- Progress is rarely perfect. Setbacks happen, but persistence is more powerful than perfection.

• Freedom is possible. No matter how heavy the backpack feels, it can be unpacked, stone by stone.

The Bigger Picture

Managing debt wisely is not just about paying balances. It's about reclaiming life. Each payment is not just money, leaving your account it's a step toward freedom, dignity, and opportunity.

The journey from debt to freedom is long, but it is also transformative. Along the way, you don't just change your finances, you change yourself. You become more disciplined, more resilient, and more intentional.

• Reinforce that debt does not define a person it's a challenge, not an identity.
• Encourage readers to take the first step, however small, and trust the process.
• End with a motivational reminder: managing debt wisely is not just about paying what you owe it's about creating space for the life you truly want.

5.7 Reflection

Debt does not define you. It is not who you are, it is simply a challenge you face. Too often, people wear debt like a label, as if the numbers in their bank account determine their worth. But debt is not an identity; it is a circumstance. And circumstances can change.

Think of someone carrying a heavy backpack filled with stones. Each stone represents a loan, a bill, or a credit card balance. At first, the weight feels unbearable. Shoulders ache, steps slow, and the journey ahead seems impossible. But then, one stone is removed. The load feels lighter. Another stone is taken out, and suddenly the path seems clearer. Eventually, the backpack is empty, and the person stands taller, walking freely. The stones never defined them as they were simply burdens carried for a season.

The same is true for you. Debt may feel overwhelming, but it is not permanent. It is not a life sentence. It is a challenge that can be overcome, one step at a time.

The first step is often the hardest. It might be as simple as writing down all your debts on a single sheet of paper. It might be making one extra payment toward the smallest balance. It might be calling a creditor to negotiate a lower rate. These steps may feel small, but they are powerful. Each one is a declaration: "I am taking control."

Progress rarely comes in giant leaps. It comes in steady, consistent steps. And with each step, confidence grows. The fear that once held you back begins to fade, replaced by hope. The shame that once silenced you is replaced by pride in your persistence.

Managing debt wisely is not just about paying what you own, it's about creating space for the life you truly want. Imagine the freedom of opening your bank account and seeing money that belongs to you, not to creditors. Imagine saying yes to opportunities without the shadow of repayment hanging over you. Imagine building savings, investing in your future, or giving generously to causes you care about. That is the life debt management makes possible.

The journey will not always be easy. There will be setbacks, temptations, and moments of doubt. But remember this: every payment is not just money, leaving your account is a step toward freedom. Every sacrifice today is an investment in tomorrow.

So take the first step. Trust the process. Celebrate the small victories along the way. And never forget debt is not your identity. It is simply a chapter in your story, and you have the power to write the ending.

The life you want, the life of stability, freedom, and choice, is waiting on the other side of persistence. Keep walking. Keep believing. And one day, you'll look back and realize the backpack is gone, the quicksand is behind you, and the path ahead is wide open.

Chapter 6: Investing for Beginners

6.1 Breakdown of Investment Vehicles

Investing can feel intimidating at first glance. The jargon equities, bonds, ETFs, diversification can sound like a foreign language. But at its core, investing is simply the act of putting your money to work so it grows over time. Think of it as planting seeds in a garden. Some seeds sprout quickly, others take years, but with patience and care, they all contribute to a harvest.

The key is understanding the different "seeds" the investment vehicles available to you. Each has its own risk, reward, and role in your financial garden. Let's break them down.

6.2 Stocks (Equities)

Stocks are like planting fruit trees. They take time to grow, but once they mature, they can bear abundant fruit year after year. When you buy a stock, you own a small piece of a company. If the company grows, so does your share. Stocks can also pay dividends, which are, like seasonal harvests, small but steady rewards that can be reinvested to grow even more fruit over time.

Unlike savings accounts, which offer slow and predictable growth, stocks carry the potential for significant wealth creation. Historically, the stock market has delivered average annual returns of around 7–10% after inflation. That means money invested in stocks has the power to double roughly every decade, thanks to the magic of compounding. But this growth doesn't happen in a straight line. Prices can swing daily, sometimes dramatically, which is why stocks are considered high-risk in the short term.

Risk: High—prices can swing daily.
Reward: High—long-term growth potential.
Best For: Long-term goals (5+ years).

Why Stocks Matter

Stocks are the growth engine of most investment portfolios. They represent innovation, productivity, and the future of businesses across the globe. When you invest in stocks, you're not just buying paper you're buying into human creativity and enterprise. Whether it's a technology company developing new software, a healthcare firm creating life-saving treatments, or a retailer expanding worldwide, stocks allow you to participate in that growth.

Benjamin Graham, in *The Intelligent Investor*, famously described the stock market as a "voting machine" in the short run but a "weighing machine" in the long run. In other words, daily prices reflect emotions and speculation, but over time, the true value of a company shines through. This is why patience is essential.

The Ups and Downs

Imagine planting an apple tree. In the first year, it may look fragile, and storms may strip away leaves. You might even wonder if it will survive. But with time, roots deepen, branches strengthen, and fruit begins to appear. Stocks behave the same way. In the short term, markets can crash like in 2008 or during the 2020 pandemic. But investors who stayed the course and held their "trees" through the storms were rewarded with abundant harvests in the years that followed.

Dividends: The Seasonal Harvest

Some companies share profits with their shareholders in the form of dividends. These are like seasonal harvests from your fruit tree. You can enjoy them as income or reinvest them to plant more trees. Over decades, reinvested dividends can account for a large portion of total returns.

Practical Example

Suppose you invest £1,000 in a diversified stock index fund. If it grows at an average of 8% per year, in 30 years that £1,000 could grow to over £10,000. That's the power of compounding your money working for you while you sleep.

Reflection on Stocks

Owning stocks is more than a financial transaction, it's a declaration of belief. When you buy a share of a company, you're not just betting on numbers or charts. You're saying, I believe in this business. I believe in its future. I want to grow with it. That's the essence of stock investing: ownership with intention.

Stocks are the heartbeat of the market. They represent innovation, risk, resilience, and reward. And while they can be volatile in the short term, over the long term, they've historically been one of the most powerful engines of wealth creation. But to benefit from that power, you must approach stocks not as a gambler, but as a builder.

Think of stocks like seeds. Some sprout quickly; others take time. Some wither; others flourish. The key is not to chase every shiny seed, but to plant wisely, water consistently, and let time do its work. Legendary investor Warren Buffett once said, "The stock market is a device for transferring money from the impatient to the patient." Patience, then, is your greatest asset.

For beginners, the stock market can feel like a storm loud, unpredictable, and intimidating. But beneath the noise lies a rhythm. Companies rise and fall. Trends come and go. But those who invest with discipline, diversify their holdings, and stay the course tend to come out ahead. The goal isn't to time the market, it's to spend time in the market.

Start with what you understand. Invest in companies whose products you use, whose missions you admire, or whose industries you believe in. Read their annual reports. Follow their leadership. Learn their story. The more you understand what you own, the less likely you are to panic when prices fluctuate.

And yes, prices will fluctuate. That's the nature of stocks. But volatility is not the enemy emotion is. Fear and greed are the twin forces that derail most investors. The antidote? A clear plan, a long-term mindset, and a commitment to learning. When you invest in stocks, you're not just growing your money, you're growing your character.

Diversification is also key. Don't put all your eggs in one basket. Spread your investments across sectors, geography, and company sizes. This reduces risk and increases resilience. And remember you don't need to pick the next Amazon to succeed. A portfolio of solid, well-managed companies can quietly build wealth over time.

Finally, investing in stocks is a journey, not a sprint. There will be highs and lows, wins and losses. But if you stay grounded in your goals, informed in your decisions, and patient in your approach, the market can become a powerful ally in your wealth-building journey.

So take a deep breath. Step into the market with curiosity, courage, and care. You're not just buying stocks you're buying into the future. And with every share you own, you're shaping a legacy of growth, ownership, and possibility.

6.3 Bonds

Bonds are essentially loans you give to governments or corporations. In return, they promise to pay you interest over time and return your principal at maturity. If stocks are like planting fruit trees that can grow tall and bear abundant harvests, bonds are more like planting sturdy hedges. They may not grow as quickly or dramatically, but they provide structure, stability, and protection to your financial garden.

Unlike stocks, which can swing wildly in value from day to day, bonds are designed to provide steadier, more predictable returns. When you buy a bond, you know in advance how much interest you'll receive and when your money will be repaid. This makes bonds attractive to investors who value security and consistency.

- Risk: Lower than stocks, but not risk-free.

• Reward: Steady, predictable income.
•Time Horizon: Medium to long-term.

Why Bonds Matter
Bonds play a crucial role in balancing a portfolio. While stocks drive growth, bonds act as a cushion. When markets tumble, bonds often hold their value or even rise, softening the blow. This is why financial advisors often recommend a mix of stocks and bonds, tailored to your age, goals, and risk tolerance.
For example, a young investor might hold 80% stocks and 20% bonds, prioritizing growth. Someone nearing retirement might flip that ratio, holding more bonds to preserve wealth and generate income.

An Example of Practice
Imagine you purchase a government bond with a face value of £1,000 and an annual interest rate of 3%. Each year, you receive £30 in interest. At the end of the bond's term say, 10 years you get your £1,000 back. While this won't make you rich overnight, it provides stability, especially during turbulent times when stock markets are falling.
Corporate bonds work similarly, though they often pay higher interest rates than government bonds because they carry more risk. A well-established company might offer a 5% bond, while a smaller or riskier company might offer 7% or more to attract investors.

Author Insight
Burton Malkiel, in his classic book A Random Walk Down Wall Street, emphasized the importance of bonds in reducing volatility. He argued that bonds act as a stabilizer, smoothing out the ups and downs of stock market investing. While they may not deliver the same explosive growth as equities, their role is to provide peace of mind and steady income.

The Bigger Picture
Bonds are not about excitement they are about reassurance. They are the part of your portfolio that lets you sleep at night, knowing that not all your money is exposed to the storms of the stock market. For beginners, bonds may seem less glamorous, but they are essential for building a resilient financial foundation.
Just as a strong hedge protects a garden from harsh winds, bonds protect your wealth from the unpredictable gusts of the market.

6.4 Mutual Funds and ETFs

Mutual funds and exchange-traded funds (ETFs) pool money from many investors to buy a diversified basket of stocks, bonds, or other assets.
• Risk: Varies depending on what the fund holds.
• Reward: Diversification reduces risk compared to individual stocks.
• Time Horizon: Flexible, but best for long-term growth.
Example: An S&P 500 index fund invests in the 500 largest U.S. companies. Instead of betting on one company, you're betting on the overall economy.
Author Insight: John C. Bogle, founder of Vanguard and author of The Little Book of Common-Sense Investing, championed index funds. He argued that most investors are better off buying low-cost index funds and holding them for decades, rather than trying to beat the market.

Mutual Funds and ETFs
If stocks are like planting individual fruit trees, then mutual funds and exchange-traded funds (ETFs) are like planting an entire orchard at once. Instead of betting on the growth of a single tree, you spread your seeds across many, ensuring that even if one tree struggles, others will thrive. This built-in diversification is what makes funds such a powerful tool for beginners.

At their core, mutual funds and ETFs pool money from many investors to buy a basket of asset stocks, bonds, or a mix of both. By investing in one fund, you gain exposure to dozens, hundreds, or even thousands of companies.

This reduces the risk of relying on a single stock's performance and makes investing more accessible to those who don't want to research individual companies.

- Risk: Medium diversification lowers risk compared to single stocks, but funds still fluctuate with the market.
- Reward: Solid long-term growth potential, often matching the broader market.
- Best For: Beginners and long-term investors seeking simplicity and balance.

The Power of Index Funds

One of the most popular types of funds is the index fund, which simply tracks a market index like the S&P 500. Instead of trying to outsmart the market, index funds mirror it. Over time, this approach has consistently outperformed most actively managed funds.

John C. Bogle, founder of Vanguard and author of The Little Book of Common-Sense Investing, was a pioneer of index funds. He argued that keeping costs low and staying invested in the market was the surest path to wealth for ordinary investors. His philosophy was simple: "Don't look for the needle in the haystack. Just buy the haystack."

An Example in Practice

Imagine you invest £1,000 in an S&P 500 index ETF. That single purchase gives you exposure to 500 of the largest U.S. companies from technology giants to healthcare leaders. If one company struggles, others balance it out. Over decades, the overall market tends to rise, and your investment grows with it.

Why Funds Work for Beginners

Funds remove the pressure of picking winners. Instead of asking, "Which company will succeed?" you're asking, "Will the economy grow over time?" History shows that despite recessions and downturns; markets trend upward in the long run. By investing in funds, you align yourself with that growth.

6.4 Reflection on Funds

Mutual funds and ETFs are the gardener's shortcut to a thriving orchard. They offer diversification, simplicity, and long-term growth without requiring constant attention. For beginners, they are often the smartest first step into investing. As Burton Malkiel noted in A Random Walk Down Wall Street, broad diversification through index funds is one of the most reliable ways to build wealth steadily over time.

But let's go deeper.

Imagine your financial life as a garden. You could try to plant every seed by hand, monitor each one obsessively, and hope for the best. Or you could invest in a well-designed orchard system. That's what mutual funds and ETFs offer: a way to grow many things at once, with less stress and more stability. Instead of betting on a single stock or trend, you're spreading your roots across an entire ecosystem industry, sectors, even countries. That's diversification. And it's one of the most powerful tools in wealth-building.

For the everyday investor, this matters. You don't need to be a stock-picking genius. You don't need to time the market. You need a plan, a habit, and a vehicle that works while you sleep. Funds especially low-cost index funds and ETFs do just that. They track the market, mirror its long-term growth, and protect you from the volatility of any one company's fate.

There's also a psychological benefit. Investing can feel overwhelming. The news is noisy. Markets rise and fall. But when you invest in a diversified fund, you give yourself permission to zoom out. You're not reacting to daily headlines you're nurturing a long-term vision. You're not chasing hype you're building quietly, steadily, with intention.

And the best part? You don't need a fortune to begin. Many platforms allow you to start with as little as £50 or

£100. The key is consistency. Monthly contributions, no matter how small, compound over time. That's the magic of the orchard: it doesn't grow overnight, but it grows. And one day, you'll look up and realize you're standing in the shade of something you planted years ago.

Of course, not all funds are created equal. Fees matter. Transparency matters. Alignment with your goals matters. So do your homework. Choose funds that reflect your risk tolerance, time horizon, and values. But don't let complexity paralyze you. Start simple. Start now.

Because the truth is, wealth isn't built in bursts it's built in seasons. And funds are one of the most elegant ways to honour that rhythm. They reward patience. They reward discipline. They reward those who plant early and stay the course.

So plant the orchard. Water it consistently. Let time do the rest. Your future self will thank you not just for the money, but for the peace of mind that comes from knowing your wealth is growing, even when you're not watching.

6.5 Real Estate

Real estate is like planting a vineyard. It requires more effort and care than scattering seeds in a field, but if tended well, it can provide both a steady harvest and long-term appreciation. Unlike stocks or bonds, which exist on paper or in digital accounts, real estate is tangible—you can see it, touch it, and walk through it. That physical presence makes it appealing to many investors, especially beginners who want to feel a sense of ownership.

At its core, real estate investment means purchasing property with the expectation that it will generate income, appreciate in value, or both. This could be a single-family home rented out to tenants, a commercial building leased to businesses, or even land held for future development.

- Risk: Medium to high property values can fluctuate, and maintenance or vacancies can eat into profits.
- Reward: Dual benefit of rental income and long-term appreciation.
- Time Horizon: Long-term (10+ years).

Why Real Estate Appeals to Investors

Real estate has a unique psychological advantage: it feels "real." While stock prices can seem abstract, a property is concrete. You can drive by it, improve it, and directly influence its value through renovations or better management. This sense of control is empowering.

Additionally, real estate often provides two streams of return:

1. Cash Flow – rental income that arrives monthly, like grapes harvested each season.
2. Appreciation – the property's value increasing over time, like a vineyard becoming more valuable as it matures.

An Example in Practice

Imagine purchasing a small rental property for £150,000. You rent it out for £900 per month, covering the mortgage and expenses while leaving a modest profit. Over the years, you raise the rent gradually, increasing your cash flow. Meanwhile, the property itself appreciates in value. After 15 years, it might be worth £250,000 or more. You've benefited both from steady income and from long-term growth.

Of course, real estate is not without challenges. Tenants may miss payments, repairs can be costly, and property values can decline during economic downturns. But for those willing to manage these risks, the rewards can be substantial.

Robert Kiyosaki, in Rich Dad Poor Dad, emphasized real estate as a cornerstone of wealth building. He argued that assets like rental properties generate income while appreciating value, creating financial freedom.

Similarly, Gary Keller, in The Millionaire Real Estate Investor, highlighted that real estate offers leverage using borrowed money to control larger assets which can accelerate wealth if managed wisely.

Real estate also acts as a hedge against inflation. As the cost-of-living rises, so do rents and property values, helping investors preserve purchasing power. For many, real estate becomes not just an investment but a legacy something tangible to pass on to future generations.

Real estate is not a quick win; it's a long-term commitment. Like a vineyard, it requires patience, care, and resilience through seasons of drought and abundance. But for those willing to tend it, real estate can provide both steady harvests and lasting wealth.

6.6 Retirement Accounts

Retirement accounts are like planting oak trees. They take decades to mature, but once they do, they provide shade, shelter, and security for the rest of your life. Unlike other investments you might dip into along the way, retirement accounts are designed to grow quietly in the background, protected by tax advantages that accelerate their growth.

At their core, retirement accounts are simply containers. Inside them, you can hold stocks, bonds, mutual funds, ETFs, or even real estate, depending on the type of account. What makes them special is the way governments encourage long-term saving by offering tax breaks. These incentives are like fertilizer for your oak tree helping it grow faster than it would in ordinary soil.

- Risk: Varies depending on the investments chosen within the account.
- Reward: High, thanks to tax benefits and decades of compounding.
- Time Horizon: Long-term (until retirement).

Why Retirement Accounts Matter

The biggest advantage of retirement accounts is compounding. When your investments grow tax-deferred (or even tax-free in some cases), the snowball effect is magnified. For example, if you invest £200 a month into a retirement account earning an average of 7% annually, in 30 years you could have over £240,000. Without the tax advantages, that number would be significantly lower.

Retirement accounts also create discipline. Because they are designed to discourage early withdrawals, they help you resist the temptation to spend your long-term savings on short-term desires. This "lockbox" effect ensures that your future self is protected, even if your present self is tempted.

Imagine a young professional who begins contributing £150 a month to a retirement account at age 25. By age 65, assuming steady growth, that account could be worth more than half a million pounds. Contrast that with someone who waits until age 40 to start the later start means they would need to contribute nearly triple the amount each month to reach the same goal. The lesson is clear: time is the most powerful ingredient in retirement investing.

Tony Robbins, in Money: Master the Game, emphasized that retirement accounts are one of the most overlooked wealth-building tools. He explained that minimizing taxes and fees is just as important as maximizing returns. John Bogle, in The Little Book of Common-Sense Investing, echoed this by urging investors to use retirement accounts to hold low-cost index funds, letting compounding and time do the heavy lifting.

Retirement accounts are not just about money they are about freedom. They represent the ability to step away from work when you choose, not when circumstances force you. They are about dignity in later years, the ability to travel, to give generously, or simply to rest without financial anxiety.

Reflection on Retirement Accounts

Planting oak trees takes patience. You won't see results overnight, but decades later, you'll be grateful for the shade. Retirement accounts are the same. Start early, contribute consistently, and let time and tax advantages work in your favour. Your future self will thank you for the seeds you planted today.

Planting oak trees takes patience. You won't see results overnight, but decades later, you'll be grateful for the shade. Retirement accounts are the same. They don't offer instant gratification, but they offer something far more powerful: long-term security, dignity, and freedom.

In a world obsessed with speed, retirement planning asks you to slow down and think ahead. It's not about chasing the next big win it's about building something that lasts. When you contribute to a retirement account whether it's a pension, a SIPP, or an ISA you're not just saving money. You're investing in your future self. You're saying, I care enough about tomorrow to act today.

The beauty of retirement accounts lies in their structure. They're designed to reward consistency and time. Tax advantages like deferred taxes on growth or tax-free withdrawals act like fertilizer for your financial soil. Compound interest becomes your silent partner, quietly multiplying your contributions year after year. The earlier you start, the more powerful this effect becomes. Even small, regular deposits can grow into something substantial over decades.

But the real gift of retirement planning isn't just financial it's psychological. Knowing that you're building a safety net gives you peace of mind. It reduces anxiety about the future. It allows you to make career choices based on purpose, not panic. It gives you the confidence to weather life's storms, knowing that your roots run deep.

Of course, the journey isn't always smooth. Markets fluctuate. Life gets busy. There will be moments when skipping a contribution feels tempting. But remember oak trees don't grow by accident. They grow because someone planted them, protected them, and trusted the process. Your retirement account deserves the same care.

And it's never too late to start. While early contributions have the most time to grow, even those who begin later in life can benefit from focused, intentional saving. The key is to start where you are, with what you have, and build from there. Automate your contributions. Increase them gradually. Review your investments annually. And most importantly, stay the course.

Think of your retirement account as a legacy project. It's not just about funding your golden years it's about modelling wisdom for your children, reducing the burden on future generations, and creating space for joy, rest, and reinvention later in life. It's about arriving at the future with options, not regrets.

So plant the oak. Water it with discipline. Let time and tax advantages do their quiet work. One day, you'll sit beneath the shade of what you started today and you'll be grateful. Not just for the money, but for the foresight, the patience, and the love you showed your future self.

Because true wealth isn't just about what you earn it's about what you preserve, protect, and prepare for. And retirement accounts are one of the most powerful tools to do exactly that.

Commodities and Alternatives

These include gold, silver, oil, or even newer assets like cryptocurrencies. They are often used to diversify portfolios and hedge against inflation.

- Risk: High (prices can be volatile).
- Reward: Potential for gains, especially during economic uncertainty.
- Time Horizon: Short to medium-term, often as a hedge.

Gold often rises when stock markets fall, making it a "safe haven" asset. Cryptocurrencies, while highly volatile, have attracted investors seeking outsized returns.

In Unshakeable, Tony Robbins noted that while alternative assets can play a role, they should never dominate a beginner's portfolio. They are spices, not the main meal.

6.7 Bringing It All Together

For beginners, the goal is not to master every investment vehicle at once. It's to understand the basics and start small. Investing is a journey, not a sprint, and the most successful investors are those who begin with simple steps and build consistency over time. Most experts agree that a straightforward, diversified portfolio often built around low-cost index funds outperforms complex strategies that try to outsmart the market. Complexity may look impressive, but simplicity wins in the long run.

The authors we've mentioned throughout this chapter Benjamin Graham, Burton Malkiel, John Bogle, Robert Kiyosaki, and Tony Robbins come from different backgrounds and eras, yet they all echo a similar truth: investing is not about chasing quick wins. It's about patience, discipline, and consistency.

- Benjamin Graham taught us to focus on value, not speculation. In The Intelligent Investor, he warned against being swayed by market moods, reminding us that the market is a "voting machine" in the short term but a "weighing machine" in the long term. His lesson is clear: don't gamble, invest with purpose.
- Burton Malkiel, in A Random Walk Down Wall Street, reminded us that markets are unpredictable. No one can consistently time them. His solution? Diversification. By spreading your investments across many assets, you protect yourself from the inevitable ups and downs.
- John Bogle, the father of index funds, showed that low-cost index investing is the simplest and most effective path to wealth. His mantra was "don't look for the needle in the haystack just buy the haystack." For beginners, this means you don't need to pick the next Apple or Amazon; you can own the whole market.
- Robert Kiyosaki, in Rich Dad Poor Dad, highlighted the power of assets that generate income. He encouraged people to think differently about money not just working for it, but letting it work for you. Real estate, businesses, and investments that produce cash flow can create long-term freedom.
- Tony Robbins, in Money: Master the Game, emphasized minimizing fees and taxes to maximize growth. He argued that what you keep matters more than what you earn. Even small reductions in costs can add up to huge differences over decades.

Together, their insights form a roadmap for beginners: start simple, stay consistent, and let time and compounding do the heavy lifting. The beauty of investing is that you don't need to be perfect. You don't need to predict the next market crash or the next big winner. You simply need to commit to the process, keep learning, and stay the course.

Think of it like planting a garden. You don't need to plant every seed at once or know exactly how each plant will grow. You just need to start with a few, water them regularly, and trust that with time, the garden will flourish.

The same is true with investing. Begin with what you understand, keep costs low, diversify, and give your investments time to grow. Over the years, the small, steady steps you take today will transform into the financial freedom you desire tomorrow.

6.8 Reflection

By now, you've walked through the garden of investment vehicles stocks, bonds, mutual funds, ETFs, real estate, retirement accounts, and even commodities. Each one has its own rhythm, its own risks and rewards, and its own role in shaping a healthy financial future. For beginners, the goal is not to master every single option at once. It's to understand the basics, choose a starting point, and begin planting seeds.

The truth is, investing doesn't reward complexity and rewards consistency. Many new investors feel pressure to chase the "perfect" strategy or to predict the next big winner. But history shows that a simple, diversified portfolio often built around low-cost index funds outperforms most complicated approaches over time. Simplicity is not a weakness; it's a strength.

The wisdom of great financial thinkers reinforces this. Benjamin Graham, in The Intelligent Investor, urged us to focus on value and discipline rather than speculation. He reminded us that the market's daily swings are like mood changes loud but fleeting. What matters is the long-term weight of a company's true value.

Burton Malkiel, in A Random Walk Down Wall Street, emphasized that markets are unpredictable. No one can consistently time them. His advice was to diversify broadly, spreading risk across many assets so that no single downturn can derail your future.

John Bogle, the father of index funds, simplified investing millions. In The Little Book of Common-Sense

Investing, he showed that low-cost index funds are the most reliable path to wealth. His mantra was simple: "Don't look for the needle in the haystack just buy the haystack."

Robert Kiyosaki, in Rich Dad Poor Dad, shifted the conversation by highlighting the power of assets that generate income. He encouraged people to think differently about money not just working for it, but letting it work for you. Real estate, businesses, and investments that produce cash flow can create long-term freedom.

Tony Robbins, in Money: Master the Game, reminded us that what you keep matters more than what you earn. By minimizing fees and taxes, you allow compounding to work at full strength. Even small savings in costs can add up to massive differences over decades.

Together, these voices form a roadmap for beginners:

- Start simple.
- Stay consistent.
- Diversify wisely.
- Keep costs low.
- Let time and compounding do the heavy lifting.

Think of your portfolio as a garden. You don't need to plant every seed at once, nor do you need to know exactly how each plant will grow. You simply need to start with a few, water them regularly, and trust the process. Over time, the garden flourishes not because of frantic effort, but because of steady care.

The same is true with investing. Begin with what you understand, commit to regular contributions, and resist the urge to chase quick wins. Your future wealth will not be built in a single season but over many years of patient growth.

This is the essence of investing for beginners: clarity over confusion, discipline over impulse, and long-term vision over short-term noise.

Part Two: Growing and Scaling Wealth

Chapter 7: Harnessing the Power of Networks

7.1 Introduction

Wealth is rarely a solo achievement. Behind every thriving business, career, or investment portfolio lies a web of relationships mentors who guide, peers who challenge, collaborators who share the load, and supporters who open doors. The myth of the "self-made" individual often overlooks the invisible scaffolding of networks that make success possible.

At its core, networking is not about collecting business cards or adding connections on LinkedIn. It's about how you show up, contribute, and create value in the lives of others. True networks are built on trust, generosity, and reciprocity. They are less about who you know and more about how you engage.

Think of wealth as a tree. Your skills, knowledge, and discipline form the trunk, but the branches the opportunities, partnerships, and resources grow outward through your relationships. Without those branches, the tree cannot spread wide or bear fruit. Networks are the ecosystem that allows your financial and personal growth to flourish.

Opportunities often flow through people, not just through markets or systems. A new job offer, an investment tip, a business partnership, or even a life-changing introduction usually comes from someone in your circle. This is why networks are sometimes called "social capital." Just as financial capital compounds when invested wisely, social capital compounds when nurtured with care.

Keith Ferrazzi, in Never Eat Alone, argues that success is built not on transactions but on generosity. When you help others without expecting immediate returns, you create goodwill that often circles back in unexpected ways. The most powerful networks are not built on self-interest but on shared growth.

Why Networks Accelerate Wealth

- Access to Opportunities: Many of the best opportunities are never advertised, they're shared within trusted circles.
- Knowledge Sharing: Networks expose you to new ideas, strategies, and perspectives that you might not encounter alone.
- Support in Setbacks: During downturns or failures, networks provide encouragement, advice, and sometimes financial lifelines.
- Credibility and Trust: Being recommended or introduced by someone respected in your field can accelerate your progress far faster than going alone.

Reid Hoffman, co-founder of LinkedIn, describes networks as "living ecosystems." They are dynamic, constantly evolving, and require ongoing care. Just as you wouldn't plant a garden and walk away, you can't build a network and neglect it. Relationships thrive on attention, authenticity, and consistency.

In the pages ahead, we'll explore three key dimensions of harnessing networks for wealth:

1. Professional and Personal Networks that Build Wealth – how to identify, nurture, and balance the circles

that matter most.
2. The Art of Making Introductions – why connecting others is one of the most powerful ways to strengthen your own influence.
3. Tips for Strategic Relationship Building – practical, actionable steps to grow your network authentically and sustainably.
This chapter is not about manipulation or superficial charm. It's about cultivating genuine relationships that enrich both sides. When you approach networking as a way to serve, contribute, and connect, wealth becomes a shared journey rather than a solitary climb.
As the African proverb reminds us: "If you want to go fast, go alone. If you want to go far, go together." Wealth, in its truest sense, is not just measured in money but in the strength of the relationships that sustain and multiply it. By learning to harness the power of networks, you're not just building wealth you're building a legacy of connection, trust, and shared success.

7.2 Professional and Personal Networks that Build Wealth

Wealth is not just built through spreadsheets and strategy it's built through people. Behind every successful entrepreneur, investor, or professional career is a constellation of relationships that shaped their path. These networks professional and personal are often the hidden engine behind financial growth. They provide access, insight, support, and leverage. And for beginners, they offer something even more valuable: momentum.

The Two Pillars of Connection

Let's begin by distinguishing the two primary types of networks:
• **Professional Networks** include colleagues, mentors, industry peers, clients, collaborators, and even competitors. These relationships are forged through shared work, mutual goals, and aligned expertise. They open doors to new opportunities, offer insider knowledge, and help you stay relevant in a fast-changing world.
• **Personal Networks** include friends, family, neighbors, community members, and social circles. These relationships are built on trust, history, and emotional connection. While they may not always speak the language of business, they often provide the first referrals, the early encouragement, and the safety net when things go wrong.
The most powerful networks blend both. A mentor becomes a friend. A cousin becomes a business partner. A former colleague becomes a co-founder. The key is to nurture both sides with equal respect and intentionality.
Social Capital: The Hidden Currency
In the world of wealth-building, relationships are a form of capital often called social capital. Just as financial capital can be invested, grown, and leveraged, so can social capital. When you build trust, offer help, and show up consistently, you create a reservoir of goodwill. That goodwill often returns in the form of referrals, introductions, collaborations, and unexpected opportunities.

Keith Ferrazzi, in Never Eat Alone, writes:
He emphasizes that networking is not about manipulation, it's about generosity. When you help others succeed, you build a reputation that attracts opportunity. The most valuable relationships are not transactional, they're transformational.

Real-Life Story: Amara's Network Effect

Consider Amara, a freelance designer in her late twenties. She had talent but struggled to find consistent work. Cold emails went unanswered. Online ads drained her budget. She felt stuck.

Instead of chasing clients, Amara shifted her focus to building relationships. She began attending local creative meetups, offering free design tips on social media, and volunteering her skills for community projects. She didn't pitch she contributed.
Over time, people noticed. A marketer she met at a meetup referred to her to a startup. A nonprofit she

volunteered for recommended her to a corporate sponsor. Within a year, Amara had tripled her income not through ads or algorithms, but through relationships.
Her story illustrates a powerful truth: networks multiply your reach. One connection led to another. One act of generosity creates a ripple. And over time, those ripples become waves.

Professional Networks: Building with Purpose
To build wealth through professional networks, you need to be intentional. Here are key strategies:
• Show Up Where Value Is Shared: Attend industry events, join online communities, participate in webinars, and engage in forums where your expertise can shine. Don't just consume contribute.
• Seek Mentors and Peers: Mentors offer wisdom, while peers offer collaboration. Both are essential. Reach out with humility, ask thoughtful questions, and express genuine interest in their journey.
• Follow Up Thoughtfully: After meeting someone, send a message that reflects something specific you appreciated. Mention a shared interest or offer a resource. This builds connection beyond the initial encounter.
• Be a Connector: Introduce people who could benefit from knowing each other. When you become known as someone who creates value through connection, your own network deepens.
Reid Hoffman, co-founder of LinkedIn and author of The Start-Up of You, describes networks as "living ecosystems." They require care, attention, and authenticity. You don't build a network by showing up only when you need something. You build it by being present, generous, and curious day after day.

Personal Networks: The Power of Trust
While professional networks often provide access, personal networks provide trust. These are the people who know your character, your story, and your values. They may not be experts in your field, but they are often your first believers.
• Start Close to Home: Share your goals with friends and family. You never know who they know. A cousin might work at a company you admire. A friend might have contact in your target industry.
• Be Transparent: Let people know what you're working on and where you need support. Vulnerability builds connection. It invites others to help.
• Celebrate and Acknowledge: When someone supports you whether through advice, a referral, or encouragement, thank them publicly. Gratitude strengthens bonds.
• Don't Overlook Community: Local groups, faith communities, and social clubs often contain untapped potential. These spaces are built on trust, and trust is the foundation of opportunity.
Robert Kiyosaki, in Rich Dad Poor Dad, emphasizes that wealth is built through assets that generate income. But he also notes that relationships often determine how quickly and effectively those assets are acquired. Your personal network may be the bridge to your first investor, your first customer, or your first collaborator.
Building networks that generate wealth is not a one-time effort, it's a long game. It requires patience, consistency, and a mindset of contribution. Here are some guided principles:
• Give First, Ask Later: Offer help, insight, or introductions before asking for Favors. This creates goodwill and reciprocity.
• Diversify Your Circles: Don't limit yourself to people in your field. Cross-industry connections often spark the most innovative opportunities.
• Stay in Touch: Relationships fade without attention. A simple message, coffee catch-up, or congratulatory note keeps connections alive.
• Be Curious, Not Calculating: Ask questions, listen deeply, and engage with genuine interest. People can sense when you're only networking for gain.

• Invest in Depth, Not Just Breadth: A few strong relationships are more valuable than dozens of shallow ones. Focus on quality over quantity.
Burton Malkiel, in A Random Walk Down Wall Street, reminds us that markets are unpredictable.

Diversification is key. The same applies to networks. A diverse, well-tended network acts as a buffer against uncertainty and a catalyst for growth.
Your network is not just a list of names, it's a living web of trust, insight, and opportunity. When you invest in people, you're investing in your future. The relationships you nurture today may become the bridges to your next breakthrough.
Whether you're just starting out or scaling your wealth, remember this: people are the greatest asset you'll ever invest in. They offer wisdom, encouragement, and access to worlds you couldn't reach alone.
So show up. Contribute. Connect. And let your network become the soil in which your financial future takes root and flourishes.

7.3 The Art of Making Introductions

Introductions are the lifeblood of strong networks. They are small gestures with outsized impact bridges between people who might never have met, but who, through your thoughtfulness, discover mutual value. Whether you're connecting a friend to a mentor, a colleague to a potential client, or two strangers with shared interests, the act of introducing is one of the most generous and strategic moves you can make.
Yet many people underestimate the power of introductions. They treat them casually or avoid them altogether, fearing awkwardness or rejection. But when done with care, introductions can elevate your reputation, deepen your relationships, and create ripple effects that benefit everyone involved including you.

Why Introductions Matter
In a world overflowing with information and noise, trust is the ultimate filter. When you introduce two people, you lend your credibility to both. You're saying, "I believe in this connection." That trust accelerates rapport, shortens decision cycles, and opens doors that might otherwise remain closed.
Introductions also position you as a connector to a person who sees potential, creates value, and builds bridges. As Adam Grant writes in Give and Take, "Givers who connect others without expecting anything in return often end up with the most expansive and resilient networks." These connectors become magnets for opportunity, not because they chase it, but because they cultivate it.

A great introduction is thoughtful, clear, and purposeful. It answers three questions:
1. Why are these two people connected?
2. What value might they offer each other?
3. What context do they need to begin the conversation?

Here's a simple structure:
This kind of message is short, respectful, and sets the stage for a meaningful exchange. It doesn't pressure either party, it simply opens the door.

Timing and Consent
Before making an introduction, always ask for consent. A quick message like, "Would you be open to connecting with someone working on a project I think you'd find interesting?" shows respect and avoids putting anyone in an uncomfortable position.
Timing also matters. Don't introduce someone during a crisis or when they're overwhelmed. Pay attention to context. A well-timed introduction feels like a gift; a poorly timed one can feel like a burden.

Real-Life Story: The Ripple Effect
Consider Daniel, a mid-level manager who introduced his former intern, Aisha, to a friend working in venture capital. Aisha was launching a startup and needed advice. Daniel didn't expect anything but in return he simply believed in her potential.
That introduction led to mentorship, which led to funding, which led to a successful product launch. Months

later, Aisha invited Daniel to join her advisory board. His simple act of connection became a career pivot. Introductions often work like that. You plant a seed, and months or years later, it blooms into something unexpected and beautiful.

7.4 Common Mistakes to Avoid

• Vague or Unclear Introductions: Don't just say, "You two should meet." Explain why. Give context.
• Unsolicited Introductions: Always ask first. Surprising someone with a connection they didn't agree to can damage trust.
• Overloading Your Contacts: Don't introduce people constantly without considering their bandwidth. Quality over quantity.
• Making It About You: The best introductions focus on the value between the two people not on your role as the connector.

Strategic Introductions: Building Influence

Introductions aren't just about kindness, they're also strategic. When you connect with people who go on to collaborate, succeed, or create impact, your reputation grows. You become known as someone who "makes things happen." This builds influence, trust, and visibility.

But the strategy must be rooted in sincerity. Manipulative introductions made solely for personal gain erode credibility. The goal is to create value for others, knowing that value will eventually return to you in ways you can't predict.

The Long-Term Impact

Introductions over time. One connection led to another. One act of generosity leads to a reputation. One moment of insight leads to a breakthrough.

Tony Robbins, in Money: Master the Game, emphasizes that relationships are one of the most overlooked assets in wealth-building. He writes, "The right relationship can compress decades of learning into days." Introductions are how those relationships begin.

Practical Tips for Mastering Introductions

• Keep a Mental Rolodex: As you meet people, note their strengths, interests, and needs. This helps you spot potential connections.
• Be Specific: When introducing, mention one or two concrete reasons why the connection makes sense.
• Follow Up: After the introduction, check in. Ask if the connection was helpful. This shows care and strengthens your bond with both parties.
• Celebrate Outcomes: If the introduction leads to something great a partnership, a job, a friendship celebrates it. Share the story. It reinforces your role as a connector.
• Don't Overthink It: Not every introduction needs to be perfect. If you believe two people could benefit from knowing each other, trust your instinct and make the connection.

7.5 The Power of Introductions

The art of making introductions is one of the most powerful, underrated tools in your wealth-building toolkit. It requires no money, no credentials, just awareness, generosity, and a willingness to connect. In a world obsessed with transactions, introductions are acts of transformation. They say, "I see you. I see them. And I believe something meaningful could happen if you met."

When you introduce two people with care and purpose, you become more than a participant in your network you become a catalyst. You help others grow, and in doing so, you grow too. You become a quiet architect of opportunity, a bridge-builder whose influence ripples far beyond the moment.

This kind of generosity doesn't just build social capital it builds legacy. Because wealth isn't only measured in assets. It's measured in impact. And sometimes, the most valuable thing you can offer is a connection.

Real-Life Resonance

Consider the story of a young entrepreneur in London who introduced her graphic designer friend to a local author seeking a book cover. That simple email led to a collaboration, then a long-term partnership, and eventually a design agency. The introducer didn't profit financially but she became part of a story that changed both lives.

Or the mentor who connected a former student to a hiring manager. The student got the job, the company gained a star performer, and the mentor became a trusted advisor. No money changed hands, but value was created, shared, and multiplied.

7.6 Strategic Generosity

Introductions work best when they're intentional. Think about alignment—shared values, complementary skills, mutual benefit. Ask yourself:

- What does each person need right now?
- What strengths or insights could they offer each other?
- How can I frame the introduction to spark curiosity and trust?

Even a short message "I thought you two should meet" can open doors. But when you add context "She's building a platform for young creatives, and I know you've mentored emerging talent" you create momentum.

Start Small, Start Sincerely

You don't need a vast network to begin. Start with one thoughtful introduction a month. Reach out to someone you admire and ask, "Is there anyone in my circle you'd like to meet?" Or reflect on your own connections who's quietly brilliant but underexposed? Who's stuck and needed a fresh perspective?

Your introductions don't need to be grand. They just need to be sincere. Because sincerity builds trust. And trust builds bridges.

In Give and Take, author Adam Grant writes, "The most meaningful way to succeed is to help others succeed." Introductions are one of the simplest, most profound ways to do that. They cost nothing but they can change everything.

So look around. Who do you know that could benefit from knowing each other? What bridges can you build today that might shape someone's tomorrow? Start small. Start sincerely. And let your introductions become the quiet sparks that ignite extraordinary change.

7.7 Tips for Strategic Relationship Building

Building relationships that support your financial growth isn't about charm or charisma it's about intention, consistency, and emotional intelligence. Strategic relationship building means cultivating connections that are authentic, mutually beneficial, and aligned with your long-term goals. It's not about networking for the sake of visibility; it's about creating a web of trust, insight, and opportunity that grows with you.

Whether you're just starting out or scaling your wealth, these tips will help you build relationships that last and that matter.

1. Show Up Consistently

Presence is power. You don't need to be everywhere, but you do need to be somewhere consistently. Choose communities, events, or platforms that align with your values and goals, and commit to showing up. This could be a monthly industry meetup, a professional Slack group, or a local entrepreneur circle.

Consistency builds familiarity, and familiarity builds trust. When people see you regularly contributing, learning, and engaging, they begin to associate your name with reliability and value.

Example: Jamal, a freelance developer, joined a small online community for ethical tech founders. He didn't pitch his services, he simply answered questions, shared resources, and encouraged others. After six months, he was invited to collaborate on a funded project. His presence not his pitch opened the door.

2. Listen More Than You Speak

In a world full of noise, listening is a superpower. When you listen deeply, you uncover what people truly need, value, and struggle with. This insight allows you to offer help that's relevant and meaningful.

Strategic relationship building isn't about impressing others it's about understanding them. Ask thoughtful questions. Reflect what you hear. Resist the urge to dominate conversations. People remember how you made them feel, and feeling heard is one of the most powerful emotional experiences you can offer.

Author Insight: Dale Carnegie, in How to Win Friends and Influence People, emphasized that being genuinely interested in others is far more effective than trying to make others interested in you.

3. Offer Help First

Generosity is the foundation of strong networks. Before asking for any advice, referrals, introductions look for ways to contribute. Share a resource. Recommend a book. Offer feedback. Make a connection.

This doesn't mean overextending yourself or giving away your time indiscriminately. It means being intentional about adding value. When you become known as someone who helps others succeed, people naturally want to support you in return.

Example: Priya, a marketing consultant, made a habit of sending personalized LinkedIn messages to people she admired, offering a quick tip or article relevant to their work. Over time, many of those people became clients not because she sold to them, but because she served them first.

4. Diversify Your Network

It's easy to stay within your comfort zone connecting only with people in your industry, age group, or background. But innovation and opportunity often come from unexpected intersections.

Make a conscious effort to diversify your network. Reach out to people in different fields, cultures, and generations. Attend events outside your niche. Join interdisciplinary communities. These connections broaden your perspective and expose you to ideas and opportunities you wouldn't find otherwise.

Author Insight: Frans Johansson, in The Medici Effect, argues that breakthrough ideas often emerge at the intersection of diverse disciplines and cultures. The more varied your network, the more fertile your idea landscape becomes.

5. Nurture, Don't Neglect

Relationships fade without attention. Strategic relationship building means tending to your connections like a garden not just planting seeds but watering them regularly.

This doesn't require grand gestures. A simple check-in message, a birthday note, or a "thinking of you" email can keep relationships alive. Use reminders, calendars, or CRM tools if needed. The goal is to stay present in people's lives without overwhelming them.

Example: Daniel, a financial advisor, set aside one hour each Friday to send five personalized messages to people in his network. Over time, this habit led to referrals, partnerships, and a reputation for thoughtfulness.

6. Be Clear About Your Values

Strategic relationships are built on alignment. When you're clear about your values, integrity, creativity, sustainability, generosity you attract people who share them. This makes collaboration smoother, trust deeper, and growth more sustainable.

Don't be afraid to express what matters to you. Share your mission. Speak openly about your goals. Let people see the heart behind your work. The right people will resonate with it and the wrong ones will self-select out.

Author Insight: Brené Brown, in Dare to Lead, emphasizes that clarity is kindness. When you communicate your values clearly, you create space for authentic connection.

7. Use Technology Thoughtfully

Digital tools can enhance relationship building but only if used with care. Social media, email, and messaging platforms allow you to stay connected across time zones and schedules. But they can also create noise and superficiality.

Use technology to deepen relationships, not just maintain them. Personalize your messages. Avoid mass outreach. Schedule video calls when possible. And don't rely solely on digital make time for in-person or voice-based connection when it matters.

Example: Aisha, a startup founder, used LinkedIn to share her journey with vulnerability and insight. Her posts attracted mentors, investors, and collaborators not because they were polished, but because they were real.

8. Protect Your Energy

Not every relationship is strategic or healthy. Part of building strong networks is knowing when to step back. If a connection drains you, disrespects your boundaries, or consistently takes without giving, it's okay to let it go. Protecting your energy allows you to invest more deeply in relationships that nourish you. Strategic relationship building is not about quantity, it's about quality.

Author Insight: Greg McKeown, in Essentialism, reminds us that saying no is a powerful act of self-respect. Focus on the relationships that align with your purpose and values.

9. Celebrate Others

One of the simplest ways to build strong relationships is to celebrate others. Acknowledge their wins. Share their work. Recommend their services. People remember who cheered for them and they often return the Favor.

Celebration builds goodwill, strengthens bonds, and creates a culture of mutual support. It's a small act with a big impact.

Example: Obinna, a writer and podcast creator, made a habit of spotlighting fellow creatives in his newsletter. Over time, those shoutouts led to collaborations, guest appearances, and a thriving creative circle.

10. Play the Long Game

Strategic relationship building is not about instant results. It's about planting seeds that may bloom months or years from now. Some of your most valuable connections will come from relationships you nurtured quietly over time.

Trust the process. Keep showing up. Keep giving. Keep listening. Don't forget yourself. The compound interest of relationships is just as powerful as the compound interest of money.

7.9 Reflection

Wealth, in its deepest sense, is not just about money, it's about connection. It's about the people who challenge you, support you, open doors for you, and walk beside you as you grow. Throughout this chapter, we've explored how networks shape opportunity, how introductions spark transformation, and how strategic relationship building becomes a quiet superpower.

But here's the truth: the most valuable relationships are not built in moments of need. They're built in moments of generosity. When you show up with curiosity, when you listen without agenda, when you connect with others without expectation you become more than a participant in your network. You become a catalyst.Think of your network as a living ecosystem. Every conversation is a seed. Every act of kindness is water. Every introduction is sunlight. You may not see the results immediately, but over time, the garden grows. And when it does, it bears fruit not just for you but for everyone you've touched along the way.

This is the quiet magic of networks: they multiply what you give. A single introduction can change someone's career. A thoughtful message can spark a collaboration. A shared insight can lead to a breakthrough. And all of it begins with intention.

So as you move forward, ask yourself:

- Who can I support today?
- What connection can I make that might help someone else grow?
- How can I show up not to impress, but to contribute?

Because when you build relationships with purpose and care, you're not just building wealth you're building legacy. You're creating a ripple effect that extends far beyond your own goals.

And in the end, that's what real wealth looks like: a life filled with meaningful connections, shared growth, and the quiet joy of knowing you helped others rise.

Chapter 8: Entrepreneurship Essentials

8.1 Introduction

Entrepreneurship has long been painted as the great adventure of wealth, creating a daring leap into the unknown, where visionaries build empires from scratch. But behind the glossy headlines and "overnight success" stories lies a more grounded truth: entrepreneurship is less about sudden brilliance and more about persistence, problem-solving, and the courage to keep moving forward when the path is uncertain.

At its core, entrepreneurship is about creating value. It begins with a simple question: What problem can I solve? Every thriving business, from the corner café to the global tech giant, started with someone noticing a gap, a frustration, or an unmet need and deciding to do something about it. Entrepreneurs are not just dreamers; they are builders. They take ideas and give them form, testing, refining, and adapting until those ideas serve real people in meaningful ways.

For beginners, the entrepreneurial journey can feel overwhelming. There are so many moving parts business plans, funding, marketing, operations, legal structures that it's easy to freeze before even starting. But the truth is, no one begins with all the answers. The most successful entrepreneurs didn't wait until everything was perfect; they started small, learned quickly, and grew steadily. Entrepreneurship is not about knowing everything about being willing to learn everything you need along the way.

This chapter is designed to strip away the myths and provide a clear, practical foundation. We'll explore a roadmap to business success, breaking down the essential steps from idea to execution. We'll also share startup stories and resources that illustrate how ordinary people turned small beginnings into sustainable ventures. These stories will remind you that entrepreneurship is not reserved for the elite or the exceptionally gifted it's available to anyone willing to take the first step.

Entrepreneurship also requires a shift in mindset. Unlike traditional employment, where security often comes from a paycheck, entrepreneurship demands that you create your own security by building systems, products, and services that others value. It's a path that requires resilience, creativity, and adaptability. Failures are not dead ends but steppingstones each one teaching lessons that refine your approach.

Author Insight: Michael Gerber, in the E-Myth Revisited, argues that many small businesses fail because their founders confuse technical skill with entrepreneurial skill. Being a great baker doesn't automatically make you a great bakery owner. Entrepreneurship requires learning how to work on the business, not just in it. This distinction is crucial for anyone hoping to build something that lasts.

Finally, entrepreneurship is not just about money. It's about freedom, the freedom to shape your own path, to align your work with your values, and to create impact in your community and beyond. For some, that means building a global company. For others, it means running a small, profitable business that supports their family and lifestyle. Both are valid. Both are powerful.

As we step into this chapter, remember entrepreneurship is not a destination, but a journey. It's a process of growth, discovery, and creation. And like any journey, it begins with a single step the decision to start.

8.2. Roadmap to Business Success

Entrepreneurship is often compared to climbing a mountain. From the base, the summit looks impossibly far away. The air is thinner at the top, the terrain is unpredictable, and the climb demands stamina. But with the right roadmap, the journey becomes less daunting. You may not know every twist and turn, but you'll have a compass to guide you.

This roadmap is not a rigid formula, it's a framework. Every entrepreneur's path is unique, but the milestones are remarkably consistent. Whether you're starting a side hustle or building a scalable company, these steps will help you move from idea to impact.

Step 1: Identify a Problem Worth Solving

All great businesses begin with a problem. Entrepreneurs are problem-solvers at heart. They notice frustrations others accept as normal and ask, "What if there's a better way?"

Case Study: Airbnb began when two friends couldn't afford rent in San Francisco. They noticed a problem with expensive hotels and limited lodging and offered a simple solution: air mattresses in their apartment. That humble idea grew into a global hospitality platform.

Practical Tip: Keep a "problem journal." Write down daily annoyances you or others face. Patterns will emerge, and within them lie opportunities.

Step 2: Validate the Idea

Ideas are cheap; validation is priceless. Too many entrepreneurs fall in love with their ideas without testing if anyone else cares. Validation means asking: Is this problem real, and will people pay for a solution?

• Minimum Viable Product (MVP): Build the simplest version of your idea that delivers value. It could be a landing page, a prototype, or even a conversation.

• Customer Conversations: Talk to potential users. Ask about their pain points, not just if they "like" your idea.

Author Insight: Eric Ries, in The Lean Startup, stresses the "build-measure-learn" cycle. Don't wait for perfection launch small, gather feedback, and adapt quickly

Step 3: Build a Business Model

A business without a model is like a car without fuel, it won't go far. A business model answers: How will this idea make money?

• Revenue Streams: Will you charge subscriptions, one-time fees, or rely on ads?

• Cost Structure: What are your fixed and variable costs?

• Value Proposition: Why should customers choose you over alternatives?

Case Study: Netflix began as a DVD rental service by mail. Its subscription model disrupted Blockbuster's pay-per-rental approach. The model, not just the product, created the advantage.

Step 4: Secure Resource

Resources are more than money. They include skills, time, and networks.

• Bootstrapping: Funding your business with personal savings or early sales. This builds discipline but limits speed.

• Investors: Angel investors or venture capital can accelerate growth but often require giving up equity.

• Grants and Loans: Government programs and banks can provide non-dilutive funding.

Practical Tip: Map your resource gaps. Do you need technical expertise, marketing skills, or capital? Then decide whether to learn, hire, or partner.

Step 5: Launch and Iterate

Perfection is the enemy of progress. Many entrepreneurs delay launching until everything feels flawless. But markets reward speed and adaptability, not perfection.

• Soft Launch: Release to a small group of users. Gather feedback.

• Iterate Quickly: Use feedback to refine your product or service.

• Embrace Failure: Each misstep is data. Failure is not the opposite of success it's part of the process.

Case Study: Instagram started as a location-based app called Burbn. Users ignored most features but loved the photo-sharing tool. The founders pivoted, focusing solely on photos. That pivot created one of the most influential apps of the decade.

Step 6: Scale Strategically

Scaling is about multiplying success without multiplying chaos. Growth is exciting, but uncontrolled growth can sink a business.
• Systems and Processes: Document workflows. Automate where possible.
• Team Building: Hire for culture and values, not just skills.
• Market Expansion: Enter new markets only after proving success in your core.
Author Insight: Michael Gerber, in the E-Myth Revisited, warns that many small businesses fail because founders work in the business, not on it. Scaling requires stepping back to design systems that run without you.

Step 7: Sustain and Adapt
Markets evolve. Customer needs shift. Competitors emerge. The final step is not an endpoint but a cycle: sustaining and adapting.
• Continuous Innovation: Keep improving your product.
• Customer Relationships: Loyal customers are your best defense against competition.
• Agility: Be willing to pivot when the landscape changes.
Case Study: Netflix pivoted again from DVDs to streaming, and later into original content. Each adaptation kept it ahead of disruption.

8.3 The Entrepreneurial Mindset

Beyond the steps, success requires mindset. Entrepreneurs must cultivate resilience, curiosity, and patience. They must learn to see setbacks as feedback, not failure.
• Resilience: Every entrepreneur faces rejection. The difference lies in persistence.
• Curiosity: Ask questions, seek feedback, and stay open to learning.
• Patience: Wealth through entrepreneurship is rarely quick. It's built over years of consistent effort.
Author Insight: Simon Sinek, in Start with Why, reminds us that businesses built on purpose endure longer. When your "why" is clear, it fuels resilience during tough times.
The roadmap to business success is not a straight line it's a winding path with detours, setbacks, and surprises. But each step builds momentum. Identify a problem. Validate it. Build a model. Secure resources. Launch. Scale. Adapt.
Think of entrepreneurship like planting an orchard. The first seed may take years to bear fruit, but once it does, it provides harvests for decades. The key is to plant, nurture, and keep tending even when the seasons are harsh.
Your journey won't look exactly like anyone else's. But with this roadmap, you'll have a compass. And with persistence, you'll not only build a business, but you'll also build freedom, impact, and legacy.

Startup Stories and Practical Resources
Entrepreneurship can feel abstract until you see it lived out in real stories. Theories and frameworks are important, but it's the journeys of real people ordinary individuals who turned small beginnings into thriving ventures that make the path tangible. These stories remind us that entrepreneurship is not reserved for the elite or the exceptionally gifted. It's for anyone willing to notice a problem, take a risk, and persist through uncertainty. Alongside these stories, practical resources provide scaffolding to help you build your own venture with confidence.

8.4 Startup Stories: Lessons from the Frontlines

Airbnb: From Air Mattresses to Global Hospitality
In 2007, Brian Chesky and Joe Gebbia couldn't afford rent in San Francisco. A design conference was in town, hotels were fully booked, and they saw an opportunity. They bought a few air mattresses, set up a simple website, and offered "Air Bed and Breakfast" to attendees. Their MVP was as scrappy as it gets three guests sleeping on the floor. But it validated a problem: people needed affordable, flexible lodging.

Fast forward, Airbnb is now a multi-billion-dollar company. The lesson? Start small, solve a real problem, and don't be afraid to test with the simplest version of your idea.

Spanx: Persistence Over Perfection

Sara Blakely started with Spanx with $5,000 in savings and an idea for footless pantyhose. She faced rejection after rejection from manufacturers, most of whom dismissed her idea. But she persisted, eventually convincing one factory owner to take a chance. Blakely did her own marketing, hustled to get her product into stores, and even sent samples to Oprah Winfrey who later endorsed Spanx on her show.

Spanx became a billion-dollar brand, and Blakely became the world's youngest self-made female billionaire. Her story underscores the power of resilience, creativity, and belief in your product—even when others don't see it yet.

Innocent Drinks: A Market Stall Beginning

In London, three friends Adam Balon, Richard Reed, and Jon Wright blended fruit smoothies and sold them at a music festival. They put up a sign asking customers: "Should we quit our jobs to make these full-time?" with bins labeled "Yes" and "No." By the end of the weekend, the "Yes" bin was overflowing. That grassroots validation gave them the courage to launch Innocent Drinks, which grew into one of the UK's most beloved beverage brands.

The takeaway? Sometimes the simplest form of market research asking people directly can provide the clarity you need to take the leap.

Local and Everyday Entrepreneurs

Not every success story makes headlines. Consider the baker who starts selling sourdough at a weekend market, then expands into a café. Or the fitness trainer who begins with a few clients in a park, then builds an online coaching business. These stories remind us that entrepreneurship doesn't always mean unicorn startups. It can mean building a sustainable, profitable business that supports your family and aligns with your values.

Practical Resources for Entrepreneurs

Stories inspire, but resources are equipped. Here are practical tools, communities, and guides to help you on your journey:

Books to Build Your Foundation

• The Lean Startup by Eric Ries – A must-read for learning how to test, iterate, and pivot quickly.
• Zero to One by Peter Thiel – Encourages thinking about innovation and creating something truly new.
• The E-Myth Revisited by Michael Gerber – Explains why most small businesses fail and how to build systems that scale.
• Start With Why by Simon Sinek – Helps you clarify your purpose, which fuels resilience and attracts loyal customers.

Online Learning Platforms

• Y Combinator Startup School – Free online curriculum from one of the world's top accelerators.
• Coursera & edX – Offer entrepreneurship courses from universities like Stanford, MIT, and Harvard.
• Udemy – Affordable, practical courses on everything from digital marketing to business finance.

Funding and Support

• British Business Bank (UK) – Provides loans, grants, and guidance for small businesses.
• SCORE (US) – Free mentoring and resources for entrepreneurs.
• Crowdfunding Platforms like Kickstarter and Indiegogo – Allow you to validate demand and raise capital simultaneously.

Communities and Networks

- Indie Hackers – An online community of entrepreneurs sharing transparent stories about building businesses.
- LinkedIn Groups – Industry-specific groups where you can connect, learn, and collaborate.
- Local Chambers of Commerce – Offer networking events, mentorship, and resources.
- Co-working Spaces – Provide not just desks, but communities of like-minded builders.

Tools to Get Started

- Canva – For creating professional designs without a designer.
- Shopify – For launching an e-commerce store quickly.
- Notion or Trello – For organizing projects and tasks.
- QuickBooks or Xero – For managing finances and bookkeeping.
- Slack or Microsoft Teams – For team communication and collaboration.

Bringing Stories and Resources Together

The stories of Airbnb, Spanx, Innocent Drinks, and countless local entrepreneurs show that beginnings are often humble. What matters is not where you start, but how you persist, adapt, and grow. The resources listed here are your toolkit, the scaffolding that supports your climb.

But remember resources are only as powerful as the action you take with them. Reading The Lean Startup won't build your business. Joining a community won't guarantee success. The magic happens when you combine inspiration with execution when you take the lessons from stories and apply them with the tools at your disposal.

Entrepreneurship is not about waiting for the perfect idea, the perfect timing, or the perfect plan. It's about starting where you are, with what you have, and learning as you go. The stories remind us that ordinary people can build extraordinary things. Resources remind us that we don't have to do it alone.

So as you step into your own entrepreneurial journey, carry with you both: the inspiration of those who've gone before, and the practical tools that will help you carve your own path.

Because the truth is, the next great startup story could be yours.

8.5 Reflection

Entrepreneurship is not a straight road it's a winding path filled with detours, setbacks, and unexpected breakthroughs. The roadmap you've just explored offers structure, the stories remind you that ordinary people can achieve extraordinary things, and the resources give you the tools to begin. But the most important ingredient is your willingness to take the first step.

Every great business began as a fragile idea. Airbnb was once just air mattresses on a floor. Spanx was once sketched in a notebook. Innocent Drinks was once a blender at a music festival. What transformed these small beginnings into global successes was not perfection, but persistence. The founders dared to test, to fail, to learn, and to try again.

Entrepreneurship is less about having the "perfect" plan and more about cultivating the courage to act. You don't need to know everything before you start. You don't need vast resources or a flawless strategy. What you need is clarity of purpose, resilience in the face of obstacles, and the humility to learn as you go.

Think of entrepreneurship as planting an orchard. The first seed may take years to bear fruit, but once it does, it provides harvests for decades. Each decision, each experiment, each connection is a seed. Some will sprout quickly, others will take time, and some may never grow at all. But if you keep planting, nurturing, and adapting, the orchard will flourish.

And remember entrepreneurship is not only about money. It's about freedom, the freedom to shape your own path, to align your work with your values, and to create impact in your community. It's about building something that outlives you, something that carries your vision into the future.

Chapter 9: Real Estate as a Wealth Vehicle

9.1 Introduction

Real estate is more than land, bricks, and mortar. It is the ground beneath our feet, the walls that shelter our families, the spaces where dreams are nurtured and futures are built. To own property is to hold a tangible piece of the world a stake in something that endures beyond the fluctuations of markets and the passing of time.

For centuries, property symbolized stability, security, and belonging. In ancient civilizations, land ownership was the measure of wealth and power. Kings and nobles were defined not by the coins in their coffers but by the acres they controlled. Even today, in a world of digital assets and intangible investments, real estate retains its primal allure. It is solid. It is visible. It is something you can touch, walk through, and improve with your own hands.

But real estate is not only about economics. It is deeply emotional. Think of the first place you called home. Perhaps it was a modest apartment, a childhood house, or even a rented room. The walls may have been plain, the space small, but within those walls' memories were made meals shared, laughter echoed, tears shed. A home is not just a structure; it is a container for life itself.

This is why the journey from renting to ownership feels so profound. Renting provides shelter, but it is temporary, borrowed. Ownership, by contrast, represents permanence. It is the moment when you stop paying into someone else's dream and begin building your own. The first down payment, the first mortgage signed, the first set of keys in your hand these are not just financial milestones, but emotional ones. They mark the shift from transience to rootedness, from being a guest in someone else's story to becoming the author of your own.

Real estate teaches patience. Unlike stocks that can rise or fall in a day, property grows slowly, steadily, often imperceptibly. It requires stewardship maintenance, care, and foresight. A house left untended will crumble; a building ignored will decay. But with attention, properties appreciate, neighborhoods flourish, and wealth compounds. This patience is not passive, it is active, a discipline of tending to something that grows over years, even decades.

It also teaches vision. When you look at a run-down house or an empty lot, do you see what it is, or do you see what could be? Entrepreneurs in real estate are visionaries. They imagine a family gathering in a once-abandoned home, a thriving business in a vacant storefront, a community revitalized by investment. Real estate invites us to see beyond the present into the potential.

And yet, real estate is not without its fears. The commitment of a mortgage can feel daunting. The responsibility of ownership repairs, taxes, tenants can weigh heavily. Many hesitate at the threshold, wondering if they are ready. But within that hesitation lies the very reason real estate is such a powerful teacher: it forces us to grow. Ownership demands responsibility, discipline, and courage. It stretches us into new roles landlord, investor, steward.

Consider the symbolism of keys. To rent is to borrow keys that must one day be returned. To own is to hold keys that are truly yours. Keys unlock not only doors but futures. They represent access, autonomy, and authority. The jingling of keys in your pocket is the sound of independence.

Real estate also connects us to legacy. Unlike many investments, property can be passed down. A home becomes an inheritance, a gift to the next generation. Families often speak of "the old house" or "the land" as more than assets they are repositories of history, identity, and continuity. To invest in real estate is to plant seeds that may bear fruit long after you are gone.

There is also a communal dimension. Property anchors communities. Streets lined with homes create neighborhoods. Commercial buildings create hubs of commerce and culture. When you invest in real estate, you are not only shaping your own wealth, you are shaping the fabric of society. A well-kept property uplifts a street; a thriving business revitalizes a block. Real estate is wealth that radiates outward.

Psychologically, real estate satisfies a deep human need for security. Abraham Maslow placed shelter at the base of his hierarchy of needs, alongside food and water. Without a safe place to live, higher aspirations creativity, purpose, self-actualization are difficult to pursue. This is why property ownership feels so empowering: it secures the foundation upon which everything else is built.

But real estate is also aspirational. It is not only about survival but about flourishing. The dream of a bigger home, a better neighborhood, or a portfolio of properties is not just about money it is about growth, progress, and possibility. Each property acquired is a step forward, a marker of achievement, a testament to vision turned into reality.

And yet, the true power of real estate lies not in the properties themselves but in what they represent. A house is not just walls; it is safety. An office is not just space; it is opportunity. A shop is not just square footage; it is livelihood. Real estate is wealth translated into human terms.

As you step into this chapter, pause for a moment. Imagine the first place you called home. Picture the walls, the smells, the sounds. Now imagine the pride of walking into a space that is truly yours knowing that every payment builds equity, every improvement adds value, every year deepens your stake. That feeling that blend of security, freedom, and possibility is why real estate has always been, and will always remain, one of the most powerful vehicles for wealth.

So let this meditation settle in real estate is not just about money. It is about meaning. It is about anchoring yourself in the world, creating stability for your family, and leaving a legacy for those who come after you. It is about turning spaces into stories, investments into impact, and ownership into empowerment.

When you hold the keys to a property, you hold more than access to a building. You hold access to a future.

9.2 Comparing Residential and Commercial Property

Real estate is one of the oldest and most enduring wealth vehicles in human history. From ancient civilizations that measured power by land ownership to modern investors who diversify portfolios with property, the principle remains the same: land and buildings hold value because they meet fundamental human needs. But not all real estate is created equal. Broadly, property investment falls into two categories residential and commercial and each offers distinct opportunities, risks, and rewards.

Understanding the differences between these two paths is essential for anyone considering real estate as part of their wealth-building journey. Residential property often feels more accessible, while commercial property can appear intimidating but potentially more lucrative. Let's explore both in detail.

Residential Property: The Familiar Starting Point

Residential property refers to homes where people live in single-family houses, apartments, duplexes, and small multi-unit buildings. For many investors, this is the first step into real estate because it feels familiar. Everyone has lived in a home, so the concept is tangible. You understand what makes a space loveable, what tenants might value, and how neighborhoods shape lifestyle. That emotional connection makes residential property one of the most accessible and intuitive entry points into wealth-building through real estate.

Unlike commercial property, which can feel intimidated with its jargon, zoning laws, and business leases, residential real estate speaks a language most people already know. You've likely paid rent, dealt with repairs, or imagined your dream home. That lived experience becomes a quiet advantage when stepping into property investment.

Why Residential Property Works for First-Time Investors

One of the biggest benefits of residential property is its relative simplicity. Financing is often easier to secure, especially for owner-occupiers or first-time buyers. Banks are familiar with residential mortgages, and government schemes may support your purchase. Managing a residential unit also tends to be more straightforward, especially if you start with a single property or use a letting agent.

There's also consistent demand. People always need places to live. Whether it's students, families, professionals, or retirees, the rental market remains active across economic cycles. Even during downturns, residential property tends to hold its value better than more volatile assets.

Emotional and Practical Rewards

Beyond financial returns, residential property offers emotional rewards. You're not just investing in bricks and mortar you're providing shelter, stability, and community. Many investors find satisfaction in improving a property, welcoming tenants, and watching their investment grow over time.

It's also a flexible asset. You can rent it out long-term, offer short-term stays, renovate and sell, or even live in it yourself while building equity. That versatility makes residential property a dynamic tool in your wealth-building toolkit.

Consider a young investor in London who purchased a two-bedroom flat in a growing neighborhood. She lived in one room and rented out the other to cover her mortgage. Over time, the property appreciated, and she used the equity to buy a second flat. What began as a modest step became a foundation for financial independence.

This kind of story is common and powerful. Residential property allows you to start small, learn as you go, and scale when ready.

Residential property is more than a financial asset it's a familiar starting point. It offers a blend of emotional resonance, practical simplicity, and long-term potential. For new investors, it's a way to enter the world of real estate with confidence, clarity, and a sense of purpose.

Start where you are. Use what you know. And let your first property become the seed of something much bigger.

Advantages of Residential Property

- Lower Barrier to Entry: Buying a single apartment or small house requires less capital than purchasing an office block or warehouse.
- Steady Demand: People always need a place to live. Even during economic downturns, housing remains essential.
- Financing Options: Banks are often more willing to lend for residential purchases, with lower interest rates and longer repayment terms.
- Emotional Connection: Many investors like the idea of owning homes because they can imagine themselves or their families living there.

9.3 Challenges of Residential Property

- Tenant Turnover: Leases are often short (6–12 months), which means more frequent vacancies and the need to find new tenants.
- Management Intensity: Residential tenants may call for repairs, maintenance, or disputes more often than commercial tenants.
- Lower Yields: While residential property can be appreciated steadily, the rental yields are often smaller compared to commercial.

Case Study: The First Rental Home

Consider James, a young professional in Manchester who bought a two-bedroom flat as his first investment. He rented it to students, generating modest but steady income. Over time, the property appreciated, and he refinanced to buy a second flat. James's story illustrates how residential property can be a manageable entry point, especially for beginners.

9.4 Commercial Property: The Scalable Wealth Builder

Commercial property includes office buildings, retail shops, warehouses, industrial spaces, and large multi-family complexes. These properties are used for business purposes, not personal living and that distinction makes all the difference. While residential property often feels familiar and emotionally grounded, commercial real estate is where scalability, structure, and strategic wealth-building come into sharper focus.
For many investors, commercial property represents the next level. It's not just about owning space it's about owning systems. Businesses rent these properties to operate, serve customers, store inventory, or house employees. That means longer leases, more predictable cash flow, and often higher returns. But it also means deeper due diligence, larger upfront investments, and a more professional approach to management.

Why Commercial Property Scales

One of the biggest advantages of commercial real estate is its scalability. A single commercial lease can generate the same income as multiple residential units without the turnover or emotional labor of managing individual tenants. Lease terms often span 3 to 10 years, and tenants (especially in retail or industrial spaces) may be responsible for maintenance, insurance, and property taxes under full repair and insuring (FRI) leases. This structure creates a more passive, predictable income stream. You're not chasing rent every month or fielding calls about broken boilers. Instead, you're managing contracts, reviewing performance, and optimizing returns.

9.5 Types of Commercial Property

• Office Buildings: Ranging from small suites to corporate towers, these spaces cater to professionals and service providers. Demand may fluctuate with remote work trends, but prime locations remain valuable.
• Retail Shops: From high street storefronts to shopping centers, retail properties depend on foot traffic, visibility, and local demographics. They can be lucrative but sensitive to economic cycles and consumer habits.
• Warehouses and Industrial Units: These are the backbone of logistics, manufacturing, and e-commerce. With the rise of online shopping, demand for storage and distribution space has surged.
• Large Multi-Family Complexes: Though residential in use, these are managed as commercial assets due to their scale. They offer consistent rental income and economies of scale in maintenance and operations.
A property investor in Manchester purchased a small warehouse and leased it to a local distribution company. The lease was for five years, with rent reviews built in. The tenant handled most upkeep, and the investor enjoyed steady income with minimal involvement. Over time, the property appreciated, and the investor used the equity to acquire a second industrial unit doubling his cash flow without doubling his workload.
This is the power of commercial property: once the system is in place, it can grow with you.
Commercial property isn't just a bigger investment it's a smarter one. It requires more planning, more capital, and more strategy but it offers scale, stability, and long-term wealth potential. For investors ready to move beyond familiarity and into structured growth, commercial real estate is a powerful vehicle.

It's not about owning buildings it's about building systems. And systems, when designed well, create freedom.

Advantages of Commercial Property

• Higher Income Potential: Commercial leases often generate significantly higher rental yields than residential.
• Longer Leases: Businesses typically sign multi-year leases, providing stability and predictable cash flow.
• Professional Tenants: Commercial tenants are usually businesses that maintain the property well, since it reflects their brand.
• Value Based on Income: Commercial property is often valued on the income it generates, meaning improvements that increase rent can directly raise the property's market value.

9.6 Challenges of Commercial Property

• Higher Barriers to Entry: Purchasing a warehouse or office block requires substantial capital or partnerships.
• Economic Sensitivity: Commercial spaces can sit vacant during recessions if businesses close or downsize.
• Complex Management: Commercial leases and regulations are more complex, often requiring legal expertise and professional property managers.
• Financing Difficulty: Banks may require larger deposits and charge higher interest rates for commercial loans.

Case Study: The Warehouse Investor
Nneoma, an entrepreneur in Birmingham, purchased a small warehouse on the outskirts of the city. She leased it to a logistics company on a 10-year contract. The rental income was significantly higher than what she could have earned from a residential property of similar value. However, she also faced higher upfront costs and needed legal support to negotiate the lease. Nneoma's story shows the potential rewards and risks of commercial real estate.

9.6 Residential vs. Commercial: A Side-by-Side Comparison

Feature	Residential Property	Commercial Property
Entry Cost	Lower (single homes, small units)	Higher (offices, retail, warehouses
Risk Level	Moderate (tenant turnover)	Higher (economic cycles, vacancies)
Cash Flow	Steady but smaller	Larger, with longer leases
Financing	Easier, lower interest rates	Harder, higher deposits required
Management	Often self-managed	Usually requires professionals
Tenant Type	Individuals, families, students	Businesses, corporations
Emotional Factor	High (people live in them)	Low (purely business use)

Which Path Is Right for You?

The choice between residential and commercial property depends on your goals, resources, and appetite for risk.
• If you're a beginner: Residential may be the best starting point. It's easier to understand, finance, and manage.
• If you're seeking higher returns and have capital: Commercial can accelerate wealth but requires expertise and resilience.
• If you want balance: Many investors diversify, holding both residential and commercial properties to spread risk and opportunity.

9.7 Blending the Two: Hybrid Strategies

Some investors bridge the gap by starting with residential and gradually moving into commercial. For example:
• Buying a duplex (residential) and renting one unit while living in the other.
• Transitioning into small multi-family buildings (technically commercial if more than four units).
• Partnering with others to invest in a small retail space or office.
This gradual approach allows investors to build confidence and capital before tackling larger commercial projects.

Author Insights

- Robert Kiyosaki (Rich Dad Poor Dad): Emphasizes that real estate is about cash flow, not just appreciation. He often highlights commercial property as a faster wealth builder but acknowledges residential as a practical entry point.
- Barbara Corcoran (real estate investor and Shark Tank star): Notes that residential property often provides emotional satisfaction, while commercial requires a more analytical, business-minded approach.
- Sam Zell (billionaire property investor): Built his empire on commercial real estate, stressing the importance of understanding cycles and being willing to buy when others are fearful.

Residential and commercial real estate are like two sides of the same coin. One offers accessibility, familiarity, and steady growth. The other offers scale, higher returns, and complexity. Neither is inherently better; they simply serve different purposes.

The key is alignment: aligning your choice with your resources, your risk tolerance, and your vision for the future. Some investors find joy in owning homes that families live in. Others thrive on negotiating leases with businesses. Both paths can lead to wealth, but the journey will look different.

As you consider your own path, remember this: real estate is not just about property. It's about people families seeking homes, businesses seeking spaces, communities seeking growth. When you invest in property, you're not just buying walls and land. You're investing in human stories. And that, more than anything, is what makes real estate such a powerful vehicle for wealth.

9.8 From Renting to Ownership: A Personal Story

For years, Daniel lived in a rented flat in South London. It was two modest bedrooms, a small kitchen, and a view of the train tracks but it was home. He paid his rent on time, kept the place tidy, and even painted the walls a calming shade of blue. Yet every month, as he transferred money to his landlord, a quiet frustration grew. He was investing in someone else's future, not his own.

Daniel wasn't reckless with money. He saved diligently, tracked his expenses, and dreamed of owning a place he could truly call his own. But the idea of buying property felt distant. London prices were intimidating, and the process seemed wrapped in mystery mortgages, deposits, stamp duty, surveys. It was easier to stay put, to keep renting, to postpone the leap.

Then one winter evening, everything shifted.

Daniel received notice that his rent would increase by £250 per month. The landlord was renovating the building and passing the costs on to tenants. Daniel stared at the letter, heart sinking. He calculated the new annual rent and realized he'd be paying nearly £20,000 a year for a flat he didn't own, couldn't improve, and might be asked to leave at any time.

That night, he made a decision. He would stop renting and start owning.

The First Steps

Daniel began researching obsessively. He read blogs, watched videos, and spoke to friends who had bought homes. He learned about Help to Buy schemes, first-time buyer incentives, and shared ownership options. Slowly, the fog began to lift. The process wasn't easy, but it was navigable.

He set a goal: save £30,000 for a deposit within two years. That meant cutting back fewer nights out, no holidays, and a side hustle tutoring students on weekends. It was hard, but the vision of ownership kept him going.

During this time, Daniel's mindset began to shift. He stopped seeing property as a distant dream and started seeing it as a strategic move. He wasn't just buying a home he was building equity, creating stability, and laying the foundation for future wealth.

The Purchase

Two years later, Daniel had saved enough. He found a one-bedroom flat in a quiet part of Croydon—close to transport, with potential for appreciation. The place wasn't perfect. The kitchen was outdated, and the bathroom needed work. But it was his.

The day he received the keys, Daniel stood in the empty living room and cried. Not because the journey had been hard (though it had), but because he had crossed a threshold. He was no longer a tenant. He was an owner.

Ownership brought new responsibilities. He learned about boiler maintenance, council tax, and service charges. He spent weekends fixing things, painting walls, and budgeting for repairs. But every improvement added value. Every mortgage payment-built equity. Every decision was his to make.

The Shift to Investor

After three years, Daniel's flat had been appreciated by nearly £60,000. He had built equity not just through payments, but through market growth and smart renovations. He refinanced, pulled out some equity, and used it as a deposit for a second property, a small two-bedroom flat he planned to rent out.

Becoming a landlord was a new challenge. He learned about tenancy agreements, insurance, and property management. He treated his tenants with respect, kept the property in good condition, and built a reputation for fairness. The rental income covered the mortgage and provided modest profit.

Daniel was now an investor.

Emotional Milestones

The journey from rent to ownership wasn't just financial it was emotional. Daniel had moved from uncertainty to stability, from dependence to autonomy. He no longer feared sudden rent hikes or eviction notices. He had control. He had options.

He also had pride. When friends visited, he showed them the improvements he'd made to the new floors, the custom bookshelves, the herb garden on the balcony. His home reflected his personality, his values, and his journey.

And perhaps most importantly, he had hope. Property ownership had opened doors he hadn't imagined. He was building wealth not just for himself, but for his future family. He was creating something that could be passed down, something that would outlast him.

Lessons from Daniel's Story

Daniel's journey is not unique. Thousands of people make the transition from renting to ownership every year. But his story highlights key lessons:

- Start with a decision: The turning point was not money it was mindset. Daniel chose to take control of his financial future.
- Educate yourself: Knowledge replaced fear. Once he understood the process, it became manageable.
- Sacrifice is temporary: The two years of saving were hard, but they unlocked decades of benefit.
- Ownership is empowerment: Beyond financial gain, owning property gave Daniel autonomy, pride, and peace of mind.
- Real estate is a journey: Daniel didn't stop at one property. Ownership became a steppingstone to investment.

The path from renting to ownership is not linear. It's filled with doubts, delays, and decisions. But each step forward builds momentum. Each sacrifice lays a brick. Each choice shapes the foundation of a future.

Daniel's story reminds us that real estate is not just about wealth it's about agency. It's about turning passive payments into active investment. It's about transforming shelter into strategy.

Whether you're renting now or already own a home, the journey continues. There are always new thresholds to cross, new properties to explore, new ways to grow. And with each step, you move closer to a life built not just on income but on equity, stability, and legacy.

9.9 Key Points Highlighted in Tables

Real estate is a complex field, but clarity is power. After exploring the emotional journey from renting to ownership and comparing residential and commercial property, it's time to distill the essentials. These tables are designed to help you quickly grasp the differences, weigh your options, and make informed decisions based on your goals, resources, and risk tolerance.

Each table below captures a core theme from this chapter whether you're choosing between renting and owning, residential and commercial, or preparing for your first investment. Think of these as your reference sheets: simple, direct, and ready to guide your next step.

Renting vs. Owning

Aspect	Renting	Owning
Flexibility	High – easy to relocate	Lower – tied to location
Monthly Cost	Often lower upfront	Higher due to mortgage + maintenance
Wealth Building	None – paying landlord's mortgage	Builds equity over time
Responsibility	Minimal – landlord handles repairs	Full – you manage upkeep
Security	Limited – subject to lease terms	High – long-term control
Emotional Impact	Temporary, borrowed space	Pride, permanence, autonomy
Long-Term Benefit	No asset accumulation	Asset that appreciates and cash flows

Insight: Renting may suit short-term needs or transitional phases, but ownership transforms housing into a wealth-building tool. The emotional shift from paying someone else's mortgage to building your own equity is profound.

9.10 Residential vs. Commercial Property

Feature	Residential Property	Commercial Property
Entry Cost	Lower (single homes, small units)	Higher (offices, retail,
Risk Level	Moderate (tenant turnover)	Higher (economic cycles, vacancies)
Cash Flow	Steady but smaller	Larger, with longer leases
Financing	Easier, lower interest rates	Harder, higher deposits required
Management	Often self-managed	Usually requires professionals
Tenant Type	Individuals, families, students	Businesses, corporations
Emotional Factor	High (people live in them)	Low (purely business use)
Lease Duration	Short – 6 to 12 months	Long – 3 to 10 years
Value Drivers	Location, condition, emotion	Income, lease terms, ROI

Insight: Residential property offers accessibility and emotional satisfaction, while commercial property provides scale and higher returns. The choice depends on your capital, comfort level, and long-term strategy

9.11 First-Time Buyer Checklist

Step	Action Item	Why It Matters
Assess Finances	Review savings, income, credit score	Determines affordability and loan terms
Set a Budget	Include deposit, fees, taxes, and emergency buffer	Prevents overextension
Research Locations	Compare prices, transport, schools, growth potential	Location drives value and lifestyle
Explore Loan Options	Fixed vs. variable rates, government schemes	Impacts monthly payments and flexibility
Get pre-approved	Secure mortgage approval before house hunting	Strengthens offers and speeds process
Hire Professionals	Solicitor, surveyor, broker	Ensures legal and structural soundness
Inspect Thoroughly	Look beyond aesthetics – check plumbing, wiring, roof	Avoids costly surprises post-purchase
Plan for Maintenance	Budget for repairs, insurance, and upgrades	Ownership includes ongoing costs

Insight: Buying property is not just about finding the right home, it's about preparing wisely. A checklist keeps emotions in check and ensures you're building wealth, not stress.

9.12 Property Investment Snapshot

Strategy	Description	Ideal For
Buy-to-Let	Purchase property to rent out	Steady income seekers
Flipping	Buy, renovate, and sell quickly	High-risk, high-reward investors
House Hacking	Live in one unit, rent out others	First-time buyers with limited capital
REITs (Real Estate Investment Trusts)	Invest in property via shares	Passive investors, low entry barrier
Commercial Leasing	Rent to businesses with long-term contracts	Experienced investors with capital
Land Development	Buy raw land, build or sell	Visionaries with planning expertise

Insight: There's no one-size-fits-all approach to property investment. Choose a strategy that aligns with your lifestyle, risk tolerance, and financial goals

9.13 Emotional vs. Strategic Ownership

Ownership Lens	Emotional Ownership	Strategic Ownership
Motivation	Based on personal attachment	Based on ROI (Return on Investment) and market data

Decision Making	Buy, renovate, and sell quickly	High-risk, high-reward investors
Property Selection	Dream home, familiar neighbourhood	High-yield areas, undervalued assets
Renovation Choices	Personal taste, comfort	Value-adding upgrades, tenant appeal
Exit Strategy	Rarely sells, holds for life	Sells or refinances based on performance

Insight: Both lenses matter. Emotional ownership builds roots; strategic ownership builds wealth. The most successful investors learn to balance both.

9.14 Residential vs. Commercial ROI Example

Metric	Residential Flat (London)	Commercial Unit (Manchester)
Purchase Price	£300,000	£500,000
Annual Rent	£15,000	£50,000
Yield (%)	5%	10%
Vacancy Risk	Moderate	Medium to High
Appreciation Potential	Steady	Variable

Insight: Commercial property can offer higher returns, but with greater complexity and risk. Residential offers stability and ease of entry. Choose based on your capacity to manage and adapt.

9.15 Decision Matrix: Which Path Is Right for You?

Question	Residential Property	Commercial Property
Do you have limited capital?	☑ Yes	✕ No
Do you prefer hands-on management?	☑ Yes	✕ No
Are you seeking higher cash flow?	✕ No	☑ Yes
Do you want emotional satisfaction?	☑ Yes	✕ No
Are you comfortable with complexity?	✕ No	☑ Yes
Do you want long-term leases?	✕ No	☑ Yes

Insight: Use this matrix to reflect on your preferences and readiness. Real estate is not just about numbers it's about fit.

Tables simplify what life complicates. They offer clarity, but they don't replace wisdom. As you review these comparisons, remember that real estate is both art and science. It's about numbers, yes but also about timing, emotion, and vision.

Let these tables guide your thinking but let your values guide your decisions. Whether you're buying your first home or investing in commercial property, the goal is not just to accumulate assets but to build a life of stability, freedom, and impact.

Which Path Is Right for You?

9.16 Reflection

Real estate is more than an investment—it's a declaration. A declaration that you are ready to take root, to build something lasting, to shape your future with intention. Whether you're buying your first home, exploring rental income, or stepping into commercial property, the decision to engage with real estate is a decision to participate in one of the oldest and most enduring forms of wealth creation.

But this chapter has shown that real estate is not just about money. It's about meaning. It's about the pride of holding your own keys, the quiet confidence of knowing your rent won't suddenly rise, the joy of watching a space you own come to life under your care. It's about the stories that unfold within walls you've chosen, improved, and protected.

You've seen the contrasts residential versus commercial, renting versus owning, emotional versus strategic. You've walked with Daniel from tenant to owner to investor. You've studied the tables, weighed the options, and perhaps begun to imagine what your own journey might look like.

And that's the point: this chapter isn't just about information. It's about imagination. It's about seeing yourself not just as a consumer of space, but as a creator of value. Not just as someone who pays for shelter, but as someone who builds equity, stability, and legacy.

Real estate rewards those who think long-term. It teaches patience, resilience, and vision. It asks you to look beyond the surface to see potential where others see problems, to invest in places and people, to believe that what you build today can serve generations tomorrow.

So whether your next step is saving for a deposit, researching your first buy-to-let, or walking through a commercial space with fresh eyes, know this: you are not just buying property. You are buying possibility. You are anchoring your wealth in something solid. You are planting seeds that will grow. You are stepping into a story that is yours to shape.

Chapter 10: Mastering the Stock Market

10.1 Understanding the rhythms of wealth creation.

The stock market is one of the most misunderstood areas in personal finance. To some, it's a high-stakes casino unpredictable, intimidating, and best avoided. To others, it's a playground for the rich, a place where insiders win and ordinary people lose. These perceptions are not just inaccurate, they're limiting. They keep people from engaging in one of the most powerful tools for long-term wealth creation.

The truth is that the stock market is neither a game of chance nor a privilege reserved for the elite. It's a system one built on patterns, principles, and psychology. And like any system, it can be learned, navigated, and mastered. But mastery doesn't begin with charts or jargon. It begins with mindset.

This chapter is not just about strategies, it's about perspective. It's about shifting your relationship with risk, redefining your understanding of value, and learning to think like an investor, not a gambler. Because the most successful investors don't chase trends, they cultivate discipline. They don't react to headlines, they follow principles. And they don't panic in downturns they see opportunity.

To truly master the stock market, you must first master yourself. That means understanding your goals, your tolerance for risk, and your emotional triggers. It means learning to separate noise from signal, hype from substances. It means developing the patience to let your investments grow, and the wisdom to know when to pivot.

In this chapter, we'll explore the foundational concepts of stock market investing from how stocks work, to how portfolios are built, to how wealth is grown over time. But more importantly, we'll study the mindset of the masters. We'll look at how legendary investors like Warren Buffett, Peter Lynch, and Cathie Wood approach the market not just with skill, but with clarity, conviction, and long-term vision.

You'll learn how to:

- Read the market without being ruled by it.
- Build a portfolio that reflects your values and goals.
- Avoid common traps that derail new investors.
- Use downturns as opportunities, not disasters.
- Think in decades, not days.

Whether you're a beginner or someone who's dabbled in investing before, this chapter will give you the tools and insights to approach the stock market with confidence. Not because you'll predict every move, but because you'll understand the principles that guide smart decisions.

The stock market is not a place to get rich quick. It's a place to grow wealth steadily, intentionally, and with purpose. And once you learn its rhythms, it becomes more than a financial tool it becomes a mirror of your mindset, your discipline, and your belief in the future.

Let's begin.

1. Building a Diverse Portfolio

Diversification is the cornerstone of smart investing. It's the art of not putting all your eggs in one basket spreading your investments across sectors, geography, and asset types to reduce risk and smooth returns. John Bogle, founder of Vanguard, revolutionized this idea. He believed most investors should own the entire market through low-cost index funds. His advice was simple:

Bogle's philosophy was rooted in humility. He knew that even professionals struggled to beat the market consistently. By owning a broad slice of the market, investors could benefit from overall growth without trying

to predict winners.
Peter Lynch, legendary manager of the Fidelity Magellan Fund, took a slightly different approach. He believed in investing in what you know. Lynch famously said:
He encouraged investors to look around at the shops they frequent, the brands they trust, the trends they notice. His portfolio was diverse, but it was also personal. He believed that everyday observations could lead to extraordinary returns.
Practical Tip: Start with a mix of index funds (for broad exposure), sector ETFs (for targeted growth), and a few individual stocks you understand deeply. Rebalance annually and match your risk level to your time horizon.

2. Lessons Learned from Market Setbacks

Every investor faces downturns. The question is not if the market will fall but how you'll respond when it does.
Warren Buffett, perhaps the most famous investor of all time, built his fortune by staying calm when others panicked. His strategy? Buy great companies at fair prices and hold them for decades. During the 2008 financial crisis, while many fled the market, Buffett invested billions in companies like Goldman Sachs and General Electric. His belief in long-term value never wavered.
Buffett's mentor, Benjamin Graham, taught him the principles of value investing buying stocks below their intrinsic value and ignoring short-term noise. Graham's book The Intelligent Investor remains a timeless guide. He wrote:
This means that while prices may fluctuate wildly based on emotion, over time, true value wins.

But even the greats stumble.

Bill Ackman, a prominent hedge fund manager, made headlines for his bold bets. In 2015, he invested heavily in Valeant Pharmaceuticals, believing it was undervalued. The stock collapsed amid scandal, and Ackman lost billions. His mistake? Overconfidence and lack of diversification.
Lesson: No investor is immune to error. The key is to learn, adapt, and never let ego override discipline.

3. Practical Investment Tips

The masters offer timeless wisdom, but how do you apply it today?
• Start Small, Start Now: Don't wait for the "perfect" moment. Begin with what you have. Even £50 a month can grow meaningfully over time.
• Automate Your Investments: Use dollar-cost averaging investing a fixed amount regularly regardless of market conditions. This removes emotion and builds consistency.
• Avoid Timing the Market: As Lynch said, "Far more money has been lost by investors preparing for corrections than in the corrections themselves."
• Understand Fees: High fees eat into returns. Choose low-cost funds and platforms.
• Stay Informed, Not Overwhelmed: Follow a few trusted sources. Avoid hype and panic-driven headlines.
• Know Your Exit Strategy: Are you investing in retirement, a home, or financial freedom? Your goals shape your timeline and risk tolerance.

Charlie Munger, Buffett's longtime partner, adds a final piece of wisdom:
Patience is not passive, it's strategic.

10.2 Investor Profiles: Wisdom and Wounds

Let's meet a few more icons whose journeys illuminate the path:

Ray Dalio

Founder of Bridgewater Associates, Dalio built one of the world's largest hedge funds. His philosophy blends macroeconomic insight with radical transparency. He believes in understanding cycles and preparing for downturns.

Dalio's book Principles outlines his belief in thoughtful decision-making and learning from mistakes. He once lost everything early in his career and had to borrow money from his father. That failure became the foundation of his future success.

Cathie Wood
Founder of ARK Invest, Wood is known for bold bets on disruptive innovation Tesla, genomics, AI. Her approach is high-risk, high reward. During bull markets, her funds soared. During downturns, they plummeted. Her story teaches us that conviction matters but so does timing and risk management.

George Soros
Famous for "breaking the Bank of England," Soros made billions by betting against the British pound in 1992. His strategy? Deep analysis, bold action, and a willingness to go against the crowd.
But Soros also emphasizes reflexivity with the idea that markets are shaped by human behavior, which is often irrational. His success came not just from data, but from understanding psychology.
The stock market is not a place of certainty it's a place of possibility. The greatest investors didn't succeed because they predicted the future. They succeeded because they prepared for it. They diversified, stayed disciplined, learned from mistakes, and invested with purpose.
You don't need to be a genius to invest well. You need humility, patience, and a willingness to learn. The market will test you. It will tempt you. But if you stay grounded if you follow the wisdom of those who've walked the path before you'll find that the stock market is not a gamble. It's a garden.
Plant wisely. Tend patiently. And let time do its work.

10.3 Building a Diverse Portfolio

- Why diversification matters: Reduces risk, smooths return and protects against market shocks.
- Asset types: Stocks, ETFs, mutual funds, bonds, REITs, and international exposure.
- Sectors and industries: Technology, healthcare, energy, consumer goods, etc.
- Growth vs. value investing: Balancing high-potential stocks with stable, undervalued picks.
- Time horizon and risk tolerance: Matching investments to personal goals and emotional bandwidth.
- Sample portfolio breakdowns: For beginners, mid-level investors, and long-term planners.

Author Insight: John Bogle, founder of Vanguard, championed low-cost index funds as the simplest way to diversify and grow wealth over time.

1. Building a Diverse Portfolio
If the stock market is a garden, then your portfolio is the soil. What you plant and how you mix your seeds determines what grows. A diverse portfolio is not just a safety net against volatility; it's a strategy for resilience, growth, and peace of mind. It allows you to participate in multiple stories of progress while protecting yourself from the risks of any single one.
Diversification is the practice of spreading your investments across different asset types, industries, geographies, and risk levels. It's the antidote to overexposure. Instead of betting everything on one company, one sector, or one trend, you build a mosaic each piece contributing to the whole.

Why Diversification Matters
Markets are unpredictable. Even the most promising companies can stumble. A tech boom can be followed by a crash. A global crisis can shake entire economies. Diversification doesn't eliminate risk, but it helps you manage it. When one part of your portfolio dips, another may rise. The goal is balancing not perfection.
Diversification is the financial equivalent of not putting all your eggs in one basket. It's the strategy of spreading your investments across different asset classes, sectors, and geographies to reduce the impact of any single failure. Think of it as building a financial ecosystem. If one tree in the forest falls, the others still stand. If one crop fails, the harvest isn't lost.

At its core, diversification is about resilience. It acknowledges that we can't predict the future with certainty. No one knows which stocks will soar or which sector will slump. But by owning a mix of investments stocks, bonds, real estate, funds, and more you create a buffer. You give your portfolio the ability to absorb shocks and keep growing.

John Bogle, the legendary founder of Vanguard, was a fierce advocate for this approach. He believed that trying to beat the market was a fool's errand for most investors. Instead, he championed broad diversification through low-cost index funds. His advice was simple but powerful: "Don't look for the needle in the haystack. Just buy the haystack." In other words, own the entire market. Let the winners and losers balance each other out. Over time, the market tends to rise and so will your wealth.

Diversification also helps manage emotional risk. When your portfolio is concentrated in one area say, tech stocks or cryptocurrency every headline can feel like a crisis. Fear and greed take over. But a diversified portfolio gives your perspective. It reminds you that no single investment defines your success. It encourages patience, discipline, and long-term thinking.

There are many ways to diversify:

- Across asset classes: Mix stocks, bonds, real estate, and cash.
- Across sectors: Invest in technology, healthcare, energy, consumer goods, etc.
- Across geographies: Include international and emerging markets alongside domestic ones.
- Across time: Use dollar-cost averaging to invest consistently, regardless of market conditions.

The goal isn't to avoid all losses, it's to avoid catastrophic ones. It's to create a portfolio that can weather storms and still move forward. Diversification is your financial seatbelt. You may still hit bumps, but you're far less likely to crash.

So as you build your investment strategy, remember you don't need to predict the future. You just need to prepare for it. Diversification is how you do that. It's not flashy. It's not exciting. But it works. And in the world of wealth-building, consistency beats brilliance every time.

Follow Bogle's wisdom. Buy the haystack. Trust the process. And let diversification be the quiet force that protects your future.

10.4 Types of Diversification

Let's break down the key dimensions of a diverse portfolio:

1. Asset Class Diversification: The Foundation of a Resilient Portfolio

Asset class diversification is the cornerstone of smart investing. It's the practice of spreading your investments across different types of assets each with its own risk profile, return potential, and role in your financial strategy. Just as a well-built house rest on multiple pillars, a strong portfolio relies on a mix of asset classes to weather economic storms and seize opportunities.

Different asset classes respond differently to market conditions. When one zigs, another may zag. By diversifying across them, you reduce the risk that a downturn in one area will derail your entire financial plan.

Stocks: Growth with Volatility

Stocks represent ownership in companies. They offer high growth potential, especially over the long term, but they also come with higher volatility. Market sentiment, earnings reports, and global events can cause sharp swings in value.

Role: Capital appreciation and long-term wealth building.

Tip: Younger investors often allocate more to stocks because they have time to recover from market dips. Over time, this allocation can be gradually reduced to preserve capital.

Bonds: Stability and Income
Bonds are essentially loans to governments or corporations. In return, you receive regular interest payments and the return of your principal at maturity. They're generally less volatile than stocks and provide a steady income stream.
Role: Capital preservation and income generation.
Example: During a stock market downturn, bonds often hold their value or even rise, helping to cushion your portfolio.

ETFs and Mutual Funds: Instant Diversification
Exchange-Traded Funds (ETFs) and mutual funds pool money from many investors to buy a diversified mix of assets. They can focus on specific sectors, regions, or strategies or offer broad market exposure.
Role: Simplified diversification and professional management.
Tip: Low-cost index ETFs are a popular choice for passive investors seeking broad exposure with minimal fees.

REITs: Real Estate Without the Hassle
Real Estate Investment Trusts (REITs) allow you to invest in property markets without owning physical buildings. They typically pay dividends from rental income and can offer both income and growth.

Role: Inflation hedge and income generation.
Real-Life Example: A London-based investor added REITs to her portfolio to gain exposure to commercial property. When inflation rose, her REITs helped offset the impact on her bond holdings.

Cash and Equivalents: Liquidity and Safety
Cash, savings accounts, and money market funds offer low returns but high liquidity and safety. They're essential for emergency funds and short-term needs.

Role: Liquidity buffer and capital preservation.
Tip: Keep 3–6 months of living expenses in cash equivalents to avoid selling investments during market downturns.

Putting It All Together
A balanced portfolio might include 60% stocks, 30% bonds, and 10% cash or alternatives. This mix can be adjusted based on age, goals, and risk tolerance. Younger investors may lean more heavily into stocks for growth, while older investors may prioritize bonds and cash for stability.

10.5 Sector Diversification: Spreading Risk Across the Economic Landscape

The economy is not a monolith, it's a mosaic of sectors, each with its own rhythm, risks, and rewards. From technology and healthcare to energy, finance, and consumer goods, every sector responds differently to market cycles, political shifts, and global events. Sector diversification is the strategy of investing across multiple industries to reduce exposure to any single area's volatility.
Think of your portfolio as a well-balanced meal. Relying too heavily on one ingredient no matter how trendy it can leave you nutritionally imbalanced. Similarly, overloading on one sector, even if it's booming, can make your portfolio vulnerable to sudden downturns.

Technology: The Innovation Engine
Tech stocks often lead during periods of innovation and economic expansion. Companies in this sector ranging from software giants to AI startups can deliver rapid growth and outsized returns. However, they're also sensitive to interest rate hikes, regulatory scrutiny, and investor sentiment.
Example: During the 2020–2021 tech boom, many investors saw huge gains. But when inflation fears and rate hikes hit in 2022, tech valuations dropped sharply. Those who were overexposed felt the full brunt of the

correction.

Healthcare: The Defensive Pillar

Healthcare tends to be more stable, even during recessions. People need medical care regardless of economic conditions, making this sector a defensive anchor in turbulent times. It includes pharmaceuticals, biotech, hospitals, and medical device companies.
Tip: Healthcare can provide a cushion when growth sectors falter. It's especially valuable for conservative investors or those nearing retirement.

Energy: Volatile but Strategic

Energy stocks, oil, gas, renewables are highly sensitive to geopolitical events, supply chain disruptions, and commodity prices. They can be volatile, but also profitable during inflationary periods or global supply shocks.
Real-Life Example: An investor in London held a diversified portfolio but added energy exposure in 2022 amid rising oil prices. While tech and consumer sectors dipped, energy stocks surged, offsetting losses elsewhere.

Finance, Consumer Goods, and Beyond

- Finance includes banks, insurers, and investment firms. It often benefits from rising interest rates but can suffer during credit crises.
- Consumer Goods (both staples and discretionary) reflect household spending. Staples like food and hygiene products are recession-resistant, while discretionary items (luxury goods, travel) thrive in strong economies.
- Industrials, Utilities, and Real Estate also play key roles, each with unique cycles and sensitivities.

Practical Tip: Balance Is Strength

Don't overload on one sector, even if it's trending. A well-diversified portfolio typically includes exposure to at least 4–5 sectors. This spreads risk and ensures that no single downturn derails your entire strategy.

Author Insight: In Common Stocks and Uncommon Profits, Philip Fisher warns against "falling in love" with one industry. He advocates for understanding the broader economic picture and maintaining flexibility.

10.6 Geographic Diversification: Expanding Your Financial Horizon

Markets behave differently around the world. Political climates shift, currencies fluctuate, and economic cycles vary. Geographic diversification is the strategy of spreading your investments across multiple regions to reduce risk and capture global growth. It's not just a financial tactic, it's a mindset. It says, "I believe opportunity exists beyond my borders."
When you invest globally, you protect yourself from regional downturns and gain access to innovation, expansion, and resilience in other parts of the world. It's like building a house with multiple foundations if one cracks, the others hold firm.

Domestic Stocks: Familiar Ground

Domestic stocks companies based in your home country are often the starting point for investors. They're easier to research, follow in local news, and feel more predictable. In the UK, this might include firms like Tesco, BP, or Barclays.

Role: Stability, familiarity, and ease of access.

Limitation: Over-reliance on domestic stocks can expose you to concentrated risk. If the UK economy falters due to political instability, inflation, or regulatory shifts, your entire portfolio may suffer.

International Stocks: Global Growth Engines

International stocks offer exposure to dynamic markets in Asia, Africa, Latin America, and beyond. These regions often experience faster growth due to younger populations, expanding middle classes, and technological leapfrogging.

Real-Life Example: An investor in London held a portfolio heavily weighted in UK equities. During Brexit-related volatility, her return stagnated. After adding exposure to Indian tech firms and Brazilian infrastructure companies, her portfolio rebounded driven by growth in emerging markets.

Tip: Use international ETFs or mutual funds to simplify access and reduce currency risk.

Global Funds: Built-In Diversification
Global funds automatically spread investments across countries and sectors. They're ideal for investors who want broad exposure without managing individual international holdings.

Benefits:
• Professional management
• Balanced risk across regions
• Simplified reporting and tax treatment
Example: If the UK market dips due to political instability, your holdings in U.S. or Asian companies may balance the impact. A global fund might include Apple, Samsung, Nestlé, and Tata—all in one basket.

Author Insight
In The Little Book of Common-Sense Investing, John C. Bogle emphasizes that "diversification is not only the key to reducing risk it's the key to capturing opportunity." Geographic diversification, he argues, allows investors to benefit from the global economy, not just their local one.
Similarly, in Unshakeable, Tony Robbins advocates global exposure as a hedge against uncertainty. "The world is your portfolio," he writes. "Don't limit your wealth to one postcode."
Geographic diversification is how your future proofs your portfolio. It's how you say, "I trust the world to grow even if my region stumbles." It's not about abandoning your roots it's about expanding your reach.
When your investments span continents, your wealth becomes more resilient, more dynamic, and more reflective of the world we live in. Because legacy isn't local it's global.

10.7 Risk Level Diversification: Balancing Stability and Opportunity

Not all investments carry the same risk and that's precisely why a well-constructed portfolio should include a mix of risk levels. Risk level diversification is the art of balancing stability with growth, predictability with potential. It's not about avoiding risk altogether it's about managing it intelligently.
Think of your portfolio like a football team. You need defenders (low-risk assets), midfielders (moderate risk), and strikers (high-risk, high-reward). Each plays a role. Together, they create a strategy that can perform across different market conditions.

Blue-Chip Stocks: The Stalwarts
Blue-chip stocks are shares in large, established companies with a history of stable earnings, strong balance sheets, and reliable dividends. These are your portfolio's anchors companies like Unilever, Shell, or HSBC in the UK. They may not deliver explosive growth, but they offer resilience during downturns and steady returns over time.

Role: Stability, long-term reliability, and lower volatility.
Investor Insight: Peter Lynch, legendary fund manager of the Fidelity Magellan Fund, referred to these as "stalwarts" companies that grow steadily and help cushion your portfolio when markets wobble.

Growth Stocks: The Fast Growers
Growth stocks are companies expected to grow earnings faster than the market average. They often reinvest profits rather than pay dividends, aiming for expansion. Think of tech startups, biotech firms, or innovative disruptors.

Role: Capital appreciation and long-term upside.

Risk: Higher volatility, especially during economic uncertainty.

Real-Life Example: An investor in London allocated 20% of her portfolio to growth stocks like renewable energy firms and AI startups. While some dipped during market corrections, others doubled in value boosting her overall returns.

Dividend Stocks: The Income Generators

Dividend stocks pay regular income to shareholders, often from mature companies with consistent profits. They're ideal for retirees or anyone seeking passive income.

Role: Income generation and moderate growth.

Tip: Look for companies with a history of increasing dividends annually this signal financial health and shareholder commitment.

Speculative Picks: The Wildcards

Speculative investments include small-cap stocks, cryptocurrencies, or emerging market ventures. These carry high risk but also the potential for outsized returns. They should occupy only a small portion of your portfolio (typically under 5–10%).

Role: Strategic upside, innovation exposure.

Warning: Never invest more than you're willing to lose. These assets can be thrilling but they're not the foundation of a legacy.

Investor Insight: Peter Lynch believed in owning a mix of "stalwarts" and "fast growers," but he cautioned against chasing hype. His advice: "Know what you own and know why you own it." Risk level diversification isn't just about numbers it's about understanding the nature of each asset and its role in your plan.

10.8 Rebalancing: The Art of Maintenance

Diversification isn't a one-time act it's a living process. Like tending a garden, your portfolio needs regular pruning and reshaping to stay healthy. Over time, some assets will grow faster than others, skewing your original balance. Rebalancing is the discipline of restoring that balance—selling what's overgrown and reinvesting in what's underweight. It's not about chasing performance; it's about preserving strategy.

Imagine your portfolio as a well-built house. Each asset class stocks, bonds, property, cash is a structural beam. If one beam expands disproportionately, the house becomes lopsided. Rebalancing restores symmetry, ensuring your financial foundation remains strong and aligned with your goals.

Why Rebalancing Matters

Without rebalancing, your portfolio can drift into unintended risk. For example, if tech stocks surge and now makes up 50% of your portfolio (when your target was 30%), you're now more exposed to market volatility than you intended. A downturn in that sector could disproportionately impact on your wealth.

Rebalancing helps you:

- Maintain your desired risk level
- Lock in gains from outperforming assets
- Reinforce discipline and long-term thinking
- Avoid emotional decision-making during market swings

When and How to Rebalance

Tip: Rebalance annually or when allocations shift by more than 5–10%. This keeps your portfolio aligned without overreacting to short-term fluctuations.

There are two main approaches:

• Calendar-Based Rebalancing: Review and adjust your portfolio at regular intervals—typically once a year. This method is simple and consistent.
• Threshold-Based Rebalancing: Rebalance only when an asset class deviates from its target by a set percentage (e.g., 10%). This method is more responsive to market movements.
Real-Life Example: A couple in London had a balanced portfolio of 60% stocks and 40% bonds. After a strong bull market, stocks grew to 75% of their holdings. They rebalanced by selling some equities and reinvesting in bonds and international funds. This move preserved their risk tolerance and locked in gains without trying to time the market.
Author Insight in the Bogle heads' Guide to Investing, Taylor Larimore emphasizes that "rebalancing is not market timing it's risk control." It's a way to stay true to your plan, not chase trends. Similarly, in Unshakeable, Tony Robbins advocates for rebalancing as a tool to "buy low and sell high automatically "removing emotion from the equation.

Practical Tips
• Use automated tools or robo-advisors to simplify rebalancing
• Avoid excessive trading stick to your thresholds
• Consider tax implications when selling assets
• Reinvest proceeds into underweight areas, not just cash
• Review your target allocation as your life stage or goals change

10.9 Common Mistakes to Avoid

Building wealth is not just about what you do it's also about what you avoid. Even well-intentioned investors can fall into traps that quietly erode returns, increase risk, or complicate their financial lives. These mistakes often stem from enthusiasm, overconfidence, or lack of strategic clarity. By recognizing them early, you can protect your portfolio and ensure your decisions reflect both wisdom and purpose.

1. Over-Diversification: When Variety Becomes a Burden
Diversification is essential but too much of it can backfire. Owning dozens of funds, properties, or stocks may feel safe, but it often dilutes impact and complicates management. You end up tracking too many assets, duplicating holdings, and losing sight of your overall strategy.
Real-Life Example: A retiree in London held 45 different mutual funds across three platforms. Many overlapped in holdings, and some had high fees. When she tried to rebalance, the complexity was overwhelming. A financial advisor helped her consolidate into a streamlined portfolio with fewer, more efficient funds improving performance and reducing stress.
Author Insight: In The Intelligent Investor, Benjamin Graham warns against "diworsification" the tendency to add assets without improving risk-adjusted returns. Simplicity, when strategic, is often more powerful than complexity.

2. Sector Bias: Betting Too Heavily on One Industry
Investing heavily in a single sector like technology, real estate, or energy can expose your portfolio to concentrated risk. If that industry faces regulatory changes, market shifts, or economic downturns, your entire portfolio suffers.
Real-Life Example: A young investor in Manchester allocated 80% of his portfolio to tech stocks during a boom. When the sector corrected, he lost nearly half his gains. Diversifying into healthcare, consumer goods, and global equities helped him recover and build a more resilient strategy.
Tip: Use sector ETFs or broad index funds to maintain exposure while avoiding overconcentration.

3. Neglecting International Exposure

Focusing solely on domestic markets limits growth potential and increases regional risk. Global diversification allows you to benefit from emerging economies, currency variation, and different economic cycles.
Real-Life Example: A UK-based investor avoided international stocks due to unfamiliarity. During a period of local stagnation, her portfolio underperformed. After adding global funds including exposure to Asia and North America, her returns improved, and volatility decreased.
Author Insight: In Unshakeable, Tony Robbins emphasizes that international diversification is not optional, it's essential. "The world is your playground," he writes. "Don't limit your wealth to one postcode."

4. Ignoring Fees: The Silent Drain on Returns
High expense ratios, trading costs, and hidden fees can quietly erode your returns, especially in actively managed funds. Over time, even a 1–2% fee difference can cost thousands.
Tip: Compare fund fees before investing. Look for low-cost index funds or ETFs with transparent pricing.
Real-Life Example: A couple in Birmingham switched from actively managed funds (1.8% fees) to passive index funds (0.2% fees). Over 10 years, the savings compounded into tens of thousands without sacrificing performance.

10.10 Emotional Benefits of Diversification

1. Beyond numbers, diversification offers emotional stability. It helps you sleep better during market dips. It reduces panic and impulsive decisions. It reminds you that your wealth is not tied to one company, one headline, or one moment.
Investor Insight: Charlie Munger, Warren Buffett's partner, said:
The balance lies in thoughtful selection not randomness.
Building a diverse portfolio is like composing a symphony. Each instrument plays a role. Some are bold, others subtle. Together, they create harmony. Your investments should reflect your goals, your values, and your temperament.
Diversification is not just a strategy, it's a philosophy. It's the belief that wealth is best built not through bold bets, but through balanced choices. It's the discipline to spread risk, the wisdom to embrace variety, and the patience to let time do its work.
So as you build your portfolio, think like a gardener. Plant different seeds. Tend them with care. And trust that, with time, your financial garden will flourish.

2. Lessons Learned from Market Setbacks
Every investor, no matter how seasoned, faces moments of doubt. The stock market, by nature, is cyclical rising with optimism, falling with fear. But setbacks are not failures. They are teachers. They reveal our emotional triggers, test our discipline, and shape our long-term strategy.

Let's begin with a story.
In 2008, during the global financial crisis, millions watched their portfolios shrink overnight. Among them was a young investor named Priya. She had just started investing £10,000 in a mixture of tech and retail stocks. When the market crashed, her portfolio lost nearly half its value. Panicked, she sold everything, locking in her losses.
Years later, Priya revisited those same stocks. Had she held on, her portfolio would have more than doubled. That experience taught her a powerful lesson: reacting emotionally to short-term volatility can sabotage long-term growth.

She wasn't alone.
Warren Buffett, one of the most successful investors in history, famously said:
During downturns, Buffett doesn't retreat he invests. In 2008, while others fled, he bought shares in Goldman Sachs and General Electric, securing favorable terms and long-term gains. His strategy is simple: buy great

companies at fair prices and hold them through storms.
Ray Dalio, founder of Bridgewater Associates, emphasizes understanding economic cycles. He believes setbacks are inevitable and that preparation, not prediction is key. Dalio once lost everything early in his career, a humble moment that led him to build one of the world's largest hedge funds.

Key Takeaways from Setbacks:

- Markets recover: Historically, every major crash has been followed by a rebound. The dotcom bust, the 2008 crisis, the COVID-19 dip all eventually gave way to growth.
- Emotions mislead: Fear leads to panic selling. Greed leads to overexposure. Discipline is the antidote.
- Time is your ally: The longer you stay invested, the more you benefit from compounding and recovery.
- Diversification cushions the blow: A balanced portfolio reduces the impact of any single asset's decline.
- Setbacks are buying opportunities: When prices fall, value often rises. Savvy investors see dips as discounts.

Practical Tip: Create an investment plan with clear goals and risk tolerance. When markets dip, revisit your plan not the headlines. If your goals haven't changed, your strategy shouldn't either.
Setbacks are not the end of your investing journey they're part of it. They build resilience, sharpen your strategy, and deepen your understanding. The investors who succeed are not those who avoid losses, but those who learn from them. Stay steady. Stay curious. And let every dip become a step forward.

10.11 Practical Investment Tips

Investing in the stock market doesn't require genius, wealth, or perfect timing. It requires consistency, curiosity, and a willingness to learn. The most successful investors aren't those who chase trends, they're the ones who build habits. This section offers practical tips to help you start strong, stay steady, and grow wisely.

You don't need thousands to begin. Even £50 a month can grow meaningfully over time. The earlier you start, the more time your money has to compound. Waiting for the "perfect moment" often leads to missed opportunities. Markets rise and fall, but time in the market beats timing the market.

Tip: Choose a simple index fund or ETF to begin. These funds track broad market indexes like the FTSE 100 or S&P 500, giving you exposure to hundreds of companies in one investment. They're low-cost, diversified, and ideal for beginners.

Real Life Example: Take Sarah, a 26-year-old teacher in Manchester. She started investing £75 a month into a global index ETF in 2015. She didn't know much about the market, but she committed to learning and stayed consistent. By 2025, her portfolio had grown to over £13,000 not because she picked the perfect stocks, but because she started early, stayed steady, and let compounding do the heavy lifting.

Emotion is the enemy of consistency. When markets dip, fear can tempt you to pull out. When they soar, greed can push you to overextend. Automating your contributions monthly deposits into your investment account removes the temptation to time the market or skip a month.

Strategy: Use dollar-cost averaging. This means investing a fixed amount regularly, regardless of market conditions. When prices are high, you buy fewer shares. When prices are low, you buy more. Over time, this smooths out volatility and builds discipline.

Most investment platforms allow you to set up automatic transfers from your bank account. Treat it like a bill you pay to your future self. The less you have to think about it, the more likely you are to stay consistent.

The market rewards those who stay engaged. Read books, follow trusted financial educators, and ask questions. You don't need to become an expert overnight but the more you understand, the more confident you'll feel.

Start with the basics: What is a stock? How do dividends work? What's the difference between active and passive investing? Each answer builds your foundation.
Before you invest, define your goals. Are you saving for retirement, a home, or financial independence? Your goals shape your strategy. When markets get rocky and they will revisit your plan, not the headlines. If your goals haven't changed, your strategy shouldn't either.

Avoid Timing the Market

Trying to predict highs and lows is a losing game. Even professionals get it wrong. Focus instead on time in the market not timing the market.
Investor Insight: Peter Lynch said, "Far more money has been lost by investors preparing for corrections than in the corrections themselves."

Understand Fees

Fees may seem small, but over decades they eat into your returns. A fund with a 1.5% fee versus one with 0.2% can cost you tens of thousands over time.
Tip: Choose low-cost index funds or ETFs. Platforms like Vanguard, Fidelity, and iShares offer excellent options.
Use Trusted Platforms
Choose brokers or apps with transparent fees, strong security, and user-friendly interfaces. Look for platforms that offer educational resources and allow fractional investment.
Examples: In the UK, platforms like Free trade, Hargreaves Lansdown, and AJ Bell are popular among beginners and seasoned investors alike.

Stay Informed, Not Overwhelmed

The news cycle thrives on drama. Markets rise and fall daily but your strategy should be built for years. Avoid reacting to every headline.
Tip: Follow a few trusted sources. Read quarterly updates, not hourly alerts. Focus on fundamentals, not hype.

Know Your Exit Strategy

Investing isn't just about buying it's about knowing when and why to sell. Are you investing for retirement, a home, or financial freedom? Your timeline shapes your decisions.

Tip: Revisit your goals annually. Rebalance your portfolio if needed. Don't sell out of fear sell with intention.
Investing is not a sprint it's a marathon. The tools are simple. The challenge is emotional. Build habits, stay curious, and trust the process. The market may fluctuate, but your commitment to growth can remain steady. And that steadiness, over time, becomes wealthy.

10.12 Reflection

The stock market is not just a place where money moves it's where belief meets discipline. Every share you buy is a vote of confidence in a company, a vision, a future. And every decision you make as an investor shape not only your financial destiny, but your emotional resilience.
You've learned how to build a diverse portfolio, how to weather setbacks, and how to invest with clarity.
You've walked alongside legends Buffett, Bogle, Lynch, Dalio each offering a different lens, but all pointing to the same truth: success in the market is not about brilliance. It's about behavior
It's about staying calm when others panic. About investing consistently, even when the headlines scream uncertainty. About choosing strategy over emotion, and purpose over hype.
The market will test you. It will rise and fall. But if you stay grounded if you invest with patience, humility, and curiosity you'll find that the stock market is not a gamble. It's a garden. And you are the gardener.
So plant wisely. Tend patiently. Diversify with care. Learn from the storms. And trust that, over time, your portfolio will not only grow it will reflect your values, your vision, and your journey.

Chapter 11: Safeguarding Your Assets

11.1 Introduction

Wealth, once built, must be protected. It's easy to focus on growth investing, earning, scaling but without safeguards, even the most impressive financial achievements can unravel. A single lawsuit, accident, or unexpected event can pierce through years of progress. That's why asset protection isn't just a technical topic, it's a deeply personal one.

Consider the story of a small business owner who had spent a decade building her brand. She had loyal clients, a growing team, and a steady income. But when a legal dispute arose over a contract misunderstanding, everything was at risk. Without a proper legal structure, her personal savings, home, and retirement funds were exposed. The stress was overwhelming not just financially, but emotionally. She survived, but barely. Had she set up a limited company or secured liability insurance, the damage would have been contained.

Or take the couple who had just welcomed their second child. Life was full of joy and plans. Then came the unexpected a serious illness that left one partner unable to work for months. With no income protection insurance, their savings drained quickly. Mortgage payments became a source of dread. They leaned on family, cut expenses, and eventually recovered. But the experience left scars. Later, they made sure to review every policy, every contingency, and every legal document. They never wanted to feel that vulnerable again.

These stories aren't rare. They're reminders that wealth is fragile when left unguarded. And protection isn't just for the wealthy it's for anyone who's worked hard to build something meaningful.

Asset protection is about foresight. It's about asking, "What if?" before the crisis hits. It's about creating buffers, legal, financial, and emotional that allow you to weather storms without losing everything. It's not about paranoia. It's about stewardship.

This chapter will guide you through the essential tools, insurance, legal structures, and planning strategies, that shield your assets from common threats. You'll learn how to separate personal and business finances, how to use trusts and wills to control your legacy, and how to prepare for incapacity with grace and clarity.

You'll also hear stories of near disasters that were averted, moments where preparation turned potential tragedy into manageable challenges. These examples aren't just cautionary tales. They're proof that protection works.

Because safeguarding your assets isn't just about money. It's about peace of mind. It's about knowing that what you've built your home, your business, your investments can withstand uncertainty. It's about protecting not just your wealth, but your future, your family, and your freedom.

11.2 Tools for Risk Management: Building Confidence, Not Fear

Wealth is fragile when left unprotected. A single lawsuit, accident, or unexpected event can unravel years sometimes decades of hard work. Risk management is the discipline of anticipating those threats and putting safeguards in place. It's not about living in fear it's about building confidence. It's about ensuring that what you've built can withstand storms, not just sunshine.

As financial author Suze Orman writes in The Courage to Be Rich, "True wealth is not just about what you accumulate it's about what you protect." Risk management is the quiet, often invisible layer of wisdom that separates sustainable wealth from fleeting fortune.

Insurance: The First Line of Defense

Insurance is often underestimated until it's needed. It doesn't prevent crises, but it absorbs their financial impact, allowing you to recover without losing everything. It's the financial equivalent of a seatbelt: you hope you never need it, but you're grateful when you do.

Here are key types of insurance every wealth builder should consider:

1. Home and Property Insurance
This protects against fire, theft, vandalism, and natural disasters. Whether you own a single home or a portfolio of rental properties, comprehensive coverage is essential.
Real-Life Example: A young family in Kent had just bought their first home. Months later, a fire caused by faulty wiring destroyed half the property. The emotional toll was heavy, but financially they were spared—comprehensive home insurance covered repairs and temporary accommodation. Without it, they would have faced debt and displacement. Insurance didn't erase the trauma, but it gave them stability when they needed it most.

2. Life Insurance
Life insurance provides financial security for your dependents if you pass away. It can cover funeral costs, pay off debts, and replace lost income ensuring your loved ones aren't left vulnerable.
Tip: Term life insurance is often the most cost-effective option for young families, while whole-of-life policies can support long-term estate planning.

3. Income Protection
If illness or injury prevents you from working, income protection replaces a portion of your earnings. This is especially vital for self-employed individuals or those without employer benefits.
Author Insight: In Your Money or Your Life, Vicki Robin emphasizes that financial independence isn't just about earning it's about resilience. Income protection ensures that your financial plan doesn't collapse under the weight of a health crisis.

4. Critical Illness Cover
This pays a lump sum upon diagnosis of serious conditions like cancer, stroke, or heart disease. It can fund treatment, cover living expenses, or allow you to take time off work without financial stress.

5. Liability Insurance
For business owners, landlords, and freelancers, liability insurance is essential. It protects against legal claims for injury, negligence, or property damage.
Real-Life Example: A freelance web designer in London was sued by a client over a missed deadline and alleged data loss. Her professional indemnity insurance covered legal fees and settlement costs saving her from bankruptcy.

6. Umbrella Policies
These provide an extra layer of protection beyond standard policies. They're especially useful for high-net-worth individuals or those with multiple properties, businesses, or public exposure.

11.3 Beyond Insurance: Other Risk Management Tools

While insurance is foundational, it's not the only tool in the risk management toolkit. Consider these additional strategies:

- Legal Structures: Use limited companies, trusts, and LPAs to separate personal and business assets. This creates legal boundaries that shield your wealth from lawsuits or business failures.
- Emergency Funds: Maintain 3–6 months of living expenses in an accessible savings account. This buffer protects you from job loss, medical emergencies, or unexpected repairs.
- Diversification: Spread your investments across asset classes, sectors, and geographies. This reduces the impact of any single market downturn.

• Cybersecurity Measures: In an increasingly digital world, protecting your identity, data, and online accounts is a form of financial risk management. Use strong passwords, two-factor authentication, and secure cloud storage.
• Estate Planning: Wills, trusts, and advance directives ensure your wishes are honored and your loved ones are protected if you're incapacitated or pass away.

What Other Experts Say

In The Millionaire Next Door, Thomas J. Stanley and William D. Danko found that most self-made millionaires are not risk-takers, they're risk managers. They ensure their assets, plan for contingencies, and avoid unnecessary exposure. Their wealth isn't built on luck it's built on discipline.
Similarly, in Unshakeable, Tony Robbins emphasizes that "the best investors don't just focus on returns they obsess over risk." He advocates for downside protection as a core principle of financial freedom.
And in Family Wealth, James E. Hughes Jr. argues that protecting wealth across generations requires more than financial acumen it requires governance, communication, and legal foresight. Risk management, in this context, becomes a form of love a way to shield your family from unnecessary pain.
Risk management is not glamorous. It doesn't make headlines or spark excitement. But it's the quiet strength behind every enduring legacy. It's the difference between a setback and a collapse, between a crisis and a catastrophe.
The right tools insurance, legal structures, diversification, and emergency planning form a protective shield around your wealth. They don't eliminate risk, but they make it survivable. And in doing so, they give you the confidence to build boldly, give generously, and live fully.
Because true wealth isn't just what you accumulate it's what you preserve. And preservation begins with protection.

11.4 Legal Structures: Building Walls Around Wealth

Wealth, once built, must be protected. Legal structures act as the walls around that wealth defining boundaries, absorbing shocks, and preventing one problem from consuming everything. Whether you're an entrepreneur, investor, or legacy planner, the right legal framework can mean the difference between resilience and ruin.
Many people assume legal structures are only for large corporations or ultra-wealthy families. They're essential for anyone with assets, dependents, or responsibilities. They don't just shield wealth; they preserve peace of mind.

Limited Companies: Separating Business from Personal Risk

One of the most common and effective structures is the limited company. By incorporating your business or investment activity, you create a legal entity that's separate from you personally. If the company faces a lawsuit, bankruptcy, or debt, your personal savings and home are generally protected.
Real-Life Example: A property investor in London owned several rental units under her personal name. When a tenant slipped on a broken stair and sued, her entire portfolio was at risk. The legal claim extended beyond the property to her personal bank accounts and savings. After that scare, she restructured each property in a separate limited company. Years later, another legal dispute arose, but this time only one company was affected. Her other properties and personal finances remained untouched. The lesson was clear: structure matters.

Trusts: Control with Protection

Trusts are powerful tools for transferring ownership while retaining control. They can shield assets from probate, reduce inheritance tax, and protect wealth from creditors or family disputes. Trusts are especially useful in estate planning, allowing you to set conditions for how and when assets are distributed.

Tip: A discretionary trust can provide flexibility, allowing trustees to allocate funds based on changing needs or circumstances.
Author Insight: In Wealth Secrets of the Affluent, Christopher R. Jarvis and David B. Mandell emphasize that trust is not just for passing on money they're for passing on values. When structured well, they become vehicles for legacy, not just protection.

Pension Schemes: Hidden Shields

In many jurisdictions, pensions are legally protected from creditors. This makes them one of the safest places to grow long-term wealth. Contributions often come with tax advantages, and the funds are typically inaccessible to claimants in lawsuits or bankruptcy proceedings.
Strategy: Maximize pension contributions annually, especially if you're self-employed or own a business. It's a way to build retirement security while insulating assets from external threats.

Lasting Power of Attorney (LPA): Planning for Incapacity

An LPA allows you to appoint someone you trust to manage your financial or medical affairs if you lose capacity. Without it, your loved ones may face delays, legal hurdles, or court-appointed decisions that don't reflect your wishes.
Real-Life Example: A business owner in Birmingham suffered a stroke and was unable to manage his affairs. Because he had an LPA in place, his wife was able to access accounts, pay bills, and make medical decisions without delay. The structure didn't just protect wealth, it protected dignity.

11.5 Estate Planning: Preparing for the Inevitable

Estate planning isn't just for the ultra-wealthy, it's for anyone who wants clarity, dignity, and control over what happens when they're no longer here. It's not about anticipating death with fear; it's about preparing for it with wisdom. Because while we can't predict the future, we can shape how our legacy unfolds.
Without a plan, even modest estates can become tangled in legal delays, family disputes, and financial strain. With a plan, your wishes are honored, your loved ones are protected, and your legacy is preserved with intention.

Essential Tools for Every Estate Plan

- **Wills:** A will is the cornerstone of estate planning. It outlines how your assets property, savings, heirlooms should be distributed after your death. Without one, the state decides, often in ways that don't reflect your values or relationships.
- **Trusts:** Trusts offer more control and privacy. They allow you to set conditions for how and when assets are distributed, reduce inheritance tax liabilities, and avoid probate delays. Trusts are especially useful for blended families, business owners, or those with complex assets.
- **Guardianship Designations:** If you have minor children, naming a legal guardian is critical. Without this, the courts decide who raises your children potentially against your wishes.
- **Advance Directives:** These include living wills and lasting powers of attorney. They ensure your medical and financial decisions are handled according to your preferences if you become incapacitated.

Two Families, Two Outcomes

Consider the story of a father of three in London who passed away suddenly without a will. His estate was frozen for months while the courts determined how to distribute his assets. Family members, already grieving, began to argue over what he "would have wanted." Legal fees mounted. Relationships fractured. The emotional toll was compounded by financial chaos.
Now contrast that with another family who had prepared a comprehensive estate plan. The parents had a will, a trust, and guardianship designations in place. When tragedy struck, the transition was smooth. Assets transferred without delay. The children were cared for by the designated guardian. The family could focus on

healing, not paperwork.

Planning didn't remove the grief, but it prevented unnecessary suffering.

Author Insight: In The Seven Stages of Money Maturity, George Kinder writes, "When we plan for death, we are really planning for life, for the lives of those we love." Estate planning is an act of care. It's not about control, it's about compassion.

Estate planning is not a luxury, it's a responsibility. It's how we protect our loved ones, honour our values, and ensure that our final chapter is written with clarity, not confusion.

Start with a simple will. Add layers as your life evolves. Review your plan every few years. And most importantly, talk to your family. Because the greatest gift you can leave behind isn't just wealth it's peace.

11.6 Estate Planning Checklist

Build Confidence, Not Fear

Step 1: Clarify Your Intentions

- Define your legacy goals (e.g. protect family, minimize taxes, support causes)
- Identify key beneficiaries (family, charities, business partners)
- Reflect on values: What do you want your wealth to represent?

Step 2: Organize Your Assets

- List all major assets (property, investments, savings, business interests)
- Note ownership structure (individual, joint, trust-held)
- Gather documentation (titles, deeds, account statements)

Step 3: Choose Your Tools

- Draft or update your Will
- Consider a Living Trust for privacy and probate avoidance
- Assign Power of Attorney for financial and medical decisions
- Create an Advance Directive (living will)
- Review Life Insurance policies and beneficiaries
- Explore Gifting Strategies (annual exclusions, charitable donations)

Step 4: Protect Your Plan

- Consult an estate planning attorney or financial advisor
- Review tax implications (inheritance, capital gains, estate tax thresholds)
- Store documents securely and share access with trusted individuals
- Schedule annual reviews to update based on life changes

Step 5: Communicate Your Wishes

- Talk to your family about your plan
- Clarify roles (executor, guardians, trustees)
- Leave a legacy letter or ethical will (values, stories, intentions)

11.7 Visual Estate Planning Roadmap

From Chaos to Clarity

1. The Starting Point: Awareness

You realize estate planning isn't just for the wealthy, it's for anyone who wants peace of mind. You begin by listing your assets and intentions.

2. The Crossroads: Choosing Your Tools

You explore will, trusts, powers of attorney, and insurance. Each tool is a path toward protection. Hermes-style wisdom: choose with foresight, not fear.

3. The Fortress: Legal and Financial Protection
You build your estate fortress, consulting experts, reviewing taxes, and securing documents. This is your shield against uncertainty.

4. The Bridge: Communication
You cross the emotional bridge, sharing your plan with loved ones, clarifying roles, and leaving behind more than money: meaning.

5. The Legacy Temple: Ongoing Stewardship
You revisit your plan yearly, adjusting as life evolves. Your estate becomes a living reflection of your values, not just your assets.

11.8 Contracts and Agreements: Clarity as Protection

Many risks in business and personal finance don't arise from malice, they stem from misunderstanding. Expectations go unspoken. Roles blur. Memories differ. And when money, property, or reputation is involved, even the closest relationships can unravel. That's why clear contracts are not just legal tools, they're instruments of trust, clarity, and protection.
A contract is a mirror. It reflects what each party understands, expects, and agrees to. Without it, assumptions and so do disputes.

Real-Life Example: The Cost of a Handshake
Two friends in London started a catering business with a handshake agreement. In the early days, everything felt fair. They split tasks informally and reinvested profits. But as the business grew, tensions surfaced. One felt she was going to do more work. The other believed she had contributed more capital. Without a written agreement, there was no clear record of roles, ownership, or exit terms. The dispute escalated into court, costing them not just money but their friendship.
Contrast this with another pair of entrepreneurs in Manchester. Before launching their brand wellness, they drafted a detailed partnership agreement. It outlined each person's responsibilities, profit-sharing ratios, decision-making protocols, and exit strategies. When one partner later chose to pursue a different career, the transition was smooth. The agreement had already anticipated the possibility. There was no drama, just clarity. The difference wasn't lucky. It was foresight.

11.9 Best Practices for Contractual Clarity

• Always use written agreements.
Whether it's a business partnership, rental arrangement, freelance project, or joint investment, put it in writing. Verbal agreements may feel friendly, but they're fragile. Written contracts protect everyone involved.

• Define roles, responsibilities, and exit strategies.
Who does what? Who owns what? What happens if someone wants to leave? These questions must be answered upfront. A good contract doesn't just celebrate the beginning it anticipates the end.

• Review contracts with legal professionals. Templates are helpful, but every situation is unique. A solicitor or legal advisor can ensure your agreement is enforceable, fair, and future proof.

Author Insight: In The E-Myth Revisited, Michael E. Gerber emphasizes that most small business failures stem from unclear systems and expectations. Contracts, he argues, are part of building a business that works, not just one that feels good. They create structure, accountability, and resilience.

Similarly, in The Founder's Dilemmas, Noam Wasserman highlights how early-stage partnerships often collapse due to misaligned expectations. He advocates for written agreements as a tool to surface assumptions and prevent future conflict.

And in Family Wealth, James E. Hughes Jr. reminds us that legacy planning without documentation is like sailing without a compass. Contracts and governance documents preserve not just wealth but relationships.

Clarity is kindness. A well-crafted contract doesn't signal distrust, it signals respect. It says, "Let's protect what we're building. Let's honor each other's contributions. Let's prepare for change."

Because in the end, the strongest legacies aren't built on handshakes, they're built on shared understanding, documented with care, and reviewed with wisdom.

11.10 Geographic and Asset Diversification

Risk management isn't just about insurance or emergency funds; it's about how you structure your wealth. One of the most effective strategies for long-term resilience is diversification. When your assets are concentrated in one region, one sector, or one type of investment, you expose yourself to unnecessary volatility. Diversification doesn't eliminate risk, but it cushions the blow. It turns potential collapse into manageable turbulence.

Think of your wealth like a garden. If you plant only one crop and a storm hits, you lose everything. But if you plant a variety of plants, some in different soil, some in different climates, you increase your chances of survival and growth.

Geographic Diversification

Holding property or investments in different cities or countries protects you from regional economic shocks. A downturn in one area doesn't necessarily affect another. This is especially relevant in real estate, where local markets can vary dramatically.

Real-Life Example: A woman in Leeds placed all her savings into local property. For years, the market was strong. But when the regional economy declined due to industry closures, property values plummeted. Her portfolio lost nearly 40% of its value, and she had no other assets to fall back on.

Contrast that with an investor in London who held property in Manchester, Edinburgh, and Lisbon. When one market dipped, others remained stable or grew. Her geographic spread acted as a buffer preserving her overall wealth.

Market Diversification

Investing in both domestic and international markets broadens your exposure to different economies, currencies, and growth cycles. While UK stocks may be affected by local politics or inflation, global equities offer access to emerging markets, tech innovation, and alternative growth drivers.

Tip: Use global index funds or ETFs to gain exposure without needing to pick individual international stocks. This simplifies the process while maintaining diversification.

Asset Class Diversification

Balancing your portfolio across asset classes stocks, bonds, real estate, and cash reduces reliance on any single type of performance. Each asset class behaves differently under various economic conditions.

- Stocks offer growth but can be volatile.
- Bonds provide stability and income.
- Real estate offers tangible value and rental income.
- Cash ensures liquidity and safety during downturns.

Real-Life Example: A business owner in Birmingham diversified her wealth across rental properties, global equities, and government bonds. When property values dipped during a housing slowdown, her bond income and stock growth offset the loss. She didn't escape volatility, but she avoided collapse.

Diversification is not just a financial tactic, it's a mindset. It reflects humility: the recognition that no one can predict the future perfectly. It reflects wisdom: the understanding that resilience comes from balance, not bravado.

So spread your roots. Plant your seeds in different soil. Because when the winds change and they always do diversification ensures your legacy stands strong.

11.11 Planning for Incapacity

We often plan for death but forget incapacity. Yet illness or accidents can leave us unable to manage our affairs.

Tools:

A, Lasting Power of Attorney (LPA): Appoints someone to handle finances or healthcare decisions.

B, Advance Healthcare Directives: Clarify medical preferences.

A successful consultant suffered a stroke and could no longer sign documents. Without an LPA, her family struggled to access bank accounts and pay bills. Months of legal delays followed. Another consultant, who had prepared an LPA, ensured her spouse could step in immediately. The difference was not fate—it was preparation.

Best Practices in Risk Management

A, Conduct Annual Asset Audits: List assets, liabilities, and vulnerabilities.

B, Review Insurance Regularly: Update coverage as life changes.

C, Separate Personal and Business Finances: Use distinct accounts and entities.

D, Protect Intellectual Property: Register trademarks, copyrights, and patents.

E, Seek Professional Advice: Accountants, solicitors, and planners can spot gaps you might miss.

Risk management is not about pessimism—it's about stewardship. It's about honouring the effort it took to build your wealth by ensuring it endures. Insurance absorbs shocks. Legal structures build walls. Estate planning creates clarity. Contracts prevent disputes. Diversification spreads risk. Together, they form a fortress around your future.

Think of it this way: building wealth is like constructing a house. Risk management is the foundation, the locks, the fire alarms, and the insurance policy. Without them, even the most beautiful house is vulnerable. With them, it becomes a home that can withstand storms.

11.12 Averted-Disaster Anecdotes

We often learn best not from theory, but from stories. Real lives, real crises, and the choices people made in those moments reveal the true value of safeguarding assets. These anecdotes are not about fear they are about foresight. They show how preparation transforms disaster into inconvenience, and how neglect can turn a small problem into a life-altering event.

The Business Lawsuit That Didn't Break a Family

A small business owner had built her consultancy from scratch. She worked late nights, poured her savings into marketing, and finally began to see steady profits. Then came the letter: a client was suing for breach of contract. The claim was exaggerated, but the legal fees alone could have bankrupted her.

Fortunately, she had structured her business as a limited company and carried professional liability insurance. The insurer covered the legal costs, and her personal savings, home, and children's education funds were untouched. The case was eventually dismissed, but the lesson was clear: without those protections, years of sacrifice could have been wiped out in months.

The Family Who Survived a Health Crisis

A young couple with two children lived comfortably on dual incomes. Then one partner suffered a sudden illness that left them unable to work for nearly a year. The household income was cut in half overnight. Mortgage payments loomed, bills piled up, and fear set in.

But years earlier, they had taken out income protection insurance. Each month, a steady payment arrived, covering essentials and keeping the family afloat. They still faced emotional challenges, but they didn't lose their home or their dignity. When recovery came, they were able to rebuild without the shadow of crushing debt.

The Entrepreneur Who Avoided Probate Chaos

An entrepreneur with multiple properties passed away unexpectedly. Because she had prepared a will and placed her assets in a trust, her estate transferred smoothly to her children. There were no frozen accounts, no bitter disputes, no drawn-out court battles. Her foresight gave her family clarity and peace at a time of grief. Contrast this with another family who had no such planning. When their loved one died intestate, the estate was tied up in legal wrangling for over a year. Siblings argued, lawyers billed, and the family fractured. The difference between the two outcomes was not wealth, it was preparation.

The Landlord and the Broken Stair

A landlord rented out a small block of flats. One winter, a tenant slipped on a broken stair and filed a lawsuit. The landlord feared losing everything. But because each property was held in a separate limited company, only one asset was exposed. The others remained safe. Liability insurance covered the settlement, and the landlord's personal finances were untouched. The scare was real, but the damage was contained.

The Car Accident That Didn't Derail a Future

A young professional was driving home late one night when a collision occurred. Though no one was seriously injured, the other driver sued him for damages. The claim exceeded the limits of her standard auto insurance. Fortunately, she had purchased an umbrella policy, a relatively inexpensive add-on that extended her coverage. The insurer handled the claim, and her savings and investments were preserved. Without that policy, her financial future would have been derailed by a single accident.

The Partnership That Didn't Collapse

Two friends started a catering business. Unlike many who rely on handshake agreements, they drafted a detailed partnership contract with the help of a solicitor. Years later, when one partner wanted to exit, the process was smooth. The contract outlined buyout terms, responsibilities, and timelines. There was no bitterness, no lawsuits, no collapse. The business continued, and the friendship endured. Their foresight turned what could have been a disaster into a graceful transition.

The Consultant Who Planned for Incapacity

A successful consultant suffered a stroke and could no longer manage her finances. Because she had established a Lasting Power of Attorney, her spouse immediately stepped in to handle accounts, pay bills, and manage investments. The transition was seamless. Compare this to another case where no LPA existed: the family had to petition the court for access, enduring months of delay and stress. The difference was not luck—it was planning.

Lessons from These Stories

These anecdotes highlight recurring themes:

- Legal Structures Protect: Limited companies, trusts, and contracts create boundaries that shield personal wealth.
- Insurance Absorbs Shocks: From income protection to umbrella policies, insurance turns catastrophe into inconvenience.

- Planning Prevents Chaos: Wills, LPAs, and estate planning ensure clarity when life takes unexpected turns.
- Diversification Reduces Risk: Spreading assets across entities, sectors, and geographies prevents one crisis from sinking into everything.
- Preparation Creates Peace: Beyond money, these tools provide emotional stability in times of crisis.

Disasters will come. Illness, accidents, lawsuits, and loss are part of life. But they don't have to destroy what you've built. The difference between devastation and resilience often lies in preparation. The families and entrepreneurs in these stories didn't avoid hardship but they avoided ruin. They turned potential tragedies into survivable challenges.

Safeguarding your assets is not about expecting the worst. It's about ensuring that when the worst happens, you and your loved ones can still stand. It's about building not just wealth, but resilience. And resilience, in the end, is the truest form of security.

11.13 Highlighted Best Practices

Safeguarding assets is not a one-time task, it's a lifelong discipline. The wealth you build is like a garden: it needs tending, pruning, and protection from storms. Best practices are the habits and structures that keep your financial garden flourishing. They are not glamorous, but they are powerful. They turn uncertainty into resilience and fear into foresight.

Conduct Regular Asset Audits

What it means:

At least once a year, list all your assets property, investments, savings, intellectual property, and business holdings. Then ask: What risks threaten each one?

Author Insight: In The Millionaire Next Door, the authors emphasize that wealthy individuals are not just good at making money, they are meticulous at tracking and protecting it. They know where every pound is, and they know how vulnerable it is.

A family owned several rental properties but never reviewed their insurance or legal structures. When a flood damaged one property, they discovered their policy was outdated and didn't cover water damage. The repair costs drained their savings. Another landlord, who conducted annual audits, had updated coverage and a contingency fund. The flood was disruptive but not devastating.

Best Practice: Create a yearly "asset protection day." Review insurance, legal documents, and financial structures. Adjust as your life evolves.

Separate Personal and Business Finances

What it means:

Keep your personal accounts distinct from your business. Use separate bank accounts, credit cards, and legal entities.

Author Insight: Robert Kiyosaki, in Rich Dad Poor Dad, stresses the importance of treating your finances like a business. He argues that the wealthy build structures around their money, while others leave it exposed.

A freelance designer mixed personal and business funds. When a client dispute escalated, her personal savings were dragged into the legal battle. Another freelancer, who had set up a limited company, faced the same challenge but emerge intact her personal finances were untouchable.

Best Practice: Even if you're a sole trader, consider forming a limited company or LLC. It's not just about taxes, it's about protection.

Create a Will and Consider a Trust

What it means:

A will ensure your assets are distributed according to your wishes. A trust adds privacy, control, and protection from probate delays.

Author Insight: Suze Orman, in The Road to Wealth, insists that estate planning is an act of love. She writes that failing to plan is not just careless it's unfair to those left behind.

Storytelling Example:
Two siblings lost their father. In one case, there was no will. The estate was frozen, and bitter disputes erupted. In another, the father had created a trust. Assets transferred smoothly, and the family could grieve without financial chaos.
Best Practice: Draft a will, and if your estate is complex, establish a trust. Review these documents every few years.

Review Insurance Annually
What it means:
Life changes so should your coverage. Marriage, children, new property, or business ventures all require updates.
Author Insight: In Against the Gods: The Remarkable Story of Risk, Peter Bernstein explains that insurance is one of humanity's greatest inventions. It transforms uncertainty into manageable cost. A couple bought life insurance when they married but never updated it after having children. When tragedy struck, the payout was far less than their family needed. Another couple reviewed their policies annually, ensuring coverage matched their growing responsibilities. Their foresight spared their children financial hardship.
Best Practice: Schedule an annual review with your insurer or advisor. Don't let outdated policies leave you exposed.

Plan for Incapacity
What it means:
Establish a Lasting Power of Attorney (LPA) for both health and financial affairs. This ensures someone you trust can act on your behalf if you lose capacity.
Author Insight: In The Intelligent Investor, Benjamin Graham reminds us that the greatest risk is not market volatility it's our own inability to act wisely under stress. Planning for incapacity is an extension of that wisdom. A consultant suffered a stroke and could no longer manage her accounts. Without an LPA, her family endured months of legal delays. Another consultant, who had prepared an LPA, ensured her spouse could step in immediately. The difference was not fate, it was foresight.
Best Practice: Don't wait until it's too late. Draft an LPA while you're healthy.

Protect Intellectual Property
What it means:
If you own a business, your brand, designs, and ideas are assets. Register trademarks, copyrights, and patents. A small bakery created a unique logo and slogan but never trademarked them. A larger competitor copied the design, and the bakery had no legal recourse. Another bakery, which had registered its intellectual property, successfully defended its brand and even received compensation.
Best Practice: Treat intellectual property like physical property. Protect it legally.

Diversify Across Assets and Geographies
What it means:
Don't concentrate all your wealth in one sector, one country, or one type of asset.
Author Insight: In Unshakeable, Tony Robbins highlights that diversification is the only free lunch in investing. It reduces risk without reducing opportunity.
An investor placed all her savings into local property. When the regional economy declined, her portfolio collapsed. Another investor spread her wealth across property, global equities, and bonds. When property

values dipped, her other assets cushioned the blow.

Best Practice: Aim for balance. Diversify across asset classes, sectors, and regions.

Seek Professional Advice
What it means:
Solicitors, accountants, and financial planners can spot risks you might miss.
A business owner drafted her own contracts to save money. When a dispute arose, the vague wording cost her thousands. Another owner invested in professional legal advice. When challenged, her airtight contracts protected her.
Best Practice: See professional advice as an investment, not an expense.
Best practice is not dramatic. They don't make headlines. But they are the quiet guardians of wealth. They are the habits that prevent chaos, the structures that preserve dignity, and the foresight that turns vulnerability into resilience.
Authors across generations from Graham to Orman, from Kiyosaki to Robbins agree on one thing: wealth without protection is fragile. The stories in this section prove it. Preparation doesn't eliminate hardship, but it transforms it. It ensures that when storms come, your foundation holds.
Safeguarding your assets is not just about money. It's about peace of mind. It's about love for those who depend on you. It's about honoring the effort it took to build what you have. And it's about ensuring that your wealth your legacy endures.

11.14 Reflection

Building wealth is an act of courage. Protecting it is an act of wisdom. Too often, people pour their energy into growth chasing investments, scaling businesses, buying property while neglecting the quiet discipline of protection. Yet history, and the stories we've explored in this chapter, remind us that unprotected wealth is fragile. A single lawsuit, accident, or unexpected illness can undo decades of effort.
The families and entrepreneurs we've met in these pages show us two paths. On one path, neglect leads to chaos: frozen states, bitter disputes, financial collapse. On the other, foresight creates resilience: insurance cushions the blow, legal structures shield personal savings, wills and trusts bring clarity, and diversification prevents collapse. The difference is not luck it's preparation.
Authors across generations echo this truth. In The Millionaire Next Door, wealth is described not as flashy spending but as careful stewardship. In The Road to Wealth, estate planning is framed as an act of love. In Against the Gods, insurance is celebrated as humanity's way of taming uncertainty. These voices remind us that safeguarding assets is not just technical, it's moral. It's about responsibility to yourself, your family, and your legacy.
Think of your wealth as a fortress. The walls are your legal structures. The moat is your insurance. The watchtowers are your audits and reviews. And inside that fortress is your future secure, stable, and ready to grow. Without defenses, even the strongest castle can fall. With them, even in storms, it stands.
So as you move forward, let this chapter be a turning point. Don't see risk management as dull paperwork or unnecessary expense. See it as the foundation of freedom. See it as the quiet strength that allows you to take bold steps in business, investing, and life knowing that if storms come, you are prepared.
Because true wealth is not just about what you build. It's about what you protect. And protection, in the end, is what allows your wealth to endure, your family to thrive, and your legacy to last.

Chapter 12: Tax Strategies for Retaining Wealth

12.1 Wealth isn't just earned, it's preserved.

When most people think about building wealth, they focus on income: earning more, scaling up, increasing revenue. But true financial growth isn't just about what comes in it's about what stays. And one of the biggest threats to that staying power is taxes.

Taxes are often the largest recurring expense in a person's financial life, yet they're rarely treated with the same strategic attention as income or investment. Many people file their returns reactively, hoping for a refund or bracing for a bill, without ever asking: How can I plan ahead to keep more of what I earn?

This chapter is about shifting that mindset. It's about understanding that tax planning isn't just for the wealthy it's for anyone who wants to build and retain wealth over time. With foresight, education, and ethical strategy, you can reduce your tax burden and redirect those savings toward your goals: investing, saving, giving, or growing your business.

The Power of Planning

Smart tax strategy begins with intentionality. It's not about loopholes or avoidance, it's about alignment. When your financial decisions are made with tax implications in mind, you gain control. You stop reacting and start designing.

Consider this:

• A self-employed writer who sets up a limited company may pay less tax than if they operated as a sole trader.

• A family that contributes to tax-advantaged savings accounts (like ISAs in the UK or Roth IRAs in the US) can grow wealth-free.

• A business owner who reinvests profits strategically may defer taxes while accelerating growth.

These aren't tricks, they're tools. And they're available to anyone willing to learn and apply them.

Emmanuel, a freelance consultant in Manchester, earned a steady £60,000 annually. But each year, he found himself paying more in taxes than expected. After working with a financial advisor, he restructured his business as a limited company, began contributing to a pension scheme, and tracked allowable expenses more diligently.

The result? He legally reduced his tax liability by over £8,000 in the first year. That money didn't disappear, it was redirected into investments, savings, and a family holiday he'd postponed for years.

Best Practices for Retaining Wealth

• Know your tax brackets: Understand how your income is taxed and where thresholds change.

• Use tax-advantaged accounts: ISAs, pensions, and other vehicles can shield growth from taxation.

• Track expenses: If you're self-employed or run a business, keep detailed records of allowable costs.

• Plan charitable giving: Donations can reduce taxable income while supporting causes you care about.

• Get professional advice: A good accountant or tax advisor can help you uncover opportunities you might miss alone.

Taxes are inevitable but overpaying is not. By treating tax strategy as a core part of your wealth-building journey, you empower yourself to keep more, grow more, and give more. This chapter isn't about fear, it's about freedom. And the more you understand the rules, the better you can play the game.
Let's explore the tools and tactics that make that possible.

12.2 Table of Tax-Saving Opportunities

Here's a clear, scannable table of common tax-saving opportunities available in the UK (though many principles apply globally). These are legitimate, HMRC-approved strategies not loopholes or evasions, but ways to use the system as it was designed.

Strategy	How It Works	Who Benefits Most	Example
Personal Allowance	First £12,570 of income (2025/26) is tax-free.	All taxpayers	Earning £20,000? Only £7,430 is taxed.
Marriage Allowance	Transfer unused allowance to spouse/civil partner.	Couples with one low earner	Saves up to £252 per year.
ISAs (Individual Savings Accounts)	Tax-free growth on savings and investments (limit £20,000/year).	Savers and investors	£20,000 in an ISA grows tax-free, unlike in a standard account.
Pension Contributions	Contributions receive tax relief at marginal rate.	Employees, self-employed, high earners	£5,000 contribution costs £4,000 for a basic-rate taxpayer.
Salary Sacrifice	Exchange salary for benefits (e.g., pension, childcare, cycle-to-work).	Employees with supportive employers	Sacrifice £1,000 salary for pension; save tax + NI.
Capital Gains Allowance	First £3,000 of gains (2025/26) tax-free.	Investors, landlords	Sell shares gradually to use allowance each year.
Dividend Allowance	First £500 of dividends tax-free.	Shareholders, small business owners	Useful for directors paying themselves via dividends.
EIS/SEIS Investments	Tax relief for investing in early-stage companies.	High earners, risk-tolerant investors	30–50% income tax relief, plus CGT deferral.
VCTs (Venture Capital Trusts)	30% income tax relief + tax-free dividends.	Experienced investors	£10,000 invested = £3,000 tax relief.
Charitable Donations (Gift Aid)	Donations extend basic-rate band, reclaim higher-rate relief.	Higher-rate taxpayers	£1,000 donation reduces taxable income.
Rent-a-Room Relief	Earn up to £7,500 tax-free by renting furnished rooms in your home.	Homeowners	Renting spare room to lodger.

Business Expenses	Deduct allowable expenses (travel, equipment, home office).	Self-employed, business owners	Laptop for business deducted from taxable profit.
Inheritance Tax Planning	Use annual gift allowances, trusts, and pensions to reduce IHT.	Families with estates over £325,000	£3,000 annual gift allowance reduces estate value.

Insight: Tax efficiency is not about dodging responsibility it's about using the rules wisely. As one tax adviser put it: "Paying less tax isn't about avoidance schemes. It's about using the rules properly."

12.3 Navigating Tax Law Through Real Stories

Tax law can feel abstract until you see it in action. These stories illustrate how ordinary people used (or failed to use) tax strategies, and the difference it made.

The Employee Who Overpaid Without Knowing
A teacher noticed her payslip seemed unusually low. She assumed it was normal until a friend suggested checking her tax code. It turned out she was on an emergency code after changing jobs, paying hundreds more than necessary each month. Once corrected, she received a refund and higher take-home pay.
Lesson: Always check your tax code. Errors are common, especially after job changes or multiple income sources.
The Couple Who Saved Through Marriage Allowance
One partner worked part-time, earning below the personal allowance. The other was a higher-rate taxpayer. By transferring unused allowance, they saved over £200 annually. It wasn't life-changing, but it covered a family holiday each year.
Lesson: Small allowances add up. Don't ignore them.

The Freelancer Who Missed Out on Expenses
A self-employed designer diligently filed her taxes but didn't claim home office expenses, mileage, or equipment. She thought it was "too complicated." Over five years, she missed out on thousands in deductions. When she finally hired an accountant, her tax bill dropped significantly.
Lesson: Claim every legitimate expense. Keep receipts, track mileage, and use HMRC's simplified expenses if needed.

The Investor Who Used ISAs Wisely
An investor maxed out her ISA allowance each year. Over a decade, her portfolio grew substantially. Because it was inside an ISA, she paid no capital gains tax or dividend tax. A friend with a similar portfolio outside an ISA faced a hefty tax bill.
Lesson: Tax wrappers like ISAs and pensions are powerful. Use them fully before investing elsewhere.

The High Earner Who Discovered Pension Relief
A consultant earning over £100,000 was shocked to learn her personal allowance was tapering away, creating an effective 60% tax rate on part of her income. By making pension contributions, she reduced her taxable income, restored her allowance, and boosted her retirement savings.
Lesson: Tax planning isn't just about saving now it's about aligning with long-term goals.

The Family Who Avoided Inheritance Tax Pain
A family patriarch passed away with an estate worth £1 million. Because he had made annual gifts, set up a

trust, and used pension planning, the taxable estate was reduced significantly. His heirs avoided a large inheritance tax bill, and his legacy was preserved.

Lesson: Inheritance tax planning is not just for the ultra-wealthy. Even modest estates can benefit.

12.4 Essential Tips for Tax Efficiency

Retaining wealth is not just about how much you earn it's about how much you keep. Tax efficiency is one of the most overlooked yet powerful strategies for long-term financial growth and legacy building. It's not about evasion, it's about education. When you understand the rules, you can play the game wisely and ethically. Here are five essential habits that help individuals and families across the UK protect their wealth through smart, proactive tax planning.

1. Check Your Tax Code Annually
Your tax code determines how much income tax is deducted from your earnings. Yet errors are surprisingly common especially after job changes, retirement, or receiving multiple income streams.
Real-Life Example: A man in London discovered he was on the wrong tax code after switching from full-time employment to part-time consultancy. He had overpaid by nearly £2,000. A quick call to HMRC and a corrected code led to a refund and better monthly cash flow.
Tip: Review your tax code on your payslip or pension statement each year. If something looks off, contact HMRC directly.

2. Maximize ISAs and Pensions First
ISAs (Individual Savings Accounts) and pensions are two of the most tax-efficient vehicles available in the UK. ISAs allow tax-free growth and withdrawals, while pensions offer tax relief on contributions and defer income tax until retirement often at a lower rate.

Strategy:
- Use your full ISA allowance each year (£20,000 as of 2025).
- Contribute to your pension up to the annual allowance (£60,000 or 100% of earnings, whichever is lower).
- If you're a higher-rate taxpayer, pension contributions can significantly reduce your tax bill.

Real-Life Example: A couple in their 40s used ISAs to save for their children's university fees and pensions to reduce their taxable income. Over a decade, they built a six-figure education fund tax-free.

3. Claim All Allowances
Many people miss out on allowances they're entitled to. These include:
- Marriage Allowance: Transfer unused personal allowance to a spouse (worth up to £252/year).
- Rent-a-Room Scheme: Earn up to £7,500 tax-free by letting a furnished room in your home.
- Dividend Allowance: Receive up to £1,000 in tax-free dividends (2025 threshold).
- Savings Allowance: Basic-rate taxpayers can earn £1,000 in interest tax-free.

Tip: Review HMRC's full list of allowances annually. Small claims add up.

4. Track Expenses
If you're self-employed, a landlord, or run a side hustle, tracking expenses is essential. Every legitimate business cost from travel to software can reduce your taxable profit.
Tools: Use apps like QuickBooks, Xero, or even a simple spreadsheet. Log receipts, mileage, and subscriptions consistently.
Real-Life Example: A freelance designer in Birmingham saved over £3,000 in taxes by properly recording home office expenses and travel mileage.

5. Time Your Gains

Capital gains tax (CGT) applies when you sell assets like shares or property. But you can reduce your liability by spreading sales across tax years to use your annual CGT allowance (currently £3,000 per person in 2025).

Strategy:
- Sell part of an asset before 5 April, and the rest after.
- Use both your and your spouse's allowances.
- Offset gains with losses from other investments.

Author Insights: Benjamin Franklin famously said, "In this world nothing can be said to be certain, except death and taxes." While we can't escape either, we can prepare for both. And when it comes to taxes, smart planning can soften the blow, preserve your earnings, and accelerate your path to financial freedom.

Many people treat taxes as a once-a-year headache something to survive, not strategize. But the most successful investors and entrepreneurs see tax planning as an essential part of wealth building. They don't just focus on how much they earn—they focus on how much they keep.

Suze Orman reframes tax efficiency as a form of self-care: "Every pound you save in tax is a pound you can invest in your future." That mindset shift is powerful. It transforms tax planning from a chore into an act of empowerment. It reminds us that being proactive with our finances isn't selfish, it's responsible.

Robert Kiyosaki, author of Rich Dad Poor Dad, takes it a step further. He argues that the wealthy don't just earn more, they understand the tax system better than most. They know how to use tax-advantaged accounts, structure their income, and leverage deductions to legally reduce their tax burden. They play by the rules, but they know the rules better than the average person.

This isn't about loopholes or avoidance. It's about efficiency. And efficiency is legal, ethical, and encouraged. Governments create tax incentives to promote behaviors they want to see like saving for retirement, investing in businesses, or supporting charitable causes. When you take advantage of these incentives, you're not gaming the system you're using it wisely.

Mindset Shifts That Matter

- See tax planning as part of your wealth strategy. It's not an afterthought, it's a cornerstone. Just as you plan your investments, you should plan your taxes. The two are deeply connected.
- Understand the difference between avoidance and efficiency. Avoidance is about hiding. Efficiency is about optimizing. One is risky. The other is smart.
- Invest in professional advice. A good accountant or tax advisor doesn't just file your returns they help you make strategic decisions throughout the year. In many cases, they save you far more than they cost.

Practical Examples

- Use tax-advantaged accounts like ISAs or pensions to grow your investments tax-free or tax-deferred.
- Track deductible expenses if you're self-employed or running a side hustle.
- Time your income and capital gains strategically to stay within favourable tax brackets.
- Consider charitable giving not just as generosity, but as a tool for reducing taxable income.

12.5 Reflection

Taxes are one of life's certainties, but how we respond to them determines whether they become a burden or a bridge. For some, taxes feel like an endless drain, a force that erodes wealth faster than it can be built. For others, taxes are simply another system to understand, navigate, and master. The difference lies not in income, but in mindset and preparation.

This chapter has shown that tax efficiency is not about evasion or loopholes, it's about stewardship. It's about using the rules as they were designed, ensuring that your hard-earned money works for you, your family, and your future. To close this chapter, let's reflect on the deeper lessons, the stories that bring them alive, and the wisdom of authors who have studied wealth across generations.

One of the most common reasons people overpay taxes is ignorance. They simply don't know what allowances, reliefs, or structures are available. A teacher who never checks her tax code, a freelancer who forgets to claim expenses, or a family who neglects to use marriage allowance all lose money not because they must, but because they didn't know better.

Storytelling Example:
A young professional once assumed her payslip was correct. For years, she was on the wrong tax code, paying hundreds more each month. When she finally checked, she received a refund and higher take-home pay. The lesson was simple: awareness is wealth.
Author Insight: Suze Orman often reminds readers that financial empowerment begins with knowledge. In The Road to Wealth, she argues that ignorance is the most expensive mistake anyone can make. Taxes are no exception.

The Discipline of Planning
Tax efficiency is not a one-time act, it's a discipline. It requires annual reviews, adjustments, and foresight. Life changes marriage, children, promotions, property purchases—and so should your tax strategy.
A couple had their first child but never updated their life insurance or tax planning. Years later, when tragedy struck, their outdated arrangements left their family vulnerable. Another couple, who reviewed their finances annually, ensured their policies, wills, and tax strategies always matched their reality. The difference was not income it was discipline.
Peter Bernstein, in Against the Gods, describes risk management as humanity's greatest invention. Tax planning is a form of risk management it reduces the risk of overpayment, inefficiency, and unnecessary loss.

Taxes are often framed as a battle: us versus the government. But a healthier mindset is stewardship. Taxes fund schools, hospitals, and infrastructure. The goal is not to avoid them, but to pay fairly no more, no less. Stewardship means ensuring your money is used wisely, both by the state and by you.
An investor diligently maxed out her ISA allowance each year. Over a decade, her portfolio grew tax-free. She paid her fair share on other income, but she also used the system intelligently. Her wealth grew, and she contributed to society. She saw no contradiction, only balance.
Author Insight: Benjamin Franklin famously said, "In this world nothing can be said to be certain, except death and taxes." But Franklin also believed in prudence and foresight. Paying taxes is inevitable; overpaying is not.

The Role of Professional Guidance
Many people try to navigate taxes alone, fearing the cost of accountants or advisers. Yet professional advice often saves far more than it costs. A good adviser doesn't just file returns, they design strategies, spot opportunities, and prevent costly mistakes.
A small business owner once drafted her own contracts and filed her own taxes. She thought she was saving money. But vague wording in her contracts led to disputes, and missed deductions inflated her tax bill. When she finally hired a professional, her finances stabilized, and her stress lifted.
Author Insight: Robert Kiyosaki, in Rich Dad Poor Dad, emphasizes that the wealthy surround themselves with experts. They don't try to know everything they build teams. Tax advisers, accountants, and solicitors are part of that team.

The Long Game of Wealth Retention
Taxes are not just about today they're about tomorrow. Pension contributions, inheritance planning, and capital gains strategies all shape the future. The wealth you retain is not just for you it's for your children, your community, and your legacy.
A family patriarch used annual gift allowances, trusts, and pension planning to reduce his estate's tax liability. When he passed, his heirs received not just money, but clarity and peace. Another family, who neglected planning, faced frozen accounts, legal battles, and fractured relationships. The difference was foresight.
Author Insight: Thomas J. Stanley, in The Millionaire Next Door, found that true wealth is often quiet,

disciplined, and planned. Tax efficiency is one of the quiet habits that separates the wealthy from the merely high-earning.

What Other Authors Think:

• Tony Robbins, in Unshakeable, stresses that tax efficiency is one of the most overlooked aspects of investing. He argues that even small percentage savings compound into massive differences over decades.

• Dave Ramsey, in The Total Money Makeover, while focused on debt elimination, also emphasizes the importance of maximizing retirement accounts for tax efficiency. He frames it as a moral responsibility to steward resources wisely.

• Napoleon Hill, in Think and Grow Rich, though not writing directly about taxes, highlights the principle of organized planning. Tax efficiency is a modern expression of that principle organizing your finances to retain more of what you earn.

• Seth Godin, in Linchpin, reminds us that systems exist to be understood and navigated. Taxes are one such system. Those who learn the rules gain freedom; those who ignore them remain trapped.

Taxes are not the enemy. They are part of the fabric of society. But overpaying, neglecting allowances, or failing to plan is not noble, it's careless. The stories in this chapter show that awareness, discipline, stewardship, and professional guidance transform taxes from a drain into a tool. The authors remind us that wealth is not just about earning it's about retaining.

So as you move forward, let this be your mindset: every pound saved in tax is not just money kept, it's opportunity created. It's a pound that can be invested, a pound that can compound, a pound that can serve your family and your future.

Wealth is not only built in the marketplace it is preserved in the margins. And in those margins, through tax efficiency lies the quiet power to turn income into legacy.

Part Three: Sustaining and Passing on Wealth

Introduction

Wealth is not only about what you create in your lifetime, it is about what remains when you are gone, and how it continues to shape the lives of others. The first two parts of this book explored how to build and protect wealth. Now, in Part Three, we turn to the deeper question: How do you sustain it, and how do you pass it on? For centuries, families have wrestled with this challenge. Some dynasties flourished for generations, while others lost everything within a few decades. The difference was rarely just money it was vision, planning, and values. A fortune without foresight is like a house without foundations: impressive at first glance, but vulnerable to collapse. A successful merchant once left his children a thriving business and a large estate. But he left no will, no guidance, and no shared vision. Within ten years, disputes tore the family apart, the business was sold, and the wealth was gone. Contrast this with another family who, though less wealthy, created trust, wrote a family charter, and instilled values of stewardship. Their wealth endured, but more importantly, so did their unity. This is the heart of sustaining wealth: it is not just about numbers but about meaning.

The Deeper Dimension of Wealth

Authors across the field of personal finance and legacy planning echo this truth.

• Stephen Covey urged us to "begin with the end in mind." Legacy is the ultimate "end" the vision that shapes every financial decision.

• Thomas J. Stanley, in The Millionaire Next Door, showed that enduring wealth is built not on extravagance but on discipline and values passed down.

• Dave Ramsey, in The Legacy Journey, frames giving and stewardship as the highest calling of wealth.

Their message is consistent: wealth without purpose is fleeting. Wealth with purpose becomes legacy.

Why This Part Matters

Part Three is about moving from success to significance. It is about asking:

• How do I ensure my wealth outlives me?

• How do I protect my family from disputes, taxes, and mismanagement?

• How do I use my resources to make a difference in the world?

The chapters ahead will explore strategies for creating lasting impact, the role of trust and charitable giving, and the art of meaningful generosity. But more than tools, they will invite you to reflect on your values, your story, and the mark you want to leave.

Legacy is not reserved for the ultra-wealthy. It is written in every choice you make how you raise your children, how you give, how you plan. Money is only one part of it. The greater part is meaning.

As you step into this section, remember you are not just building wealth. You are building a story that will be told long after you are gone. The question is not whether you will leave a legacy, but what kind of legacy it will be.

Chapter 13: Building a Legacy

13.1 Strategies for Creating Lasting Impact

Wealth without direction is like a river without banks, it flows, but it floods and dissipates. To create a legacy that endures, you need more than money. You need clarity, structure, and intention. This section explores strategies that families, entrepreneurs, and thinkers have used to ensure their wealth becomes more than numbers on a balance sheet it becomes a story that continues long after they are gone.

Defining Your Legacy Vision

Every lasting legacy begins with a vision. Without it, wealth is vulnerable to being squandered or misused. A vision answers the question: What do I want my wealth to achieve beyond my lifetime?

A woman who built a successful chain of restaurants once gathered her children and asked them what they thought the family's wealth should stand for. Some said security, others said opportunity. Together, they crafted a family mission: to use their resources to support education and entrepreneurship. That mission became the compass for every financial decision, from investments to charitable giving.

Author Insight: Stephen Covey's principle of "begin with the end in mind" applies perfectly here. Legacy planning is not about documents, it's about direction. When the end is clear, the path becomes purposeful.

Documenting Values and Principles

Money can be transferred with a signature. Values require storytelling. Families that endure pass down not just assets, but principles. One way to do this is through a legacy letter or family charter a written document that outlines not only financial instructions, but the values, beliefs, and hopes behind them.

A grandfather left his grandchildren a letter alongside his will. In it, he explained why he valued honesty, why he believed in hard work, and why generosity mattered more than luxury. The grandchildren often said the letter was more valuable than the inheritance itself, it gave them a sense of identity and responsibility.

Author Insight: In the Legacy Journey, Dave Ramsey argues that money without meaning is dangerous. A legacy letter transforms wealth from mere inheritance into a moral compass.

Educating the Next Generation

One of the greatest risks to legacy is unprepared heirs. Studies show that most inherited wealth is lost within two generations, not because of taxes or markets, but because of poor financial education. Teaching children about money, responsibility, and generosity is as important as leaving them assets. A family began a tradition where each child receives a small sum each year to donate to a cause of their choice. At family gatherings, they explained where they gave and why. Over time, the children grew into adults who saw wealth not as entitlement, but as stewardship.

Author Insight: Thomas J. Stanley, in The Millionaire Next Door, found that enduring wealth is built by families who instill discipline, frugality, and responsibility in their children. Education is the bridge between wealth and wisdom.

Using Trusts and Structures

Vision and values need vehicles. Trusts, foundations, and charitable structures ensure that wealth is directed according to your wishes, even when you are no longer present to guide it.

- Discretionary Trusts allow flexibility, letting trustees decide how and when beneficiaries receive funds.
- Charitable Trusts ensure wealth supports causes you care about.
- Family Foundations create a platform for multi-generational giving and involvement.

A family placed their estate into a trust with clear guidelines: funds could be used for education, healthcare, and entrepreneurship, but not for luxury consumption. Decades later, the trust had funded dozens of degrees, businesses, and medical treatments. The family's wealth had not only endured it had multiplied in impact.
Author Insight: Peter Drucker once said, "The best way to predict the future is to create it." Trusts and structures are tools for creating the future you envision.

13.3 Aligning Wealth with Purpose

Legacy is not just about protecting wealth it's about aligning it with purpose. It's about asking the deeper question: Does my money reflect my values? If generosity, education, or community matter to you, your wealth should show it. When financial decisions are guided by personal meaning, wealth becomes more than a resource it becomes a reflection of who you are and what you stand for.
This alignment is not reserved for the ultra-wealthy. Whether you're managing a modest estate or a multi-generational trust, the principle remains the same: money is a tool. As Tony Robbins writes in Unshakeable, "Its highest use is not consumption, but contribution." When wealth is used to uplift others, support causes, and builds legacy, it transcends numbers and becomes a force for transformation.

A Legacy of Education

Consider the story of a couple in Manchester who had no children. They had built a comfortable life through decades of hard work and frugal living. When it came to time to plan their estate, they asked themselves, what do we want our legacy to be? The answer was clear: education.
They created an endowment that funded scholarships for disadvantaged students across Greater Manchester. They worked with local schools to identify recipients and involved their nieces and nephews in the selection process. Over the years, their endowment supported hundreds of students, many of whom became the first in their families to attend university.
Decades later, their names lived on not in stone, but in transformed lives. Their wealth didn't just protect their assets it projected their values into the future. It became a living legacy of opportunity, empowerment, and hope.

What Does Purpose Look Like?

Aligning wealth with purpose begins with reflection. Ask yourself:

- What values matter most to me?
- What causes have shaped my life or my family's journey?
- What kind of impact do I want to leave behind?

For some, purpose may mean funding education, healthcare, or the arts. For others, it may mean supporting faith communities, environmental initiatives, or local entrepreneurship. There is no single right answer, only the one that resonates with your story.

Purposeful wealth planning might include:

- Creating a donor-advised fund to support causes over time
- Establishing a charitable trust or foundation
- Leaving a bequest to a nonprofit in your will
- Funding scholarships, community centers, or mentorship programs
- Supporting family members in launching purpose-driven ventures

The key is intentionality. When giving is guided by values, it becomes more than generosity—it becomes legacy.

13.4 Communicating Openly

Purposeful wealth planning is not just about structure, it's about conversation. Many families avoid discussions about money, fearing conflict, discomfort, or entitlement. Yet silence breeds confusion. And confusion, especially around inheritance, can fracture even the closest families.
Open communication about legacy plans prevents disputes and builds trust. It allows values to be shared, expectations to be clarified, and decisions to be understood. It turns wealth transfer into a dialogue not a surprise.

Two Families, Two Outcomes
One family in London never discussed inheritance. The parents believed it was a private matter. When they passed, the siblings discovered unequal distributions, some received property, others cash, and one was left out entirely due to an outdated will. The result was years of resentment, legal battles, and broken relationships.
Another family held annual "legacy meetings." The parents explained their estate plan, shared their values, and invited questions. They discussed charitable giving, business succession, and family governance. When the time came, there were no surprises, only unity. The children understood the reasoning behind each decision and felt included in the process.

The difference wasn't wealth, it was communication.
Author Insight James E. Hughes Jr., in Family Wealth: Keeping It in the Family, argues that communication is the single most important factor in preserving wealth across generations. "Silence destroys; dialogue sustains." When families talk openly, they build trust, reduce conflict, and pass on more than money—they pass on meaning.

13.5 Practical Steps for Alignment

Here are five steps to help align your wealth with your purpose and communicate it effectively:

1. **Define Your Values**
Start by identifying the values that matter most to you. These might include generosity, education, faith, creativity, justice, or community. Write them down. Reflect on how they've shaped your life. Consider how they might guide your legacy.
Tip: Create a "legacy statement" a short document that outlines your values, intentions, and hopes for future generations.

2. **Choose Your Vehicles**
Select the financial tools that best support your purpose. These might include:
• Wills and bequests
• Donor-advised funds
• Charitable trusts or foundations
• Living giving strategies
• Family governance structures
Work with professional advisors to ensure your plan is legally sound and tax efficient.

3. **Involve Your Family**
Legacy is more powerful when it's shared. Invite your family to the conversation. Share your values. Ask for

their input. Encourage them to participate in charitable decisions or governance roles.
Real-Life Example: A family in Birmingham created a foundation to support youth development. Each generation was invited to sit on the board, review grant applications, and vote on causes. The foundation became a classroom for empathy, leadership, and shared purpose.

4. **Communicate Clearly**
Avoid ambiguity. Be clear about your intentions, expectations, and reasoning. Document your plans and discuss them openly. Use family meetings, letters, or recorded messages to share your story.
Tip: Consider hosting a "legacy dinner" once a year to review plans, celebrate giving, and reflect on shared values.

5. **Review and Adapt**
Life changes so should your legacy plan. Revisit your documents every 3–5 years or after major life events. Update beneficiaries, trustees, and charitable priorities as needed.
Author Insight: As Tony Robbins reminds us, money is a tool. Its value lies not in what it buys, but in what it builds. When wealth is aligned with purpose, it becomes a force for good a legacy that lives on in hearts, not just accounts.
Aligning wealth with purpose is not just a financial decision, it's a moral one. It's about asking, what do I want my money to say about me? It's about using resources to reflect values, uplift others, and shape a legacy of meaning.
Whether through scholarships, foundations, or family conversations, the most enduring legacies are those rooted in love, clarity, and contribution. They are not measured in pounds or properties but in lives changed, stories shared, and values passed on.
So begin today. Define your purpose. Share your vision. Build your legacy. Because when wealth is aligned with meaning, it becomes more than inheritance it becomes inspiration.

13.6 Trusts, Charitable Giving, and Real Family Stories

Legacy is not just about what you leave behind it's about how you leave it. The tools you choose to pass on your wealth can either preserve your values or unravel them. In this section, we explore how trusts and charitable giving serve as powerful vehicles for legacy, and how real families have used them sometimes wisely, sometimes not to shape the future.

Trusts: The Architecture of Intentional Wealth
A trust is more than a legal structure it's a statement of intent. It allows you to transfer assets while retaining control over how they are used. Trusts can protect wealth from taxes, creditors, and even the poor decisions of future generations.

Types of Trusts:
- Discretionary Trusts: Trustees decide how and when to distribute funds. Ideal for flexibility and protecting beneficiaries from themselves or external claims.
- Life Interest Trusts: Provide income to one person (e.g., a spouse) while preserving capital for others (e.g., children).
- Charitable Trusts: Direct assets toward causes you care about, often with tax advantages.
- Bare Trusts: Simple structures where beneficiaries have absolute rights once they reach a certain age.

A family patriarch placed his estate into a discretionary trust. One of his children later faced bankruptcy. Because the assets were held in trust, they were protected from creditors. Another child struggled with addiction the trustees were able to provide support without handing over large sums. Trust became not just a financial tool, but a compassionate safeguard.
Author Insight: In Family Wealth, James E. Hughes Jr. writes, "A trust is not just a container for money it is a

container for values." When designed thoughtfully, trust becomes a vessel for wisdom, not just wealth.

13.7 Charitable Giving: Turning Wealth into Meaning

Charitable giving is one of the most powerful ways to transform wealth into legacy. It allows you to extend your values into the world, support causes you believe in, and model generosity for future generations. At its best, giving is not just a financial transaction it's a deeply personal act of purpose, empathy, and vision.
As Dave Ramsey writes in *The Legacy Journey*, "You haven't truly lived until you've done something for someone who can never repay you." This kind of giving doesn't just benefit the recipient it transforms the giver. It shifts the focus from accumulation to contribution, from success to significance.

Forms of Giving

There are many ways to give, each offering unique benefits and opportunities for impact:

A, Gifts in Wills: Leaving a portion of your estate to charity is a simple yet profound way to ensure your values live on. It requires no immediate financial outlay and can be updated as your circumstances change.
Real-Life Example: A retired nurse in Bristol left 10% of her estate to a local domestic violence shelter. Though modest, her gift funded emergency housing for dozens of women and children. Her name is remembered not on a plaque, but in the safety, she helped provide.
B, Donor-Advised Funds (DAFs): These flexible accounts allow you to contribute assets, receive immediate tax benefits, and recommend grants over time. DAFs are ideal for families who want to involve multiple generations in making decisions.
Real-Life Example: A family in London opened a DAF and invited their teenage children to research and nominate causes each year. One year they supported refugee education, another year mental health services. The process became a cherished family ritual and a classroom for empathy.
C, Charitable Trusts or Foundations: These structured vehicles offer long-term potential, often with tax advantages. They're especially useful for those with significant assets or a desire to support causes over decades.
Real-Life Example: A couple with no children created a charitable trust to fund scholarships for underprivileged students. They involved their nieces and nephews in selecting recipients, turning the process into a family tradition. Decades later, their trust had funded hundreds of degrees. Their names lived on not in buildings, but in lives changed.
D, Living Giving: Donating during your lifetime allows you to witness the impact of your generosity. It creates opportunities for connections, feedback, and joy.
Real-Life Example: A retired builder in Manchester donated funds to renovate a youth center he once attended. He visited the site regularly, mentoring young people and sharing stories. His gift wasn't just financial, it was relational.
Charitable giving is not about how much you give it's about why you give. It's about aligning your resources with your values and using your wealth to write a story of compassion, justice, and hope.
When giving is intentional, it becomes more than generosity, it becomes legacy. And that legacy, rooted in love and purpose, is the kind that never fades.

13.8 The Quiet Giver

Not all legacies are loud. Some arrive quietly, without fanfare or headlines, yet leave a lasting imprint on the lives they touch. One such story is that of Margaret, a retired teacher in Yorkshire. She lived modestly, never married, and spent her life nurturing young minds in the classroom. She wasn't wealthy by traditional standards, but she was rich in compassion and conviction.
When Margaret passed away, her will include a modest bequest to a local hospice where her sister had

received end-of-life care. The amount wasn't large just enough to fund the renovation of a small therapy room. But that room became a sanctuary. It offered music therapy, art sessions, and a quiet space for families to grieve and heal. Her name was engraved on a small plaque by the door, but her true legacy lived in the comfort and dignity experienced by hundreds of patients and their loved ones.

Margaret's story reminds us that legacy is not about the size of the gift, it's about the heart behind it. Her quiet generosity created ripples far beyond what she could have imagined. She didn't need a statue or a wing named after her. She simply gave what she could, where it mattered most.

Lesson: Legacy is measured not in numbers, but in meaning. Even the smallest act of giving, when aligned with love and purpose, can echo for generations.

The Family Foundation That Became a School of Values

In contrast to Margaret's quiet gift, another family chose a more structured but equally meaningful path to legacy. After selling their multi-generational business, the Patel family in Birmingham decided to allocate a portion of the proceeds to establish a charitable foundation. But they didn't stop at writing cheques, they built a framework for generational learning.

Each family member, from grandparents to teenagers, was invited to sit on the foundation board. They met quarterly to review grant applications, debate causes, and vote on funding decisions. The process was democratic, inclusive, and deeply educational. Younger members learned about budgeting, due diligence, and social impact. Elders shared stories of the family's entrepreneurial journey and the values that guided their success.

Over time, the foundation became more than a giving vehicle, it became a classroom for empathy, leadership, and shared purpose. It gave the family a reason to gather, a language for legacy, and a shared mission that transcended wealth.

Lesson: Charitable structures can be tools for education and unity, not just giving. When designed with intention, they become spaces where values are passed down, voices are heard, and purpose is practiced.

13.9 Best Practices for Trusts and Giving

Trust and charitable giving are powerful tools for shaping legacy, protecting assets, and creating impact. But their effectiveness depends not just on structure but on intention, clarity, and ongoing stewardship. Whether you're building a family trust, funding a foundation, or planning a bequest, these best practices ensure your generosity is guided by wisdom and sustained across generations.

Start Early: Planning Creates Possibility

The earlier you begin, the more options you have. Early planning allows you to explore different trust structures, tax strategies, and philanthropic vehicles. It also gives you time to clarify your values, involve your family, and adjust as life evolves.

Real-Life Example: A couple in London began estate planning in their early 50s. They created a charitable remainder trust that provided income during retirement and funded scholarships after their passing. Because they started early, they were able to align their financial goals with their philanthropic vision without pressure or haste.

Involve Your Family: Legacy Is a Shared Story

Legacy becomes more powerful when it's shared. Involving your family in trust planning and charitable giving fosters transparency, unity, and purpose. It turns wealth transfer into a conversation not just a transaction. Invite your children or heirs to participate in discussions about values, causes, and responsibilities. This builds financial literacy, emotional connection, and a sense of stewardship.

Tip: Host a "legacy roundtable" once a year to review plans, share updates, and invite input. It's not just about money, it's about meaning

Be Clear About Intentions: Avoid Ambiguity

Ambiguity breeds conflict. Be explicit about your goals, expectations, and wishes. Whether it's how assets should be distributed, which causes should be supported, or who should serve as trustees clarity prevents confusion and protects relationships.
Author Insight: I've seen families torn apart not by lack of wealth but by lack of communication. A well-drafted trust is only as strong as the clarity behind it. Document your intentions but also discuss them openly.
Real-Life Example: A woman in Manchester created a donor-advised fund and wrote a "giving letter" to her children explaining why she chose certain causes. That letter became a touchstone guiding future decisions and preserving her voice long after she was gone.

Use Professional Advice: Don't Go It Alone
Trusts and giving structures are complex. Tax laws change. Legal language matters. Professional advisors' estate planners, financial advisors, philanthropic consultants can help you navigate the terrain with confidence. They ensure your plan is not only legally sound but strategically aligned with your goals. And they help you avoid costly mistakes that could undermine your intentions.
Tip: Choose advisors who understand both the technical and emotional dimensions of legacy planning.

Review Regularly: Life Evolves So Should Your Plan
Families grow. Laws shift. Priorities change. Review your trust and giving plans every 3–5 years or after major life events like births, deaths, marriages, or business changes.

Regular reviews ensure your legacy remains relevant, responsive, and resilient.
Real-Life Example: A family in Birmingham updated their trust after welcoming grandchildren. They added educational provisions and expanded their foundation's mission to include youth development reflecting their evolving values.

13.9 What Other Authors Think

• Suze Orman, in The Road to Wealth, emphasizes that trusts are not just for the rich, they're for anyone who wants control, privacy, and protection.
• Peter Drucker believed that "the purpose of wealth is to be productive." Charitable giving, in his view, is one of the most productive uses of capital.
• Stephen Covey reminds us that legacy is not what we leave for people, it's what we leave in them. Trusts and giving are tools to do both.
• Tony Robbins, in Money: Master the Game, encourages readers to give even before they feel "ready." Giving, he argues, is not about abundance, it's about alignment.
Legacy is not a transaction, it's a transmission. It's the quiet handoff between generations, the passing of not just wealth, but wisdom, values, and vision. Trust and charitable giving are often seen as technical tools, but at their core, they are instruments of meaning. They allow us to shape the future with intention, to protect what matters, and to give beyond our lifetime.
The families we've explored in this chapter remind us that legacy is not reserved for the ultra-wealthy. A modest gift in a will can build a hospice wing. A small trust can protect a child from financial ruin. A handwritten letter can echo louder than a million-pound inheritance. What matters is not the size of the estate, but the clarity of the heart behind it.
Trusts offer structure. They are the architecture of legacy, allowing you to direct your wealth with precision and compassion. They protect against the chaos of probate, the erosion of taxes, and the unpredictability of life. But more than that, they protect your intent. They ensure that your money continues to serve your value, even when you are no longer here to speak for them.
Charitable giving, on the other hand, is the soul of legacy. It transforms wealth into impact. It says, "I was here,

and I cared." Whether through a donor-advised fund, a family foundation, or a simple bequest, giving allows you to extend your story into the lives of others. It turns money into meaning.

Authors like Dave Ramsey, Suze Orman, and James E. Hughes Jr. all agree: the most enduring legacies are not built on accumulation, but on alignment. When your financial structure reflects your deepest values, your legacy becomes more than a plan, it becomes a promise.

And yet, the most powerful legacies are not written in documents alone. They are lived. They are taught at the dinner table, modelled in acts of generosity, and reinforced through open conversations. Trust without communication can breed confusion. A gift without context can create entitlement. But when legacy is shared when it is explained, discussed, and lived it becomes a source of unity, not division.

So as you reflect on your own legacy, ask not just what you want to leave behind, but who you want to become in the process. Ask how your wealth can serve, protect, and inspire. Ask how your story can continue through the lives you touch.

Because in the end, legacy is not about what you leave. It's about what you set in motion. And with the right tools, the right heart, and the right conversations, your legacy can become a living force one that outlasts you, honors you, and blesses generations to come.

13.10 Highlights on Meaningful Giving

Giving is one of the most powerful expressions of legacy. It transforms wealth into impact, turns values into action, and connects generations through shared purpose. But not all giving is created equal. Meaningful giving is intentional, aligned, and enduring. It's not just about generosity, it's about clarity, engagement, and transformation.

This section explores the principles, practices, and stories that elevate giving from transaction to legacy.

Principle 1: Clarity of Purpose

Meaningful giving begins with clarity. What causes matter most to you? What kind of impact do you want to make? Who do you want to involve?

A retired engineer decided to support environmental education. Instead of donating randomly, he partnered with a local school to fund a hands-on science lab. He visited the school, mentored students, and saw the impact firsthand. His giving wasn't just financial, it was personal, purposeful, and deeply fulfilling.

Author Insight: In The Soul of Money, Lynne Twist writes, "When we align our money with our deepest values, we experience a sense of integrity and wholeness." Giving becomes meaningful when it reflects who we are.

Principle 2: Family Engagement

Legacy giving is most powerful when it's shared. Involving family members, especially younger generations turns giving into a cultural practice, not just a financial one.

One family created a donor-advised fund and invited their children to help choose charities each year. At holiday dinners, they discussed causes, voted on grants, and reflected on impact. The fund became a classroom for empathy, leadership, and shared values.

Author Insight: James E. Hughes Jr., in Family Wealth, emphasizes that philanthropy is a tool for family unity. "Giving together," he writes, "teaches communication, decision-making, and stewardship."

Principle 3: Strategic Structure

Meaningful giving benefits from thoughtful structure. Whether through a charitable trust, donor-advised fund, or legacy bequest, the right vehicle ensures sustainability, tax efficiency, and clarity.

Giving Vehicles:

- Donor-Advised Funds (DAFs): Flexible accounts that allow families to give overtime.
- Charitable Trusts: Provide income to beneficiaries while supporting causes.

• Endowments: Permanent funds where only the income is spent, ensuring perpetual impact.
• Living Giving: Donations made during your lifetime, allowing you to witness the results.

A couple created a small endowment to support mental health services in their community. Though modest, the fund generated annual grants that continued long after their passing. Their names became synonymous with healing and hope.
Author Insight: In Money: Master the Game, Tony Robbins encourages structured giving, noting that "even small, consistent contributions can create massive impact over time."

Principle 4: Storytelling and Visibility
Sharing your story inspires others. It doesn't mean boasting it means modeling. When you explain why you give, how you choose causes, and what impact you hope to make, you invite others into the journey.
A grandmother began a tradition of giving each grandchild £100 to donate. At family gatherings, they shared where they gave and why. Over time, the grandchildren grew into adults who saw generosity not as obligation, but as joy. Her legacy lived on in their choices.
Author Insight: Seth Godin, in Tribes, reminds us that stories build movements. "People don't follow what you do," he writes. "They follow why you do it." Giving becomes contagious when it's shared with heart.

Principle 5: Humility and Alignment
Meaningful giving is not about egotism about service. It asks: How can I use my resources to make a difference? It's not about recognition, but resonance.
A man donated anonymously to fund a community garden in a low-income neighborhood. He never visited, never sought credit. But the garden became a source of food, pride, and connection. His impact was invisible but undeniable.
Author Insight: Dave Ramsey frames giving as spiritual discipline. In The Legacy Journey, he writes, "Giving breaks the power of money over your life. It reminds you that wealth is a tool, not a master."

Best Practices for Meaningful Giving

• Start Small, Start Now: You don't need millions. Begin with what you have.
• Choose Causes That Reflect Your Values: Passion fuels sustainability.
• Involve Your Family: Giving becomes legacy when it's shared.
• Use the Right Structures: DAFs, trusts, and endowments offer flexibility and longevity.
• Track Impact: Follow up with charities, ask for stories, and celebrate results.
• Review Annually: Life changes so should your giving strategy.
• Give While Living: Don't wait for your will. Experience the joy now.

13.11 What Other Authors Think

• Peter Singer, in The Life You Can Save, argues that giving is a moral imperative. He offers frameworks for effective altruism giving that maximizes impact.
• Stephen Covey reminds us that legacy is not what we leave for people, it's what we leave in them. Giving is one of the most powerful ways to do both.
• Napoleon Hill, in Think and Grow Rich, emphasizes the power of definiteness of purpose. Giving with clarity transforms wealth into mission.
• John Maxwell, in Intentional Living, writes, "We all want to make a difference. The question is: will we do it by design or by default?" Meaningful giving is design in action.
Meaningful giving is not a financial strategy it's a legacy strategy. It's how you turn wealth into wisdom, money into movement, and resources into ripple effects. The stories in this section show that giving is not reserved for the wealthy, it's available to anyone with intention.

Chapter 14: Generational Wealth Transfer

14.1 Introduction: The Turning Point of Legacy

Wealth transfer is not just a financial transaction it's a generational turning point. It's the moment when decades of discipline, sacrifice, and growth are handed to the next stewards. Done well, it preserves legacy, strengthens families, and multiplies impact. Done poorly, it can lead to confusion, conflict, and erosion of wealth.

This chapter explores the tools and stories that make generational wealth transfer successful. Whether you're preparing to pass on wealth or receive it, the strategies here will help you navigate the emotional, legal, and financial dimensions with clarity and care.

There comes a moment in every family's financial journey when the focus shifts from building wealth to passing it on. This moment is not marked by age or net worth, but by intention. It's the point where legacy becomes real, where the baton is handed from one generation to the next, and where the future is shaped not by accumulation, but by stewardship.

Generational wealth transfer is more than a legal process it's a relational one. It's about preparing heirs not just to receive, but to carry forward. It's about ensuring that the values behind the wealth are understood, honored, and preserved. And it's about creating structures that protect, guide, and empower not just for today, but for decades to come.

A father who built a successful business spent years preparing his children not just with financial education, but with stories of how the business began, the sacrifices it made, and the values it stood for. When he passed, the children didn't just inherit assets they inherited a mission. The business thrived, the family stayed united, and the legacy endured. Contrast this with another family who never spoke of money. When the parents died, the children were overwhelmed, confused, and divided. The wealth was lost, and so was the connection.

This chapter is about choosing the first path. It's about understanding the tools wills, trusts, gifts, succession plans and using them wisely. It's about preparing heirs emotionally and practically, so they can receive with gratitude and lead with wisdom. And it's about recognizing that wealth transfer is not a moment it's a process, one that begins with conversation, continues with education, and culminates in clarity.

Authors across generations have emphasized this truth:

• James E. Hughes Jr., in Family Wealth, writes that "the greatest risk to legacy is not taxes it's unprepared heirs."

• Stephen Covey reminds us that "legacy is not what we leave for people it's what we leave in them."

• Dave Ramsey frames wealth transfer as a spiritual responsibility, urging families to pass on values as intentionally as they pass on assets.

In the pages ahead, we'll explore the most effective methods for transferring wealth, from simple wills to complex trusts. We'll share real stories of families who succeeded and those who struggled. And we'll offer practical steps to ensure that your wealth becomes a blessing, not a burden.

Because in the end, generational wealth transfer is not just about what you leave behind. It's about what you set in motion. And with the right tools, the right heart, and the right preparation, your legacy can become a living force one that outlasts you, honors you, and blesses generations to come.

14.2 Table of Methods for Wealth Transfer

Here's a structured overview of the most common and effective methods for transferring wealth in the UK, including their purpose, benefits, and considerations:

Method	Purpose	Benefits	Considerations
Will	Directs asset distribution after death	Simple, flexible, widely used	Must be updated regularly; subject to probate
Trusts	Transfers assets with control and protection	Avoids probate, protects beneficiaries, tax planning	Requires legal setup and trustees; ongoing management
Lifetime Gifts	Transfers assets during life	Reduces estate size, uses annual exemptions	May trigger IHT if donor dies within 7 years
Pension Contributions	Passes pension pots tax-efficiently	Often outside estate for IHT; flexible beneficiary options	Must nominate beneficiaries; rules vary by provider
Business Succession Plans	Transfers ownership of family businesses	Can reduce IHT if structured well	May trigger CGT or stamp duty; needs legal advice
Property Transfer	Passes real estate to heirs	Investors, landlords	Sell shares gradually to use allowance each year.
Charitable Bequests	Leaves assets to charity	Reduces IHT; creates legacy	Must be clearly stated in will or trust
Donor-Advised Funds (DAFs)	Enables structured giving over time	Flexible, family involvement, tax-efficient	Requires setup; best for larger estates
Family Investment Companies	Transfers control while retaining income	Tax planning, control, succession	Complex setup; needs legal and financial advice
Life Insurance Policies	Provides tax-free lump sum to heirs	immediate liquidity; outside estate if structured well	Must be written in trust; premiums must be affordable

14.3 Preparing Heirs: Stories and Legal Steps

Passing on wealth is not just about documents, it's about people. Heirs must be emotionally, legally, and financially prepared to receive and manage what's entrusted to them. Without preparation, even the best plans can unravel.

Financial Literacy and Emotional Readiness

A family patriarch spent decades building a property portfolio. When he passed, his children inherited millions but had no idea how to manage tenants, taxes, or maintenance. Within five years, half the portfolio was sold under pressure. Another family, with similar assets, had spent years educating their heirs. They held quarterly meetings, reviewed financial statements together, and involved children in decisions. Their wealth not only endured it grew.

Author Insight: Michael Edwards, a UK estate planning solicitor, writes that "no amount of legal structuring can compensate for a lack of understanding." Financial literacy is the foundation of stewardship.

Best Practices:

Start education early budgeting, investing, taxes, philanthropy.
Use professionals' financial advisors, tutors, workshops.
Encourage hands-on experience family business, trust committees.

Open Communication and Transparency

One family never discussed inheritance. When the matriarch died, the children discovered unequal distributions and hidden trusts. Resentment grew, and legal disputes followed. Another family held annual "legacy dinners," where parents explained their plans, answered questions, and invited feedback. When the time came, there was no surprise gratitude.
Author Insight: Blackstone Solicitors notes that "transparency prevents misunderstandings and builds trust." Silence breeds conflict.

Best Practices:

Share your estate plan with heirs.
Explain your decisions and values.
Invite questions and dialogue.

Legal Structures and Succession Planning

A business owner died without a succession plan. His children disagreed on who should lead, and the company faltered. Another owner created a detailed succession plan, trained his successor, and used a trust to manage ownership. The transition was smooth, and the business thrived.
Author Insight: My Will and Probate UK emphasize that "succession planning is not just financial—it's emotional and operational." It requires foresight and structure.

Legal Steps to Consider:

Draft or update your will.
Create trust with clear terms.
Appoint executors and trustees.
Use powers of attorney for incapacity.
Plan business succession with legal and tax advice.

14.4 Governance and Family Culture

As families grow in size and complexity, so does the challenge of managing shared wealth, values, and relationships. Without intentional governance, even the most well-meaning families can drift into confusion, fragmentation, and conflict. But with the right structures in place, families can foster clarity, continuity, and connection across generations.
Governance is not about control, it's about communication. As Michael Edwards wisely notes, "Governance is not about control it's about clarity and communication." It's about creating frameworks that support dialogue, decision-making, and shared stewardship. When done well, governance strengthens family culture and transforms wealth from a source of tension into a tool for unity and impact.

Real-Life Example: A Family Council That Worked

A large family in Kent, with multiple generations and shared business interests, created a "family council" to manage assets and resolve disputes. They also formed an investment committee to oversee joint ventures and a philanthropic board to guide charitable giving. These structures gave every generation a voice and a role.
The family council met quarterly, rotating leadership and including representatives from each branch of the family. Younger members were mentored into roles, while elders shared stories and values. The investment committee reviewed opportunities with transparency, and the philanthropic board aligned giving with the

family's mission.

Over time, these structures didn't just preserve wealth, they preserved relationships. Cousins who barely knew each other became collaborators. Disagreements were handled with process, not emotion. And the family's legacy expanded beyond money into meaning.

The Cost of No Governance

Contrast this with another family also wealthy, but without governance. As the number of heirs grew, so was confusion. Decisions were made informally, often by whoever was loudest or most senior. Disputes over property, business shares, and charitable priorities became personal. Eventually, the family splintered. Some stopped speaking. Others sold off assets just to avoid conflict.

The difference wasn't money, it was structure. One family had a framework for unity. The other had none.

Governance Tools That Build Culture

• Family Council: Facilitates dialogue, decision-making, and generational inclusion. It's a space for updates, values-sharing, and strategic planning. Councils work best when they're consistent, inclusive, and guided by clear agendas.

• Investment Committee: Overseas shared assets with transparency and accountability. It ensures that financial decisions align with family goals and risk tolerance. Including diverse perspectives financial experts, entrepreneurs, and younger voices strengthen outcomes.

• Legacy Charter: Documents about the family's values, mission, and long-term goals. It's not a legal document it's a cultural one. A charter can include stories, principles, philanthropic priorities, and hopes for future generations. It becomes a compass when decisions get complex.

Governance is not a burden, it's a gift. It offers structure without rigidity, clarity without control, and unity without uniformity. It honors individuality while protecting the collective. And most importantly, it ensures that family wealth is not just preserved but stewarded with purpose.

Because in the end, family culture is the true inheritance. And governance is how we protect it.

14.5 Values, Purpose, and Philanthropy

Wealth without context can feel hollow. When inheritance arrives without meaning, it risks becoming a burden rather than a blessing. The difference between careless spending and intentional stewardship often lies in one crucial element: purpose.

Consider two heirs. One woman inherited a large estate but felt disconnected from it. Her parents had never explained its origins or purpose. She spent lavishly on luxury cars, designer wardrobes, impulsive investments only to feel regret and emptiness. The money had no story, no soul. It was a transaction, not a legacy.

Another heir was raised with stories of sacrifice and generosity. She knew how her grandparents had built their business from scratch, how they gave quietly to local charities, and how they believed wealth was a tool for impact. When she inherited, she used the funds to start a foundation focused on education and community development. Her wealth became a source of pride, purpose, and continuity.

These contrasting stories reveal a deeper truth: wealth is not just financial—it's emotional, relational, and spiritual. And when values are embedded into the transfer, money becomes a means of meaning.

Author Insight As My Will and Probate UK wisely note, "Heirs who understand the 'why' behind wealth are more likely to manage it with care." Purpose transforms entitlement into stewardship. It shifts the narrative from "What do I get?" to "What do I carry forward?"

This insight is especially relevant in families where wealth is newly created. Without intentional storytelling and value-sharing, the next generation may inherit assets but not the wisdom that built them.

Best Practices for Purposeful Wealth Transfer

To ensure that wealth becomes a source of empowerment rather than confusion, consider these practices:

• Share stories of how wealth was built.

Talk about the early struggles, the pivotal decisions, the values that guided growth. These stories humanize money and connect heirs to their roots.

• Real-Life Example: A family in Manchester created a "legacy book" documenting their entrepreneurial journey, including letters from grandparents and photos from the original shop. It became a cherished heirloom and a guide for future generations.

• Discuss values and desired impact.

What does your family stand for? What causes matter most? What kind of legacy do you want to leave? These conversations shape not just financial plans, but moral compasses.

• Tip: Host an annual "legacy dinner" where family members share updates on charitable giving, personal growth, and community involvement.

• Involve heirs in charitable giving.

Invite them to help choose causes, volunteer, or manage small grants. This builds empathy, financial literacy, and a sense of responsibility.

• Real-Life Example: A woman in London gave each of her children £1,000 annually to donate to a cause of their choice. They researched, debated, and presented their decisions turning giving into a shared learning experience.

14.6 Review and Adaptation: Stewardship Over Time

Wealth transfer is not a one-time event—it's a living process. It's not just about passing down assets; it's about preserving values, protecting relationships, and preparing for the future. Life changes. Laws evolve. Family dynamics shift. What worked five years ago may no longer serve your goals today. That's why regular review and thoughtful adaptation are essential.

Too often, families treat estate planning as a "set it and forget it" task. But true stewardship requires ongoing attention. It's about ensuring that your intentions remain aligned with reality and that your legacy continues to reflect your values.

Here's a practical checklist to guide your review process:

A. Update Wills and Trusts Every 3–5 Years

Your will and trust documents are the foundation of your wealth transfer plan. They outline who inherits what, how assets are managed, and what protections are in place. But these documents must evolve with your life.

Real-Life Example: A woman in London updated her will after launching a nonprofit. Initially, her estate plan focused solely on family heritage. But as her mission grew, she wanted to include charitable giving. Her updated will reflect both personal and philanthropic legacy.

B. Reassess Executors and Trustees

The people you appoint to manage your estate or trust play a critical role. Are they still the right fit? Do they have the time, capacity, and temperament to carry out your wishes?

Family relationships can shift. Health can decline. Priorities can change. Reassessing these roles ensures your plan is not only legally sound but emotionally sustainable.

C. Review Beneficiary Designations

Beneficiary designations on retirement accounts, insurance policies, and investment portfolios often override what's written in your will. That's why it's vital to keep them current.

Tip: After major life events like marriage, divorce, or the birth of a child review all beneficiary forms. A forgotten designation can lead to unintended consequences.

D. Adjust Plans for New Marriages, Births, or Deaths

Families grow and change. New marriages may introduce stepchildren. Birth brings new heirs. Deaths may leave gaps in your plan. Each event is a cue to revisit your documents, update your intentions, and ensure clarity.

Author Insight: I've seen families torn apart not by lack of wealth but by lack of clarity. A well-reviewed plan is a gift of peace. It prevents confusion, reduces conflict, and honors everyone involved.

E. Revisit Family Governance Structures

If your family manages shared assets like property, businesses, or trusts governance matters. Are roles and responsibilities clear? Are decision-making processes fair? Are younger generations prepared to lead? Revisiting governance structures ensures that your legacy is not just preserved but stewarded with wisdom and unity.

14.10 What You Set in Motion

Generational wealth transfer is often described in terms of numbers of assets, percentages, tax thresholds. But beneath the spreadsheets and legal documents lies something far more profound: a moment of transition, a turning point in legacy, and a chance to shape the future in ways that extend far beyond financial value.

This chapter has explored the tools and strategies that make wealth transfer effective wills, trusts, lifetime gifts, succession plans. But the heart of the matter is not the method. It's the meaning. Because what you pass on is not just money. It's memory. It's mission. It's the story of who you are and what you stand for.

Wealth Is a Story, Not Just a Sum

Every pound you've earned carries a story. Perhaps it came from long hours, bold risks, quiet sacrifices, or creative breakthroughs. Perhaps it was built slowly, through frugality and discipline. Or maybe it arrived suddenly, through inheritance or windfall. However it came, it carries your fingerprints.

When you pass on wealth, you're passing on that story. And if you don't tell me it, it may be lost. Heirs who inherit without context often feel disconnected, overwhelmed, or entitled. But those who understand the journey behind the wealth its origins, its purpose, its values are more likely to steward it wisely.

A woman inherited a large estate from her father but had no idea how he built it. She spent lavishly, disconnected from its meaning. Years later, she regretted not asking more questions. Another heir received a modest inheritance, but alongside it came a letter detailing the sacrifices, values, and hopes behind the gift. That letter became a compass, guiding her decisions and deepening her gratitude.

The greatest threat to generational wealth is not taxes, it's lack of preparation. Studies show that 70% of wealthy families lose their wealth by the second generation, and 90% by the third. The reasons are rarely financial. They're relational. They stem from poor communication, unprepared heirs, and unclear intentions.

Preparation means more than drafting a will. It means educating your heirs, involving them in decisions, and creating structures that support clarity and continuity. It means talking about money not just how much, but why it matters, what it's for, and how it should be used.

Author Insight: James E. Hughes Jr., in *Family Wealth*, writes, "The most important legacy is not financial it's intellectual and social capital." Teaching heirs how to think about wealth is more valuable than wealth itself.

Communication Is the Bridge

Silence around money is common and costly. Families avoid conversations about inheritance out of discomfort, fear of conflict, or a desire to protect. But silence breeds confusion. It leaves heirs guessing, and often, fighting.

Open communication builds trust. It allows you to explain your decisions, share your hopes, and invite dialogue. It turns wealth transfer from a surprise into a shared journey.

One family held annual "legacy dinners" where parents explained their estate plan, invited questions, and discussed values. When the time came, there were no disputes—only unity. Another family never spoke of money. When the parents died, the children discovered unequal distributions and hidden trusts. Resentment followed, and relationships fractured.

Legal tools like trust, wills, and succession plans are not just technical, they're ethical. They protect your intentions, prevent disputes, and ensure that your wealth serves its purpose.

A well-crafted trust can shield assets from creditors, support vulnerable heirs, and direct funds toward education, entrepreneurship, or philanthropy. A clear will can prevent confusion and honor your wishes. A succession plan can preserve a family business and empower the next generation.

Author Insight: Suze Orman, in *The Road to Wealth*, insists that estate planning is an act of love. "Failing to plan," she writes, "is not just careless it's unfair to those left behind."

Legacy Is Lived, Not Just Left

The most powerful legacies are not created at death they're lived in life. They're built through daily choices, shared stories, and modelled values. Giving, teaching, and involving your heirs now creates a culture of stewardship that endures.

You don't have to wait until your final will to shape your legacy. You can start today by mentoring, giving, educating, and sharing. By living your values, you make them visible. And by involving your family, you make them last.

A grandfather began a tradition of giving each grandchild £100 to donate to a cause of their choice. At family gatherings, they shared where they gave and why. Over time, the grandchildren grew into adults who saw generosity not as obligation, but as joy. His legacy was not just financial, it was cultural.

Review Is Responsibility

Life changes. Families evolve. Laws shift. A legacy plan that worked five years ago may no longer fit. Regular review is essential.

Update your will. Revisit your trust. Reassess your executors and trustees. Adjust to new marriages, births, or deaths. Revisit your family governance structures. Legacy is not static, it's dynamic. And keeping it current is an act of care.

Other Authors Think

Stephen Covey reminds us that "legacy is not what we leave for people it's what we leave in them."

Dave Ramsey, in *The Legacy Journey*, frames wealth transfer as a spiritual responsibility, urging families to pass on values as intentionally as they pass on assets.

Tony Robbins, in *Unshakeable*, emphasizes that wealth without purpose is fragile. Purpose gives wealth direction and endurance.

John Maxwell, in *Intentional Living*, writes, "We all want to make a difference. The question is: will we do it by design or by default?" Generational wealth transfer is design in action.

14.11 Reflection

Generational wealth transfer is not the end of your financial journey it's the beginning of someone else's. It's the moment when your story becomes part of theirs. When your values become their compass. When your sacrifices become their foundation.

The question is not whether you will leave a legacy. You will. The question is: what kind?

Will it be one of confusion, conflict, and erosion? Or one of clarity, unity, and growth? Will your heirs inherit money or meaning? Will your wealth fade or flourish?

The answer lies not just in your bank balance, but in your preparation, your communication, your structures, and your heart.

Wealth without wisdom is fragile. It can divide families, fuel entitlement, or disappear within a generation. But wealth anchored in purpose shared through stories, guided by principles, and protected by planning can become a force for generational empowerment.

Start by making your intentions clear. What do you want your wealth to do not just for your children, but through them? Is it to provide security? Opportunity? A platform for service? Write it down. Share it. Let your heirs understand the "why" behind the "what."

Then, build the structures that support your vision. This might include will, trust, life insurance, or family investment vehicles. But it also includes conversations honest, ongoing, sometimes uncomfortable ones. Talk about money. Talk about values. Talk about mistakes and lessons learned. The more transparent you are, the more equipped your heirs will be to carry the torch.

Education is another pillar. Teach financial literacy early. Involve your children in budgeting, investing, and giving. Let them see how wealth is built, managed, and multiplied. Let them feel the weight of responsibility not as a burden, but as a blessing.

And don't forget the emotional legacy. What stories will they talk about you? What principles will echo in their decisions? What traditions will they carry forward? These are the invisible threads that hold a legacy together. They're not written in legal documents, they're written in memories, habits, and shared meaning.

Author Insight: I once had a childhood friend who inherited a sizable estate from his father but had no guidance. No letter. No plan. No conversation. Within five years, the wealth was gone, and the family was fractured. Contrast that with another family I worked with, where the parents held annual "legacy dinners" to discuss values, goals, and stewardship. Their wealth didn't just survive, it grew, and so did their unity. Because in the end, wealth transfer is not just about what you leave behind. It's about what you set in motion. It's about planting seeds you may never see bloom but knowing they will. It's about turning your life's work into a launchpad for someone else's.

So write the letter. Have the talk. Build the plan. Share the vision. And trust that your legacy rooted in love, shaped by wisdom, and guided by intention will not only endure, but expand.

That is the true power of generational wealth. Not just inheritance but impact.

Chapter 15: Wealth and Well-being

15.1 Introduction: Redefining What It Means to Be Wealthy

Wealth is often portrayed as the goal of a destination marked by financial freedom, material comfort, and social status. But as many discover, reaching that destination doesn't always bring peace. In fact, without intentional alignment, wealth can become a source of stress, disconnection, and even burnout. This chapter invites you to pause and ask a deeper question: What does it mean to be truly well and truly wealthy?

Wealth and well-being are not opposites. They are partners. When harmonized, they create a life that is not only prosperous, but purposeful. When misaligned, they can pull us in conflicting directions toward achievement at the expense of health, toward accumulation without connection, toward success that feels strangely hollow.

Consider the entrepreneur who built a seven-figure business but found herself chronically exhausted, disconnected from her family, and unsure what all the effort was for. Her turning point came not from another financial milestone, but from a moment of clarity: she wanted her wealth to serve her life not consume it. She restructured her business, prioritized rest, and began investing in relationships and health. Her income dipped temporarily, but her joy soared. She didn't lose wealth, she redefined it.

This chapter explores how to make that shift. It's about harmonizing money with life priorities, recognizing health and relationships as forms of capital, and avoiding the burnout that often shadows high achievement. It's about reclaiming the original promise of wealth: freedom, peace, and the ability to live well.

Authors across disciplines echo this truth:

• Meir Statman, in Finance for Normal People, argues that financial decisions should serve life well-being not just economic gain.

• Joyce Marter, in The Financial Mindset Fix, shows how emotional health and financial health are deeply intertwined.

• Naval Ravikant reminds us that "a fit body, a calm mind, and a house full of love" are the real markers of wealth.

In the sections ahead, we'll explore practical strategies for aligning money with meaning. You'll learn how to audit your financial life against your values, how to treat health and relationships as investments, and how to spot and prevent burnout before it derails your success. We'll also highlight key principles that help you stay grounded as your wealth grows.

Because in the end, the richest life is not the one with the most money it's the one where money supports what matters most.

15.2 Harmonizing Money and Life Priorities

Wealth, when disconnected from life's deeper priorities, can become a source of imbalance rather than freedom. Many people chase financial success with the hope that it will eventually buy them peace, time, or happiness only to find that the pursuit itself has crowded out the very things they value most. Harmonizing money and life priorities is not about choosing one over the other, it's about aligning them so that your financial life supports your emotional, relational, and spiritual well-being.

It's easy to fall into the trap of misalignment. You set a financial goal by buying a house, reaching a certain income, building a business and pour your energy into achieving it. But somewhere along the way, the goal becomes the master. You work longer hours, sacrifice sleep, skip family dinners, and delay joy "until things settle." But things rarely do.

A tech consultant in her 30s was earning six figures and climbing fast. But she felt constantly anxious, disconnected from her partner, and unsure what she was working toward. Her turning point came during a weekend retreat where she was asked to list her top five life values. "Freedom, connection, health, creativity, and peace," she wrote. Then she looked at her calendar and saw none of them reflected. That moment sparked a shift. She didn't quit her job, but she restructured her work, set boundaries, and began aligning her money with her values. Her income dipped slightly, but her life expanded.

15.3 Aligning Life with What Matters: A Four-Step Practice

In a world full of distractions and demands, it's easy to drift away from what truly matters. This four-step practice helps you realign your time and money with your core life priorities—so your daily choices reflect your deepest values.

Step 1: Identify Your Core Life Priorities

Begin by listing the top 3–5 things that matter most to you. These are your non-negotiables—the values that give your life meaning. They might include:

- Time with family
- Health and vitality
- Creative expression
- Spiritual growth
- Community impact
- Freedom and flexibility

Be honest. Don't list what you think should matter—list what genuinely lights you up or grounds you.

Real-Life Example: A father in London named Ade listed his top priorities as: quality time with his children, physical health, and building a legacy through entrepreneurship. This clarity helped him evaluate how he was spending his energy and where he was falling short.

Step 2: Track Your Time and Spending

For one week, track how you spend your time and money. Use a journal, spreadsheet, or app. Be honest and detailed. Include everything from scrolling social media to impulse buys to time spent commuting.

This step isn't about judgment, it's about awareness. You can't change what you don't see.

Real-Life Example: A woman in Nairobi tracked her week and realized she was spending over 10 hours watching TV and nearly 30% of her income on takeout. Yet she'd been telling herself she "didn't have time" to exercise or money to invest in her writing course.

Step 3: Compare and Reflect

Now compare your actual habits with your stated priorities. Ask:

- How well do my time and money reflect what I say matters?
- Where is there alignment?
- Where is there drift?

This is where insight emerges. You may find that your calendar and bank statement tell a different story than your values. That's okay. Awareness is the first step toward change.

Real-Life Example: Ade realized he was spending more time at work events than with his kids, and more money on networking dinners than on family experiences. This disconnect became a wake-up call.

Step 4: Make One Shift

Choose one small, meaningful change that brings your time or money closer to your values. It doesn't have to be dramatic. Cancel a subscription you don't use. Block off Sunday afternoons for family. Redirect £50 a month toward a cause you care about.

Small shifts compound. They create momentum. And they signal to yourself: I'm living on purpose.
Real-Life Example: The woman in Nairobi cancelled two streaming services and used the savings to enroll in an online writing course. That one shift reignited her creativity and gave her a sense of agency she hadn't felt in years.
Author Insight: Meir Statman on Life Well-Being In Finance for Normal People, behavioral finance expert Meir Statman argues that financial decisions should serve "life well-being," not just wealth maximization. He introduces the idea of "expressive and emotional benefits" of money how we use money to express identity, feel secure, or connect with others. When we ignore these dimensions, we risk making financially sound decisions that leave us emotionally empty.
Statman's framework invites us to ask not just "Is this a good investment?" but "Does this support the life I want to live?"
One of the most powerful concepts in harmonizing money and life is the idea of "enough." In a culture that glorifies more income, more assets, more hustle defining your personal "enough" is a radical act of clarity.
A couple in their 50s had saved diligently and reached financial independence. But they kept working, driven by fear and habit. One day, their financial planner asked, "What are you waiting for?" They realized they had no clear answer. After defining their "enough" a modest home, travel, time with grandchildren they retired early and began volunteering. Their wealth didn't grow as fast, but their life did.
What does "enough" look like for you not just financially, but emotionally and relationally?

Life priorities shift with seasons.
What matters in your 30s may not be what matters in your 50s. Harmonizing money and life is not a one-time fix it's a rhythm of reflection and rebalancing.

A, what matters most to me right now?
B, is my money supporting or sabotaging that?
C, what's one change I can make this quarter?
Example:
A new parent may shift spending from travel to childcare. A retiree may shift from accumulation to giving. A mid-career professional may prioritize health over hustle. Each season invites a new alignment.

15.3 Mindset Shifts That Support Harmony

1.From Scarcity to Sufficiency
Instead of asking, "How can I get more?" ask, "How can I use what I have more meaningfully?"

2. Comparison to Clarity
Social media and peer pressure distort our sense of what's "normal." Define success on your own terms.

3. From Delay to Integration
Don't postpone joy until retirement. Find ways to integrate rest, connection, and purpose now.

What Other Authors Say
• Vicki Robin, in Your Money or Your Life, reframes money as "life energy." She encourages readers to track spending not in pounds, but in hours of life exchanged. This lens makes it easier to align money with meaning.
• Carl Richards, in The Behaviour Gap, uses simple sketches to show how our financial decisions often drift from our intentions. His message: clarity beats complexity.
• Brené Brown reminds us that "joy comes to us in ordinary moments." If our financial lives are so busy chasing extraordinary outcomes that we miss the ordinary, we've lost the plot.

Practical Tools for Alignment

1.Values-Based Budgeting

Allocate money not just by category, but by value. For example, "Connection" might include date nights, travel to see family, or shared experiences.

Time-Money Trade-off Tracker: For each major expense, ask: Does this save me time, cost me time, or give me time with people I love?

The "Why" Filter: Before any major financial decision, ask: Why am I doing this? What feeling or outcome am I hoping for?

Harmonising money and life priorities is not about perfection it's about presence. It's about noticing when your financial life drifts from your values and gently steering it back. It's about letting your money serve your life, not the other way around.

So take a breath. Revisit your values. Look at your calendar and your bank statement. And ask: Are they telling the same story?

Because in the end, the richest life is not the one with the most money, it's the one where money supports what matters most.

15.4 Health and Relationships as Wealth

We often think of wealth as something stored in bank accounts, property portfolios, or investment funds. But the most foundational forms of wealth are often invisible, our health and our relationships. Without them, financial success can feel hollow. With them, even modest means can support a deeply fulfilling life.

Health: The First Currency

Health is the foundation upon which all other forms of wealth rest. Without physical vitality or mental clarity, it becomes difficult to enjoy the fruits of financial success. Yet in the pursuit of career goals or business growth, health is often the first thing sacrificed skipped meals, sleepless nights, chronic stress.

A high-performing executive in her 40s collapsed from exhaustion during a client presentation. Years of overwork had caught up with her. In recovery, she realized she had been treating her body like a machine fueled by caffeine and adrenaline. She began to see her health not as a cost, but as an investment. She hired a nutritionist, started walking daily, and restructured her work schedule. Her energy returned and so did her creativity and joy.

Practical Insight:

View health expenses like therapy, fitness, or preventative care not as luxuries, but as essential components of your wealth strategy. A healthy body and mind are assets that are appreciated over time.

15.6 Relationships: The Emotional Portfolio

Relationships are another form of capital emotional, social, and spiritual. They provide support in crisis, amplify joy in success, and offer meaning that money alone cannot. Yet like health, relationships are often neglected in the name of productivity.

A man who had built a successful business found himself alone at his retirement party. He prioritized work over family, networking over friendship. In his later years, he began reaching out—rebuilding bonds with his children, volunteering in his community. He said, "I thought I was rich. But I was bankrupt in the places that mattered most."

Author Insight: Harvard's 80-year longitudinal study on adult development found that close relationships, not wealth or fame are the strongest predictors of long-term happiness and health. As Robert Waldinger, the study's director, puts it: "Good relationships keep us happier and healthier. Period."

Practical Insight: Schedule time for connection as intentionally as you would a business meeting. Whether it's a weekly dinner, a phone call, or a shared hobby, relationships thrive on presence and consistency.

Redefining Richness

When we expand our definition of wealth to include health and relationships, we begin to make different choices. We invest in rest, in laughter, in love. We measure success not just by what we've earned, but by how we feel and who we're becoming.

Because in the end, the richest people aren't just those with the most money. They're the ones with energy in their bodies, peace in their minds, and love in their lives.

15.7 Avoiding Burnout: Personal Insights

Burnout is the cost of misaligned ambition. It happens when the pursuit of success overrides self-care, boundaries, and joy. Many high achievers reach financial milestones only to find themselves exhausted, disconnected, and unfulfilled.

Joyce Marter, a therapist and entrepreneur, built a multi-million-pound practice but found herself in financial distress due to poor boundaries and people-pleasing. Her turning point came when she realized her mindset not her business, was the problem. By reclaiming self-worth and setting money boundaries, she transformed her life and sold her practice in an eight-figure exit.

Author Insight: In Money Boundaries That Build Wealth, Confidence and Respect, Marter emphasizes that financial health is deeply tied to emotional health. Boundaries, self-esteem, and clarity are essential to sustainable success.

Practical Tips:

Set clear limits on work hours, spending, and emotional labor.

Recognize signs of burnout: fatigue, resentment, detachment.

Reframe success to include rest, joy, and connection.

15.8 Key Highlights

To integrate wealth and well-being, consider these guided principles:

1.Wealth Is a Tool, not a Destination

Use money to support your values, not define them. Let it buy time, health, and freedom—not just status.

Health Is the Foundation; Invest in your physical, mental, and spiritual health. Without it, wealth is fragile.

Relationships Are Capital; Nurture your social and emotional connections. They are your richest assets.

Mindset Shapes Money: Your beliefs about worth, boundaries, and abundance influence your financial outcomes.

Balance Is Dynamic; Life priorities shift review and realign regularly. What served you last year may not serve you now.

2. Health and Relationships as Wealth

We often think of wealth as something stored in bank accounts, property portfolios, or investment funds. But the most foundational forms of wealth are often invisible, our health and our relationships. Without them, financial success can feel hollow. With them, even modest means can support a deeply fulfilling life.

Health: The First Currency

Health is the foundation upon which all other forms of wealth rest. Without physical vitality or mental clarity, it becomes difficult to enjoy the fruits of financial success. Yet in the pursuit of career goals or business growth, health is often the first thing sacrificed skipped meals, sleepless nights, chronic stress.

A high-performing executive in her 40s collapsed from exhaustion during a client presentation. Years of overwork had caught up with her. In recovery, she realized she had been treating her body like a machine fueled by caffeine and adrenaline. She began to see her health not as a cost, but as an investment. She hired a nutritionist, started walking daily, and restructured her work schedule. Her energy returned and so did her

creativity and joy.
Practical Insight: View health expenses like therapy, fitness, or preventative care not as luxuries, but as essential components of your wealth strategy. A healthy body and mind are assets that are appreciated over time.

3. Relationships: The Emotional Portfolio

Relationships are another form of capital emotional, social, and spiritual. They provide support in crisis, amplify joy in success, and offer meaning that money alone cannot. Yet like health, relationships are often neglected in the name of productivity.

A man who had built a successful business found himself alone at his retirement party. He prioritized work over family, networking over friendship. In his later years, he began reaching out rebuilding bonds with his children, volunteering in his community. He said, "I thought I was rich. But I was bankrupt in the places that mattered most."

Author Insight: Harvard's 80-year longitudinal study on adult development found that close relationships, not wealth or fame are the strongest predictors of long-term happiness and health. As Robert Waldinger, the study's director, puts it: "Good relationships keep us happier and healthier. Period."

Practical Insight: Schedule time for connection as intentionally as you would a business meeting. Whether it's a weekly dinner, a phone call, or a shared hobby, relationships thrive on presence and consistency.

15.9 Redefining Richness

When we expand our definition of wealth to include health and relationships, we begin to make different choices. We invest in rest, in laughter, in love. We measure success not just by what we've earned, but by how we feel and who we're becoming.

Because in the end, the richest people aren't just those with the most money. They're the ones with energy in their bodies, peace in their minds, and love in their lives.

Wealth and well-being are not opposing forces they are partners. When aligned, they create a life that is not only prosperous, but peaceful. The stories and insights in this chapter remind us that success is not just about accumulation, it's about integration.

So ask yourself: Is my wealth serving my life or consuming it? Am I investing in what truly matters? Am I rich in time, health, and love or just in numbers?

Because in the end, the richest life is one where money supports meaning, and success includes serenity.

Avoiding Burnout: Personal Insights

Burnout is the silent tax on ambition. It creeps in when the pursuit of success overrides self-care, boundaries, and joy. For many high-achievers, burnout doesn't arrive with a dramatic collapse it builds slowly, disguised as dedication, masked by productivity, and justified by financial goals. But left unchecked, it can erode health, relationships, creativity, and even the very wealth it was meant to support.

This section explores how burnout manifests, how to spot it early, and how to recover with clarity and compassion. Through personal stories and expert insights, we'll uncover how to build a life that's both prosperous and sustainable.

The Hidden Cost of Hustle

In today's culture, hustle is glorified. Long hours, constant availability, and relentless drive are seen as badges of honor. But behind the scenes, many successful people are quietly burning out physically depleted, emotionally numb, and spiritually disconnected.

Joyce Marter, a psychotherapist and entrepreneur, built a multi-million-pound counselling practice. From the outside, she was thriving. But internally, she was drowning in stress, debt, and people-pleasing. She realised that her financial struggles weren't due to lack of income they were rooted in emotional patterns: over giving, undercharging, and fear of conflict. Her turning point came when she began setting boundaries, valuing her

worth, and healing her mindset. She later sold her business in an eight-figure exit and wrote The Financial Mindset Fix to help others do the same.
Lesson: Burnout isn't just about overwork, it's about misalignment. When your financial life is driven by fear, guilt, or perfectionism, burnout becomes inevitable.

Recognizing the Signs

Burnout doesn't always look like collapse. It often shows up as:
A, Chronic fatigue, even after rest
B, Irritability or emotional numbness
C, Loss of joy in things that once mattered
D, Feeling trapped or resentful
E, Difficulty concentrating or making decisions
F, Physical symptoms like headaches, insomnia, or digestive issues
Reflection Prompt: Are you thriving or just surviving? Are you energized by your work, or drained by it? Are you building wealth or burning through your well-being?

15.10 The Role of Boundaries

Boundaries are the antidote to burnout. They protect your time, energy, and emotional bandwidth. They allow you to say yes to what matters and no to what doesn't.
A freelance designer loved her work but found herself constantly underpaid, overbooked, and emotionally exhausted. She feared losing clients if she raised her rates or declined projects. After working with a coach, she redefined her boundaries: minimum project fees, fixed working hours, and a weekly "no-client" day. Her income increased, her stress decreased, and her creativity returned.
Author Insight: In Set Boundaries, Find Peace, Nedra Glover Tawwab writes, "Boundaries are not walls—they're gates. They let the right things in and keep the harmful things out." Financial boundaries are just as vital as emotional ones.

Reclaiming Rest and Joy

Burnout thrives in environments where rest is seen as weakness and joy is postponed "until the work is done." But rest is not a reward, it's a requirement. And joy is not a distraction it's a source of resilience.
A lawyer who had reached partner status found herself emotionally flat. She had achieved every goal she'd set but felt nothing. Her therapist asked, "When was the last time you did something just for fun?" She couldn't remember. She began painting again, taking weekends off, and reconnecting with old friends. Her productivity didn't suffer it improved. Her burnout lifted not through more effort, but through more joy.
Practical Insight: Schedule joy like you schedules meetings. Block time for hobbies, connection, and rest. Treat them as non-negotiable investments in your well-being.

Reframing Success

Many people burn out chasing a version of success that isn't even theirs. They inherit goals from culture, family, or comparison bigger houses, higher income, more prestige without asking whether those goals align with their values.
A man spent 20 years climbing the corporate ladder, driven by a desire to "make his father proud." When he finally reached the top, he realized he didn't enjoy the work. He had built someone else's dream. He transitioned into coaching, took a pay cut, but found deep fulfilment. His new definition of success included time with his children, meaningful work, and peace of mind.
Reflection Prompt: Whose version of success are you chasing? What does success look like for you not just financially, but emotionally and spiritually?

What Other Authors Say

•Joyce Marter, in The Financial Mindset Fix, shows how emotional patterns like shame, scarcity, and over giving can sabotage financial health and lead to burnout.

• Brené Brown reminds us that "exhaustion is not a status symbol." Vulnerability, rest, and authenticity are markers of true strength.

• Greg McKeown, in Essentialism, argues that success requires focus and elimination. "If you don't prioritize your life," he writes, "someone else will."

• Arianna Huffington, in Thrive, reframes success to include well-being, wisdom, and wonder not just wealth and power.

Tools to Prevent Burnout

• Energy Audit: Track what activities energize vs. drain you. Adjust your schedule accordingly.

• Boundary Blueprint: List your non-negotiables working hours, communication limits, rate minimums.

• Joy Calendar: Schedule weekly joy rituals walk, art, music, connection.

• Success Redefinition: Write your own definition of success. Include emotional, relational, and spiritual metrics.

• Support System: Build a circle of mentors, therapists, and friends who support your well-being, not just your ambition.

Avoiding burnout is not about doing less, it's about doing what matters. It's about aligning your financial life with your emotional truth. It's about setting boundaries that honor your worth, reclaiming rest as a form of power, and redefining success on your own terms.

Because in the end, wealth without well-being is a hollow victory. But when your ambition is rooted in self-respect, and your success includes serenity, you build a life that's not just rich but radiant.

15.11 Key Highlights: Integrating Wealth and Well-being

This chapter has explored the deeper dimensions of prosperity how money, health, relationships, and emotional clarity intersect to shape a truly rich life. Below are the key highlights that help harmonize financial success with personal fulfilment.

1. Wealth Is a Tool, not a Destination

Money is powerful but only when it serves your values. When wealth becomes the goal rather than the means, it can lead to burnout, misalignment, and emotional emptiness. The healthiest financial lives are those where money supports freedom, connection, and purpose not just accumulation.

Takeaway: Use money to buy time, health, and joy not just things.

2. Health Is Foundational Wealth

Without physical and mental well-being, financial success loses its meaning. Health is not a luxury it's the first currency. Investing in sleep, movement, nutrition, and emotional care is not indulgent it's strategic.

Takeaway: Treat health expenses as wealth protection. Prioritize vitality over velocity.

3. Relationships Are Emotional Capital

Strong relationships are one of the most reliable predictors of long-term happiness. They offer support, meaning, and joy that money alone cannot provide. Yet they require time, presence, and intentionality especially in high-achieving lives.

Takeaway: Schedule connection. Invest in people as deeply as you invest in assets.

4. Burnout Is a Signal, not a Failure

Burnout often signals misalignment between your goals and your values, your effort and your energy. It's not a personal flaw, but a call to reassess. Boundaries, rest, and joy are not distractions from success, they are their foundations.

Takeaway: Redefine success to include serenity. Let rest be part of your strategy.

5. Alignment Is Dynamic
Life priorities shift with seasons. What mattered in your 30s may not matter in your 50s. Harmonizing money and life is not a one-time fix it's a rhythm of reflection and rebalancing.
Takeaway: Revisit your values regularly. Let your financial life evolve with your emotional truth.

15.12 Reflection: Living a Richer Life

Wealth is not just what you accumulate it's what you activate. It's the energy you bring to your days, the relationships you nurture, the health you protect, and the joy you allow yourself to feel. This chapter has invited you to look beyond the numbers and into the heart of what it means to live richly. You've explored how money can serve not sabotage your life priorities. You've seen how health and relationships are forms of capital that compound over time. You've learned how burnout can be a signal, not a failure, and how boundaries and rest are not luxuries, but lifelines. And you've gathered key principles to help you stay aligned as your financial life evolves. Now, the invitation is simple: begin living your wealth now.
Not someday. Not when the business scales. Not when the mortgage is paid off. Not when retirement arrives. Now.

Start by asking:
- What does a rich life look like for me today?
- Where can I invest not just financially, but emotionally and relationally?
- What can I release that no longer serves my well-being?

Let your calendar reflect your values. Let your spending express your priorities. Let your goals include rest, laughter, and love. Let your definition of success be wide enough to hold your whole self. Because the richest people aren't just those with the most money. They're the ones who wake up with energy, move through the day with purpose, and go to bed with peace. They're the ones whose wealth supports their well-being not the other way around.
So take a breath. Reclaim your rhythm. And remember you are allowed to be both ambitious and well. You are allowed to build wealth and protect your joy. You are allowed to succeed without sacrificing yourself.

This is your life. Make it rich in every sense.

Chapter 16: Philanthropy & Social Good

16.1 Introduction: Giving That Changes Lives and Lasts

Philanthropy is one of the most powerful expressions of legacy. It's the act of turning resources into ripple effects, of transforming personal success into shared progress. But true philanthropy goes beyond charity, it's about intentional impact. It's about asking not just "What can I give?" but "What can I change?"

In a world where inequality, climate change, and social fragmentation challenge us daily, giving back is no longer optional, it's essential. And yet, many people feel unsure where to begin. Should I donate money, time, or skills? Should I give locally or globally? How do I know if my giving is actually making a difference?

This chapter is designed to answer those questions not with formulas, but with frameworks, stories, and soul. It explores how individuals and families can engage in philanthropy that is both heartfelt and effective. Whether you're giving £10 or £10,000, whether you're mentoring a teenager or funding a scholarship, your contribution matters. And when done with intention, it can become one of the most fulfilling chapters of your financial journey.

A retired teacher in Manchester began volunteering at a literacy nonprofit. She didn't have a large estate or a foundation, but she had time, compassion, and expertise. Over five years, she helped dozens of children learn to read. One of them went on to become a teacher herself. That ripple one life touching another became a legacy far richer than any financial gift.

Philanthropy also offers a unique opportunity to involve family. Giving together builds shared values, strengthens bonds, and teaches younger generations about empathy, responsibility, and stewardship. It turns legacy into a living conversation.

Author Insight:

Peter Singer, in The Life You Can Save, argues that effective giving is not just about generosity, it's about strategy. He encourages donors to measure impact, choose causes wisely, and treat philanthropy as a moral imperative. His message is clear: giving is not just good, it's powerful.

In the sections ahead, we'll explore how to measure impact through stories and data, how to choose causes that align with your values, and how to give in ways that fit your lifestyle and resources. We'll look at donor-advised funds, volunteering, family foundations, and social entrepreneurship. And we'll share real stories of people whose giving changed lives, including their own.

Because in the end, philanthropy is not just about what you give, it's about what you set in motion. It's about using your wealth, wisdom, and heart to shape a world that reflects your deepest values. And when you give with clarity and compassion, your legacy becomes a force for good that outlasts you.

16.2 Measuring Impact Through Stories and Tables

Giving feels good but how do you know it's doing good? Measuring impact helps philanthropists move from intention to evidence. It ensures that resources are not just spent but invested. And it allows donors to refine their approach, deepen their reach, and communicate their value with clarity.

Philanthropy is one of the most powerful ways to turn personal success into collective progress. It's the act of giving not just from abundance, but from intention. Whether through financial gifts, time, skills, or advocacy, philanthropy allows us to shape the world in ways that reflect our deepest values. It's legacy in motion.

But giving is not just about generosity, it's about impact. It's about asking: What changed because I cared? In a world where needs are vast and resources unevenly distributed; thoughtful giving becomes a moral and emotional imperative. It's how we respond to suffering, support innovation, and build bridges across differences.

And yet, many people feel unsure where to begin. Should I donate to large institutions or grassroots efforts? Should I give locally or globally? How do I know if my contribution is actually making a difference? This chapter is designed to guide you through those questions not with rigid answers, but with framework, stories, and soul. A small business owner in Birmingham began donating 5% of her profits to a local youth center. Over time, she didn't just write cheques she got involved in. She mentored teens, hosted workshops, and helped fund a new computer lab. One of those teens later launched a tech startup and credited her as the spark. Her giving wasn't just financial, it was transformational.

Philanthropy also offers a unique opportunity to involve family. Giving together builds shared values, strengthens bonds, and teaches younger generations about empathy, responsibility, and stewardship. It turns legacy into a living conversation.

Peter Singer, in The Life You Can Save, argues that effective giving is not just about generosity it's about strategy. He encourages donors to measure impact, choose causes wisely, and treat philanthropy as a moral responsibility. His message is clear: giving is not just good, it's powerful.

In the sections ahead, we'll explore how to measure impact through stories and data a, how to choose causes that align with your values, and how to give in ways that fit your lifestyle and resources. We'll look at donor-advised funds, volunteering, family foundations, and social entrepreneurship. And we'll share real stories of people whose giving changed lives including their own.

Because in the end, philanthropy is not just about what you give it's about what you set in motion. It's about using your wealth, wisdom, and heart to shape a world that reflects your deepest values. And when you give with clarity and compassion, your legacy becomes a force for good that outlasts you.

Why Measurement Matters

- It validates that your giving is creating real change not just activity.
- It helps you learn what works, what doesn't, and where to improve.
- It builds trust with stakeholders, family members, and beneficiaries.
- It connects numbers to narratives making your legacy tangible.

16.3 Combining Stories and Data

According to ThinkNPC and Charity Digital UK, the most effective impact measurement combines quantitative and qualitative data:

Data Type	Purpose	Examples
Quantitative (Numbers)	Measures reach, scale, and outcomes	Attendance rates, test scores, health metrics
Qualitative (Stories)	Captures depth, emotion, and lived experience	Interviews, testimonials, case studies

Quote: "No numbers without stories, no stories without numbers." NPC Impact Seminar

A family foundation funded a literacy program for refugee children. The data showed a 30% increase in reading scores. But the real impact came through a letter from a 10-year-old girl who wrote, "Now I can read bedtime stories to my little brother." That story became the heart of the foundation's annual report and a reminder that behind every metric is a life changed.

16.4 Tools for Measurement

In any transformational journey, whether personal, organizational, or community-based measurement is essential. It's not just about proving success; it's about learning, refining, and amplifying impact. Without tools for measurement, even the most heartfelt efforts risk becoming invisible. But with the right framework, we can turn intention into insight and progress into proof.
Here are three foundational tools that help map, track, and communicate impact effectively:

Theory of Change: Mapping the Journey
The Theory of Change is a strategic blueprint. It outlines how specific inputs (resources, actions, interventions) lead to desired outcomes and long-term impact. It's not just a plan it's a hypothesis. It asks, "If we do X, will it lead to Y?" and encourages reflection on assumptions, risks, and context.
For example, a youth mentorship program might start with weekly coaching sessions (input), aiming to improve self-esteem and academic performance (outcomes), ultimately reducing dropout rates (impact). The Theory of Change helps clarify the logic behind the effort and guides evaluation.

Logic Models: Visualizing Cause and Effect
Logic models are visual frameworks that show how activities connect to outputs, outcomes, and impact. They're especially useful for teams and funders who need clarity and alignment. A good logic model includes:
• Inputs: What resources are used?
• Activities: What actions are taken?#
• Outputs: What is produced or delivered?
• Outcomes: What short- and medium-term changes occur?
• Impact: What long-term transformation is expected?
Logic models simplify complexity. They turn abstract goals into tangible steps and help identify where things are working or where they need adjustment.

Impact Dashboards: Tracking Progress in Real Time
Digital dashboards like Impact Mapper, Google Data Studio, or Power BI allow organizations to visualize progress. They can track metrics such as attendance, engagement, satisfaction, and behavioral change. Dashboards make data accessible, dynamic, and shareable.
But numbers alone aren't enough. The best dashboards combine quantitative data with qualitative insights stories, testimonials, and reflections that show the human side of change.

Key Questions to Ask
To measure impact meaningfully, ask:
• How much did we do? (Quantity: sessions held, people reached)
• How well did we do it? (Quality: satisfaction, engagement)#
• What changed as a result? (Effectiveness: behavior, mindset, outcomes)
These questions move beyond activity tracking to outcome evaluation. They help distinguish effort from effect.

Best Practices
• Use pre- and post-program surveys to measure change over time.
• Conduct focus groups to gather nuanced feedback.
• Track outcomes consistently and transparently.
• Combine hard data with human stories to create a full picture.
Real-Life Example: A social enterprise in London ran a financial literacy program for single mothers. They used a logic model to design the curriculum, pre- and post-surveys to measure confidence and budgeting skills, and Google Data Studio to visualize progress. But the most powerful insight came from a participant's story: "Before this, I didn't believe I could manage money. Now I teach my daughter how to save."

16.5 Different Ways of Giving Back

Philanthropy is often imagined as writing large cheques or founding grand institutions. But giving back is far more diverse, accessible, and personal. It can be financial, yes, but it can also be relational, creative, or systemic. The essence of philanthropy is not the size of the gift, but the intention behind it and the ripple it creates.

This section explores the many ways individuals and families can contribute to social good, offering both practical pathways and deeper reflections on how giving transforms not only communities, but also the giver.

Financial Giving: Beyond the Cheque

Financial giving remains the most visible form of philanthropy. It can take many shapes:

- One-Time Donations: Quick responses to urgent needs, such as disaster relief.
- Recurring Giving: Monthly or annual contributions that sustain organizations.
- Major Gifts: Large donations that fund capital projects, scholarships, or endowments.
- Donor-Advised Funds (DAFs): Accounts that allow donors to contribute, invest, and recommend grants over time.
- Family Foundations: Structured entities that formalize giving across generations.

A family in London created a donor-advised fund not only to support causes, but to involve their children in decision-making. Each year, the children researched charities, presented their cases, and voted as a family. The process became a classroom for empathy, critical thinking, and stewardship.

Deep Insight: Financial giving is not just about money leaving your account it's about values entering the world. When aligned with purpose, even modest donations can create outsized impact.

Time and Talent: The Currency of Presence

Not everyone has large sums to give, but everyone has time, skills, or networks. Volunteering, mentoring, and offering expertise can be as transformative as financial gifts.

- Volunteering: Serving meals, tutoring, or helping with logistics.
- Mentorship: Guiding young people, entrepreneurs, or vulnerable groups.
- Pro Bono Work: Offering professional services—legal, financial, medical—at no cost.
- Advocacy: Using your voice and influence to amplify causes.

A retired nurse began volunteering at a community health clinic. She didn't donate money, but her decades of experience improved patient care, trained younger staff, and saved the clinic thousands of pounds annually. Her gift was not financial, it embodied wisdom.

Deep Insight: Time and talent are renewable forms of wealth. Unlike money, they cannot be outsourced. When you give your presence, you give something irreplaceable.

Family and Community Philanthropy

Philanthropy is most powerful when it becomes cultural woven into the fabric of family and community life.

- Family Giving Circles: Families pool resources and decide together where to give.
- Community Funds: Neighbors or local groups create small funds for shared needs.
- Traditions of Giving: Annual rituals, such as donating on birthdays or volunteering during holidays.

A Nigerian-British family in London created a tradition where each child received £100 at Christmas—not to spend, but to donate. At the family gathering, each child explained their choice. Over time, the children grew into adults who saw generosity not as obligation, but as joy.

Deep Insight: When giving is shared, it becomes more than philanthropy it becomes pedagogy. It teaches values, builds unity, and ensures that generosity outlives the giver.

16.6 Impact Investing: Aligning Capital with Conscience

Philanthropy is evolving. Increasingly, donors are not only giving money away they are investing it in ways that

generate both financial returns and social good.
• Social Enterprises: Businesses that reinvest profits into social missions.
• Green Investments: Funding renewable energy, sustainable agriculture, or conservation.
• Affordable Housing Projects: Investments that provide both returns and community benefit.

A group of young professionals pooled their savings to invest in a start-up producing biodegradable packaging. The company grew, reduced plastic waste, and provided jobs in underserved communities. Their investment generated both profit and purpose.
Deep Insight: Impact investing blurs the line between philanthropy and business. It asks: Why should my money do good only when I give it away? Why not every time I invest it?

Creative and Cultural Giving
Philanthropy is not limited to money, time, or business. It can also be artistic, cultural, or spiritual.
• Art Donations: Supporting museums, galleries, or public art projects.
• Storytelling: Using writing, film, or podcasts to amplify causes.
• Cultural Preservation: Funding projects that protect languages, traditions, or heritage.
A poet began hosting free workshops in underserved schools, teaching children to express themselves through writing. The program didn't just improve literacy it gave children a voice.
Deep Insight: Creativity is a form of wealth. When shared, it enriches not just individuals, but entire cultures.

Everyday Philanthropy: Small Acts, Big Ripples

Not all giving is formal. Sometimes, philanthropy is as simple as kindness in action:
• Paying for someone's groceries.
• Offering a listening ear.
• Supporting a neighbor in crisis.
• Sharing knowledge freely.
During the pandemic, a group of neighbors in Leeds created a WhatsApp group to check on the elderly, deliver groceries, and share resources. What began as crisis response became an ongoing community of care.
Deep Insight: Philanthropy doesn't always wear a suit. Sometimes it wears an apron, carries a shopping bag, or shows up with a smile.

What Thought Leaders Say
• Peter Singer: Giving is a moral responsibility, and effective giving requires strategy.
• Lynne Twist (The Soul of Money): "What you appreciate appreciates." Giving expands both the giver and the receiver.
• Muhammad Yunus (microfinance pioneer): Small, structured acts of generosity can transform entire communities.
• Brené Brown: Generosity is not just about resources it's about assuming the best in others and showing empathy.

16.7 Reflection: The Legacy of Generosity

Giving back is not a single act, it's a spectrum. It can be money, time, talent, creativity, or kindness. It can be structured or spontaneous, local or global, private or public. What matters is not the form, but the heart.
The deepest insight is this: philanthropy transforms both directions. It changes the lives of those who receive, and it reshapes the soul of those who give.

So ask yourself:
• What do I have to give beyond money?
• How can I align my giving with my values?

- What legacy of generosity do I want to leave?

Because in the end, philanthropy is not just about what you give it's about who you become in the process. Philanthropy is not simply the act of giving it is the art of transforming resources into ripples of change. It is the bridge between personal success and collective progress, between what we accumulate and what we release As we close this chapter, it is worth pausing to reflect on what philanthropy truly means: not charity as obligation, but generosity as legacy.

Throughout history, the most enduring legacies have not been measured in wealth retained, but in wealth shared. A scholarship that opens the door for a first-generation student. A community garden that feeds families and fosters connection. A mentorship that sparks confidence in a young leader. These are not just acts of kindness they are investments in futures that outlast the giver. They remind us that philanthropy is not about the size of the gift, but the sincerity of the heart and the clarity of the intention.

The families and individuals we have explored in this chapter show us that giving is not reserved for the wealthy elite. It belongs to everyone. A grandmother who teaches her grandchildren to donate, a retiree who volunteers his skills, a business owner who reinvests profits into community projects all are philanthropists in their own right. Their stories remind us that generosity is not measured in pounds, but in purpose.

Philanthropy also reshapes the giver. When we give, we loosen the grip of fear and scarcity. We discover that wealth is most alive when it flows. We find joy in seeing our resources create opportunities, heal wounds, and inspire hope. In this way, philanthropy is not just about changing the world it is about changing ourselves. It deepens our empathy, clarifies our values, and connects us to something larger than our own ambitions.

Yet, effective philanthropy requires more than good intentions. It calls for reflection and responsibility. Measuring impact through both stories and data ensures that our giving is not just symbolic, but substantive. Choosing causes that align with our values ensures that our giving is not just reactive, but resonant. And involving our families ensures that our giving is not just temporary, but generational. In this way, philanthropy becomes not a one-time act, but a culture, a way of living that shapes how we see money, meaning, and legacy.

As you reflect on your own journey, consider the many forms your giving might take. It could be financial, through donations or investments. It could be personal, through time, skills, or mentorship. It could be cultural, through storytelling, art, or advocacy. Or it could be everyday acts of kindness that ripple outward in unseen ways. Whatever form it takes, let it be intentional. Let it reflect who you are and what you stand for.

Because in the end, philanthropy is not about what you give it is about what you set in motion. It is about leaving the world a little brighter, a little fairer, a little more hopeful than you found it. And when you give with clarity and compassion, your legacy becomes more than wealth, it becomes a living force for good.

Chapter 17: Lifetime Learning for Financial Growth

17.1 Introduction: The Wealth That Never Stops Growing

Financial growth is often spoken of in terms of numbers of interest rates, investment returns, and net worth. But beneath the spreadsheets lies a deeper truth: the most valuable asset you will ever own is your capacity to learn. Unlike markets, learning never crashes. Unlike assets, it cannot be stolen. Unlike wealth, it does not diminish when shared it multiply.

Lifetime learning is the engine of sustainable prosperity. It is what allows us to adapt to shifting economies, seize new opportunities, and recover from setbacks. It is the quiet force behind every story of resilience and reinvention. And it is the one form of wealth that compounds endlessly, enriching not only our finances but our character, relationships, and legacy.

Consider the story of a factory worker who lost his job when automation reshaped his industry. Instead of resigning to decline, he enrolled in evening courses in coding. Within three years, he transitioned into a career in software development, earning more than he ever had before. His financial turnaround was not the result of luck it was the fruit of learning.

This is the essence of lifetime learning: the ability to pivot, to grow, to remain relevant in a world that never stops changing.

Education as a Pathway

Formal education lays the foundation, but it is not the end of the journey. Degrees, certifications, and apprenticeships open doors, but the real key is cultivating a mindset that sees every experience as a classroom. Whether through online courses, professional workshops, or self-study, those who continue to learn remain agile in the face of disruption.

As Warren Buffett famously said, "The best investment you can make is in yourself." Education is not just about acquiring knowledge it's about expanding capacity. It builds confidence, sharpens decision-making, and equips us to navigate complexity with clarity.

Mentorship and Curiosity

Beyond classrooms and textbooks, mentorship becomes a living form of education. A mentor compresses decades of experience into moments of wisdom, offering shortcuts through mistakes and insights that no textbook can provide. And curiosity the willingness to ask, explore, and experiment—keeps the flame of growth alive long after formal education ends.

Together, mentorship and curiosity create a cycle of learning that compounds like interest. They remind us that wisdom is not a destination, but a journey.

Why This Chapter Matters

This chapter will explore three dimensions of lifetime learning for financial growth:

1. Educational Pathways and Benefits – how different forms of education open doors and build resilience.
2. Mentorship Stories and Lifelong Curiosity – how guidance and inquiry accelerate growth.
3. Highlighted Lessons for Ongoing Growth – the distilled wisdom that sustains prosperity across seasons of life.

Because in the end, financial growth is not just about what you earn it's about who you become. And the richest lives are those where learning never stops.

Wealth is not static, it grows, evolves, and adapts. And so must we. The most successful individuals are not simply those who accumulate assets, but those who cultivate a mindset of continuous learning. Financial growth is not a one-time achievement; it is a lifelong journey shaped by education, mentorship, and curiosity. This chapter explores how learning formally and informally becomes the engine of sustainable prosperity.

17.2 Educational Pathways and Benefits

Education has always been one of the most reliable levels for financial growth. Across cultures and centuries, those who invested in learning whether through formal schooling, apprenticeships, or self-directed study gained not only knowledge but also opportunities, confidence, and adaptability. In today's rapidly shifting economy, education is no longer a one-time event that ends with a diploma. It is a lifelong pathway, a renewable source of wealth that compounds over time.
This section explores the diverse educational pathways available, the benefits they bring, and the deeper ways in which learning shapes financial growth.

Formal Education: The Traditional Gateway

For generations, formal education has been the most visible route to financial advancement. Primary and secondary schooling provide the foundation: literacy, numeracy, and critical thinking. Higher education, whether university degrees or professional schools, opens doors to specialized careers, higher salaries, and leadership roles.

Benefits of Formal Education:

- Credentialing: Degrees and diplomas signal competence, making it easier to enter competitive fields.
- Networks: Universities and colleges often provide access to alumni networks, internships, and mentors.
- Confidence: Completing structured programs builds self-belief and resilience.

A first-generation student from a working-class family in Birmingham pursued a degree in accounting. The qualification not only secured her a stable career but also gave her the confidence to start her own consultancy. Her education became the bridge between her family's financial struggles and her children's financial security.
Deep Insight: Formal education is not just about knowledge, it's about access. It opens doors that might otherwise remain closed. But in today's world, it is only one part of the journey.

17.3 Vocational Training and Apprenticeships: Learning by Doing

Not everyone thrives in traditional academic settings. Vocational training and apprenticeships offer practical, hands-on learning that leads directly to employable skills. These pathways are increasingly valuable in industries like technology, healthcare, construction, and finance.

Benefits of Vocational Pathways:

- Practical Skills: Learners gain immediately applicable expertise.
- Earning While Learning: Apprenticeships often provide income while training.
- Industry Relevance: Programs are designed in partnership with employers, ensuring skills match market demand.

A young man who struggled in traditional classrooms enrolled in a digital marketing apprenticeship. Within two years, he was managing campaigns for major brands. His pathway bypassed university debt and gave him both income and independence.
Deep Insight: Vocational education challenges the myth that success requires a university degree. It proves that financial growth comes from mastery, not conformity.

Online Learning and Micro-Credentials: The New Frontier

The digital revolution has democratized education. Platforms like Coursera, Udemy, and LinkedIn Learning offer courses on everything from coding to leadership. Micro-credentials and digital badges allow learners to showcase specific skills without committing to long, expensive programs.

Benefits of Online Learning:

• Accessibility: Anyone with internet access can learn from world-class institutions.
• Flexibility: Learners can study at their own pace, balancing work and family.
• Affordability: Many courses are free or low-cost compared to traditional degrees.
A single mother in Lagos used online courses to learn data analytics. Within a year, she transitioned from administrative work to a remote role in tech, doubling her income. Her story illustrates how digital learning can break barriers of geography, cost, and circumstance.
Deep Insight: Online learning is not just supplemental, it is transformative. It allows individuals to pivot careers, upskill rapidly, and remain competitive in industries that evolve overnight.

17.4 Professional Certifications: Specialization and Authority

In many fields, certifications carry as much weight as degrees. Credentials like CFA (Chartered Financial Analyst), CPA (Certified Public Accountant), or PMP (Project Management Professional) signal expertise and commitment.

Benefits of Certifications:

• Marketability: Certified professionals often command higher salaries.
• Credibility: Certifications build trust with clients and employers.
• Global Recognition: Many credentials are portable across countries.
An IT professional pursued cybersecurity certifications while working full-time. Within three years, he moved into a senior role with a 40% salary increase. His certifications became steppingstones to financial growth and career security.
Deep Insight: Certifications are proof of mastery in a specialized area. They show not just knowledge but discipline the willingness to invest in growth beyond the basics.

Self-Education: The Wealth of Curiosity

Some of the world's most successful entrepreneurs, creators, and investors are self-taught. They didn't wait for permission or credentials they followed their curiosity. They devoured books, listened to lectures, watched tutorials, and learned by trial and error. For them, education wasn't a destination, it was a lifelong pursuit.
Self-education requires discipline, but it offers something formal education often cannot: freedom. Freedom to explore beyond rigid curricula. Freedom to follow passion over prescription. Freedom to pivot when the world changes and to change with it.

The Benefits of Self-Education

• Low Cost: In today's digital age, knowledge is more accessible than ever. Free podcasts, YouTube channels, online courses, and public libraries offer a wealth of information at little to no cost. A smartphone and an internet connection can unlock entire worlds of expertise.
• Personalization: Self-learners choose what they study, when they study, and how they study. They follow their interests, dive deep into niche topics, and build skill sets tailored to their goals. This autonomy fuels motivation and accelerates mastery.
• Agility: The self-educated are often the quickest to adapt. They're not waiting for a syllabus they're already exploring emerging trends. Whether it's blockchain, AI, or sustainable design, they're learning in real time and applying insights immediately.

Real-Life Example: Nairobi's Tech Trailblazer
A young entrepreneur in Nairobi taught himself coding through free online tutorials. He didn't attend a prestigious university or enroll in a formal bootcamp. Instead, he spent evenings watching videos, reading documentation, and building small projects. Eventually, he created an app that addressed a local transport challenge helping commuters track buses and avoid delays.
The app gained traction, attracted media attention, and was eventually acquired by a larger company. His self-education didn't just lead to financial independence it created community impact. He solved a real problem, empowered local users, and inspired others to pursue tech without traditional barriers.
Author Insight: Curiosity as Capital-Self-education proves that curiosity is capital. Those who cultivate it can create opportunities where none seem to exist. I've seen these firsthand people who began with nothing but a question and ended up with a business, a book, or a breakthrough.
One of the most powerful shifts in my own journey came when I stopped waiting to be taught and started teaching myself. I read widely finance, psychology, design, and storytelling. I followed threads of interest, not just credentials. And every time I leaned into curiosity, I uncovered new tools, new perspectives, and new possibilities.
Albert Einstein once said, "I have no special talent. I am only passionately curious." That mindset—humble, hungry, and open is the foundation of self-education. It's not about having all the answers. It's about being willing to ask better questions.

17.5 The Benefits of Lifelong Learning

Across all pathways formal, vocational, online, certified, or self-directed, the benefits of education extend far beyond financial gain. Lifelong learning is not just about acquiring credentials or climbing career ladders. It's about cultivating adaptability, building confidence, expanding networks, and leaving a legacy. It's a mindset of continuous growth, a commitment to becoming, not just achieving.

In a world that evolves faster than ever, the ability to learn new skills is no longer optional, it's essential.

Adaptability: Thriving Through Change
The modern world is defined by disruption. Industries shift. Technologies evolve. Job roles disappear and reappear in new forms. Lifelong learners are equipped to pivot. They don't cling to outdated knowledge they update their toolkit. Whether it's learning to code, mastering digital marketing, or understanding climate-conscious business practices, adaptable learners stay relevant.
Real-Life Example: A mid-career accountant in London retrained in data analytics through an online course. Within a year, she transitioned into a tech role that aligned with emerging trends. Her willingness to learn gave her a second career and renewed purpose.

Confidence: Knowledge as Inner Strength
Learning builds confidence. It replaces fear with understanding. When you know how something works whether it's a financial system, a fitness plan, or a negotiation strategy you feel empowered. You're less reactive, more intentional. You trust your ability to figure things out.
Confidence born from learning is quiet but powerful. It shows up in decisions, conversations, and moments of uncertainty. It's the voice that says, "I may not know everything, but I know how to learn."

Networks: Learning as Connection
Education connects people. Whether in classrooms, webinars, workshops, or online forums, learners meet others who share their curiosity. These connections often lead to collaborations, mentorships, and friendships that span industries and geography.
Learning environments are fertile ground for ideas. They expose you to different perspectives, challenge your assumptions, and expand your worldview. And in a globalized economy, your network can be as valuable as

your knowledge.
Author Insight: Some of my most meaningful collaborations began in learning spaces book clubs, writing workshops, and community seminars. The shared pursuit of growth created trust, synergy, and long-term partnerships.

Legacy: Learning That Lifts Others
Educated individuals often become catalysts for change in their families and communities. They model curiosity, discipline, and resilience. They pass on not just facts, but values. They inspire others to dream bigger, think deeper, and act wiser.
Whether it's a parent teaching financial literacy to their children, or a community leader organizing free workshops, the ripple effect of learning is profound. It's how legacies are built not just in wealth, but in wisdom.
Peter Drucker once said, "The only skill that will be important in the 21st century is the skill of learning new skills." This truth underscores why education is not a phase of life, but a lifelong practice. It's not something you finish it's something you live.
So read the book. Take the course. Ask the question. Because every time you learn, you grow. And every time you grow, you expand what's possible for yourself and for others. Lifelong learning isn't just a habit it's a legacy in motion.

17.6 Practical Framework: The Learning Portfolio

Think of education as a portfolio diverse, balanced, and evolving. Just as investors diversify assets to manage risk and maximize returns, learners should diversify their educational pathways to build resilience, relevance, and richness in their lives. A well-rounded learning portfolio doesn't just prepare you for a job, it prepares you for change, for leadership, and for legacy.

Let's break down the components of this portfolio:

A. Formal Education: Foundation and Structure
Formal education universities, colleges, and structured academic programs provide foundational knowledge and critical thinking skills. It teaches discipline, research, and theory. For many, it's the starting point of their learning journey. But while formal education lays the groundwork, it's only one part of a broader landscape.

B. Certifications: Credibility and Specialization
Certifications offer targeted expertise and professional credibility. Whether it's project management, data analytics, or financial planning, certifications signal competence and commitment. They're especially valuable in fast-evolving industries where employers seek proof of current skills. For career pivots or promotions, certifications can be the bridge between intention and opportunity.

C. Online Learning: Agility and Access
Online platforms like Coursera, Udemy, LinkedIn Learning, and Khan Academy make education accessible and agile. Learners can study at their own pace, explore emerging topics, and update their skills in real time. Online learning democratizes education, allowing people from Nairobi to New York to access world-class content with a click.

Real-Life Example: A woman in Manchester transitioned from hospitality to UX design by completing a series of online courses. Within a year, she landed a remote role with a global tech firm. Her agility powered by online learning reshaped her career.

D. Mentorship and Self-Education: Depth and Creativity
Mentorship and self-education bring depth, nuance, and personal transformation. Mentors compress decades of experience into moments of wisdom. Self-education through books, podcasts, and experimentation fosters

independence and creativity. These pathways are less structured but often more profound. They teach you how to think, not just what to think.

Author Insight: I've seen firsthand how mentorship and self-study can unlock breakthroughs. One mentee of mine, with no formal background in finance, built a thriving investment club simply by reading, asking questions, and applying what he learned. His curiosity became capital—and his capital became community impact.

Educational pathways are not ladders they are landscapes. Some climb through universities, others through apprenticeships, others through self-study. What matters is not the route, but the rhythm: the commitment to keep learning, keep adapting, and keep growing.

This landscape invites exploration. It allows for detours, pauses, and reinvention. It honors the learner's pace and purpose. And it reflects the truth that education is not a phase, it's a lifelong practice.

In the end, education is the one investment that never depreciates. It compounds across a lifetime, shaping not just what you earn, but who you become. A diversified learning portfolio builds intellectual capital, social capital, and emotional resilience, the true engines of long-term growth.

So build your portfolio. Balance it. Revisit it. And let it evolve with you. Because the most powerful learners are not those who know everything but those who never stop learning.

17.7 Mentorship Stories and Lifelong Curiosity

If education builds the foundation, mentorship provides the scaffolding. Mentors offer wisdom, perspective, and accountability that accelerate growth. Many successful leaders attribute their breakthroughs not to solitary effort, but to guidance received at pivotal moments.

Mentorship Stories:

A, A young banker recalled how her mentor taught her not to "fall in love with a stock pick" a lesson in emotional discipline that saved her from costly mistakes.

B, an entrepreneur credited his mentor with teaching him that "trust controls the speed of transactions." This principle shaped his business philosophy and long-term success.

C, A freelancer navigating irregular income found stability through a mentor who guided her in budgeting, investing, and planning for retirement.

Lifelong Curiosity:

Curiosity is the fuel of continuous growth. It keeps us open to new ideas, technologies, and opportunities. In finance, curiosity means asking:

A, how are markets shifting?

B, what new tools or strategies are emerging?

C, how can I adapt my approach to stay ahead?

Anthony, a Deloitte professional, described how mentorship transformed his career. His mentor didn't just teach technical skills he modelled curiosity, asking questions others overlooked. That habit of inquiry became Anthony's edge, helping him innovate and lead.

Deep Insight: Mentorship and curiosity are intertwined. A mentor sparks curiosity, and curiosity sustains learning long after the mentorship ends. Together, they create a cycle of growth that compounds like interest.

17.8 Highlighted Lessons for Ongoing Growth

The financial landscape is dynamic shaped by inflation, interest rates, technology, and global events. To thrive, we must extract lessons from experience and apply them forward.

Key Lessons:

A, Inflation Awareness: Always measure returns against inflation. Real growth matters more than nominal

gains.
B, Liquidity Matters: Maintain flexibility to adapt when interest rates or markets shift.
C, Diversification Is Essential: Spread risk across sectors, geographies, and asset classes.
D, Technology Is Transformative: Embrace fintech, AI, and digital platforms as tools for efficiency and opportunity.
E, Long-Term Perspective: Resist the temptation of short-term speculation. Wealth compounds through patience and discipline.
G, Adaptability Is Wealth: Economic shocks, pandemics, and geopolitical shifts remind us that resilience is as important as returns.
In 2024, investors who panicked during market volatility often locked in losses. Those who stayed invested, diversified, and focused on fundamentals saw recovery and growth. The lesson: discipline and perspective are the quiet engines of wealth.
Deep Insight: Ongoing growth is not about predicting the future, it's about preparing for it. By combining education, mentorship, and lessons learned, individuals build not just wealth, but wisdom.

17.9 Reflection

Lifetime learning is the ultimate investment. Unlike markets, it never crashes. Unlike assets, it cannot be stolen. It compounds endlessly, enriching not only your finances but your character, relationships, and legacy. The pathways may differ degrees, apprenticeships, mentorships, or self-study but the principle is the same: keep learning. Stay curious. Seek wisdom. Because in the end, financial growth is not just about what you earn it's about who you become in the process.

Mentorship Stories and Lifelong Curiosity

If education lays the foundation for financial growth, mentorship and curiosity are the scaffolding that help us climb higher. They are the forces that turn knowledge into wisdom, and wisdom into action. Mentorship compresses decades of experience into moments of guidance, while curiosity ensures that learning never ends. Together, they form a cycle of growth that compounds like interest, shaping not only financial outcomes but also character and legacy.

The Transformative Power of Mentorship

Mentorship is one of the most underrated accelerators of financial and personal growth. A mentor is not simply a teacher, they are a guide, a mirror, and sometimes a challenger. They help us see blind spots, avoid costly mistakes, and stretch beyond our comfort zones.

The Banker and Emotional Discipline

A young banker in London recalled how her mentor taught her a lesson she never forgot: "Don't fall in love with a stock pick." Early in her career, she had become emotionally attached to an investment, ignoring warning signs. Her mentor gently but firmly reminded her that discipline, not emotion, drives long-term success. That single insight saved her from repeating the mistake—and became a principle she carried throughout her career.

The Entrepreneur and Trust

An entrepreneur building his first company was obsessed with speed closing deals quickly, scaling fast, and outpacing competitors. His mentor told him, "Trust controls the speed of transactions." At first, he didn't understand. But over time, he realized that trust built through integrity, transparency, and consistency was the true accelerator. Deals close faster when trust was present, and slower when it was absent. That insight reshaped his leadership and became the cornerstone of his success.

The Freelancer and Stability

A creative freelancer struggled with irregular income and constant financial stress. Her mentor, a seasoned consultant, taught her how to budget for lean months, set aside taxes, and build a financial cushion. More importantly, he helped her see her work as a business, not just a passion. That shift in mindset gave her stability and confidence, allowing her to grow her practice sustainably.

Deep Insight: Mentorship is not about giving answers it's about asking better questions. The best mentors don't just tell you what to do; they help you think differently, so you can make wiser decisions long after the mentorship ends.

The Cycle of Mentorship

Mentorship is not a one-way street. Over time, mentees become mentors, passing on the wisdom they once received. This creates a cycle of growth that strengthens communities and industries.

Anthony, a Deloitte professional, described how his mentor modelled curiosity by asking questions others overlooked. Years later, Anthony became a mentor himself, teaching younger colleagues not just technical skills but the habit of inquiry. In this way, mentorship becomes generational each person both receiving and giving, both learning and teaching.

Practical Framework: The Mentorship Ladder

1. Seek Guidance – Find mentors who can help you navigate your current stage.
2. Apply Lessons – Put their wisdom into practice, adapting it to your context.
3. Reflect and Refine – Learn not just what worked, but why it worked.
4. Give Back – Mentor others, creating a ripple effect of growth.

Lifelong Curiosity: The Engine of Growth

If mentorship provides direction, curiosity provides momentum. Curiosity is the willingness to ask, explore, and experiment. It keeps us open to new ideas, technologies, and opportunities. In finance, curiosity means not just following trends but questioning them. It means asking:

- How are markets shifting?
- What new tools or strategies are emerging?
- How can I adapt my approach to staying ahead?

A mid-career professional in her 40s could have coasted on her experience. Instead, she remained curious taking courses in blockchain, attending fintech conferences, and experimenting with digital tools. When her company pivoted toward digital finance, she was not only prepared, but she was also leading the change. Her curiosity became her competitive edge.

Deep Insight: Curiosity is not about knowing everything, it's about never assuming you know enough. It is the antidote to complacency and the fuel for reinvention.

The Mindset of a Lifelong Learner

Curiosity is not just a trait, it's a mindset. It's a way of approaching the world with openness, humility, and a hunger to grow. Lifelong learners don't wait for classrooms or credentials to expand their understanding. They see every conversation, challenge, and experience as an opportunity to learn.

This mindset isn't reserved for scholars or intellectuals. It's available to anyone willing to stay curious. And those who embrace it tend to share a few powerful habits:

They Ask More Questions Than They Answer

Lifelong learners are driven by inquiry. They're not afraid to say, "I don't know." In fact, they see not knowing as the beginning of discovery. They ask questions that go beyond the surface, why does this work? What's the story behind this? How could this be improved? Their curiosity leads them to deeper understanding and more meaningful connections.

They See Failure as Feedback

To a lifelong learner, failure isn't a dead end to its data. When something doesn't go as planned, they don't internalize it as a personal flaw. They ask, what can I learn from this? This mindset transforms mistakes into steppingstones. It builds resilience, sharpens judgment, and encourages experimentation.

They Read Widely, Beyond Their Field
Lifelong learners don't limit themselves to one domain. They read across disciplines, psychology, history, science, art knowing that insight often comes from unexpected places. This cross-pollination of ideas fuels creativity and helps them see patterns others miss.

They Surround Themselves with Diverse Perspectives
Growth thrives in diversity. Lifelong learners seek out people who challenge their assumptions, who come from different backgrounds, and who offer new ways of seeing the world. They listen more than they speak. They value dialogue over debate. And they understand that wisdom is often found in the margins.

They Remain Humble
Perhaps most importantly, lifelong learners remain humble. They know that no matter how much they've achieved or studied, there is always more to learn. They don't chase mastery for ego they pursue it for impact. Their humility keeps them teachable, adaptable, and open to transformation.
Author Insight: Albert Einstein once said, "I have no special talent. I am only passionately curious." That quote has stayed with me for years. It reminds me that brilliance isn't about having all the answers, it's about being relentlessly willing to ask better questions. In my own journey, the moments of greatest growth didn't come from certainty they came from curiosity. From picking up a book outside my comfort zone. From listening to someone with a completely different worldview. From trying something new and failing forward.

17.10 Mentorship and Curiosity in Practice

Mentorship and curiosity are two of the most powerful accelerators of personal and financial growth. They are not reserved for the elite or the exceptionally gifted they are accessible to anyone willing to ask questions, seek guidance, and stay open to learning. In a world that changes rapidly, those who thrive are not necessarily the ones with the most knowledge, but the ones most committed to learning and sharing.
So how can readers cultivate mentorship and curiosity in their own lives? Let's explore five practical steps, supported by real-life examples and insights from thought leaders who've walked this path.

1. Find a Mentor: Seek Wisdom with Humility
A mentor is not just someone older or more successful, they are someone whose values, experience, and perspective align with your aspirations. The best mentorships are built on mutual respect, clarity of purpose, and a shared commitment to growth.
Practical Tip: When approaching a potential mentor, be specific. Instead of saying, "Can you mentor me?" try, "I admire how you've built your business while staying grounded in your values. I'm working on a similar path and would love to learn how you navigated your early challenges."
Author Insight: In Tribe of Mentors, Tim Ferriss emphasizes the power of asking concise, thoughtful questions. He suggests reaching out with a single, well-crafted question rather than a vague request for mentorship. "You don't need a lifelong mentor. "You need someone who can help you with one problem, one decision, one insight."
Real-Life Example: A young entrepreneur in Lagos reached out to a local businesswoman he admired, asking for 15 minutes of her time to discuss pricing strategies. That short conversation turned into a quarterly check-in, and eventually, a mentorship that helped him scale his business sustainably.

2. Be a Mentor: Teach to Learn
Mentorship is a two-way street. You don't have to be an expert to offer value. If you've overcome a challenge,

learned a skill, or gained insight, you have something to share. Teaching others not only reinforces your own learning, it deepens your empathy and sharpens your communication.
Practical Tip: Start small. Offer to help a colleague with a skill you've mastered. Volunteer to speak at a local school or community group. Share your journey on a blog or podcast. You never know who might be inspired by your story.
Author Insight: In The Prosperous Coach, Rich Litvin and Steve Chandler argue that "coaching is not about having all the answers it's about creating space for powerful questions." Mentorship, in this sense, is less about giving advice and more about helping others discover their own wisdom.
Real-Life Example: A woman in Birmingham who had paid off £20,000 in debt began mentoring others in her church community. She didn't have formal training, but her lived experience and willingness to listen made her a trusted guide. Over time, she helped several families create budgets, reduce debt, and build savings.

3. Stay Curious: Make Learning a Lifestyle
Curiosity is the engine of lifelong growth. It keeps your mind open, your skills sharp, and your perspective fresh. In a world of constant change, curiosity is not a luxury, it's a necessity.
Practical Tip: Dedicate time each week to learning. Read books outside your field. Listen to podcasts that challenge your thinking. Attend workshops, webinars, or community events. Curiosity thrives when it's fed regularly.
Author Insight: Carol Dweck, in her groundbreaking book Mindset, distinguishes between a fixed mindset and a growth mindset. Those with a growth mindset believe that abilities can be developed through effort and learning. "Becoming is better than being," she writes. Curiosity is the fuel that powers that becoming.
Real-Life Example: A retired engineer in London began learning about digital marketing in his sixties not because he needed a new career, but because he was curious. That curiosity led him to help his granddaughter launch an online business, deepening their bond and giving him a renewed sense of purpose.

4. Ask Better Questions: Shift from Answers to Insight
The quality of your questions determines the quality of your growth. Instead of asking, "What should I do?" try asking, "What am I not seeing?" or "What assumptions am I making?" These questions invite deeper reflection and open the door to new possibilities.
Practical Tip: Keep a "question journal." Each week, write down one powerful question and sit with it. Don't rush to answer it let it guide your thinking, your conversations, and your decisions.
Author Insight: Warren Berger, in A More Beautiful Question, argues that asking the right questions is more important than having the right answers. He writes, "The ability to ask beautiful questions ambitious yet actionable can be the first step in bringing about change."

Real-Life Example: A startup founder in Edinburgh was struggling with low sales. Instead of asking, "How do I sell more?" she asked, "What problem am I really solving for my customers?" That shift in perspective led her to reposition her product, clarify her messaging, and triple her revenue within six months.

5. Create a Learning Circle: Grow Together
Learning is amplified in community. A learning circle a small group of peers committed to growth—can provide accountability, inspiration, and diverse perspectives. It's a space to share books, ideas, challenges, and breakthroughs.
Practical Tip: Start with three to five people. Meet each other monthly. Choose a theme, a book, or a question to explore. Rotate leadership. Keep it consistent, but flexible. The goal is not perfection, it's progress.
Author Insight: In The Art of Gathering, Priya Parker emphasizes the power of intentional gatherings. "Gatherings that truly work don't just happen," she writes. "They are created through thoughtful design." A learning circle is one such intentional space designed for growth, connection, and transformation.
Real-Life Example: A group of friends in London formed a "wealth and wisdom circle." They meet once a month to discuss personal finance, read books like The Psychology of Money, and share their goals. Over time, each

member grew not only in financial literacy but in confidence, clarity, and community. Their collective journey became a source of strength and accountability.

17.11 The Compound Effect of Mentorship and Curiosity

Mentorship and curiosity are not isolated traits, they are catalysts. When practiced consistently, they create a compound effect: small actions, repeated over time, that lead to exponential growth. This isn't just about accumulating knowledge or building networks it's about transformation. It's about becoming someone who learns deeply, shares generously, and evolves continuously.

The compound effect begins with a single question, a single conversation, a single moment of openness. A curious mind asks, "What if?" A mentor replies, "Here's what I've learned." Together, they spark a cycle of insight, action, and reflection that ripples outward into careers, communities, and legacies.

The Power of Small Steps

Curiosity doesn't require grand gestures. It begins with reading one chapter, attending one workshop, or asking one better question. Mentorship doesn't demand perfection, it asks for presence. A five-minute conversation can shift someone's trajectory. A shared story can unlock someone's courage.

Over time, these small steps compound. The curious reader becomes a confident thinker. The mentee becomes a mentor. The learning circle becomes a movement. And the individual journey becomes a collective transformation.

In London, a young woman named Amaka joined a local entrepreneurship group with no business background just a hunger to learn. She asked questions, took notes, and volunteered to help others. One of the group's mentors noticed her drive and offered guidance. Within two years, Amaka launched a sustainable fashion brand and began mentoring others. Her success wasn't built on shortcuts it was built on consistent curiosity and the generosity of shared wisdom.

What Other Authors Say

James Clear, author of Atomic Habits, writes, "All big things come from small beginnings. The seed of every habit is a single, tiny decision." Mentorship and curiosity are habits. They grow stronger with repetition. They shape identity. They create momentum.

Simon Sinek, in Start with Why, emphasizes the importance of clarity and connection. He argues that people thrive when they understand their purpose and surround themselves with those who believe in it. Mentorship provides that clarity. Curiosity fuels that connection.

Carol Dweck, in Mindset, reminds us that growth is not a destination, it's a process. Those with a growth mindset embrace challenges, persist through setbacks, and see effort as a path to mastery. Curiosity is the heartbeat of that mindset. Mentorship is its mirror.

As you reflect on your own journey, consider this: Who has helped you grow? Who might benefit from your insight? What questions are waiting to be asked? What stories are waiting to be shared?

The compound effect of mentorship and curiosity doesn't require brilliance, it requires commitment. It doesn't demand certainty that it invites exploration. And it doesn't end with you it expands through you.

So begin again. Ask. Listen. Share. Teach. Surround yourself with people who challenge and uplift you. Because the most powerful transformations are not built in isolation they're built in connection.

And the most enduring legacies are not just what we know, but what we pass on.

17.12 Reasonable Thoughts

Mentorship and curiosity are not luxuries; they are necessities for financial and personal growth. Mentorship gives us wisdom we could not earn alone. Curiosity ensures that wisdom never stagnates. Together, they create a rhythm of learning that sustains us through every season of life.

Because in the end, the richest people are not those who know the most, but those who never stop learning. They are the ones who seek guidance, stay curious, and pass on what they've gained. They are the ones who understand that financial growth is not just about money, it's about becoming wiser, more adaptable, and more generous with each passing year.

Highlighted Lessons for Ongoing Growth

Financial growth is not a straight line it is a rhythm of expansion, contraction, and adaptation. Each season of the economy teaches us something new, and those who thrive are not the ones who predict perfectly, but the ones who prepare wisely. This section particular key lessons drawn from history, recent economic shifts, and lived experience that can guide ongoing growth.

Lesson 1: Inflation Awareness Protecting Purchasing Power

Inflation is the silent thief of wealth. Even when it moderates, its lingering effects erode purchasing power. In 2024, investors were reminded that returns must always be measured against inflation, not just in nominal terms.

A retiree who kept most of her savings in a low-interest account saw her purchasing power shrink as prices rose. Meanwhile, her neighbor, who invested in a diversified portfolio of equities and inflation-protected bonds, maintained stability. The difference wasn't income it was awareness.

Practical Insight: Always ask: What is my real return after inflation? Build portfolios that include assets resilient to inflation such as equities, real estate, or inflation-linked bonds.

Lesson 2: Liquidity Matters Flexibility in Shifting Conditions

Interest rates and market cycles shift quickly. In 2024, as central banks plateaued and even cut rates, liquidity became a lifeline. Investors with flexible cash reserves could refinance debt, rebalance portfolios, and seize opportunities.

A small business owner who had maintained a healthy cash buffer was able to expand when competitors were forced to contract. Liquidity gave him not just survival, but advantage.

Practical Insight: Liquidity is not wasted money, it is optionality. Keep a portion of assets easily accessible to adapt when conditions change.

Lesson 3: Diversification Is Essential Never Bet on One Horse

Markets are unpredictable. Diversification remains one of the oldest and most reliable lessons in finance. In 2024, volatility across equities, bonds, and property reminded investors that no single asset class is a safe haven.

An investor who had concentrated heavily in property saw returns stagnate. Another, who spread investments across global equities, bonds, and alternative assets, weathered the storm with steadier growth.

Practical Insight: Diversification is not about chasing everything it's about balancing risk. Spread across geographies, sectors, and asset classes to reduce vulnerability.

Lesson 4: Technology Is Transformative Adapt or Fall Behind

The rise of fintech, AI, and digital platforms has reshaped how we save, invest, and transact. In 2024, digital transformation accelerated further, disrupting traditional financial services.

A mid-career professional who embraced digital tools automated savings apps, robo-advisors, and blockchain-based investments found herself ahead of peers who resisted change. Her willingness to adapt gave her both efficiency and opportunity.

Practical Insight: Don't fear technology leverage it. Use digital platforms to automate good habits, access new markets, and stay competitive.

Lesson 5: Long-Term Perspective. Patience Pays
Markets rise and fall, but wealth compounds over decades. In 2024, those who panicked during volatility often locked in losses, while disciplined investors who stayed on the course saw recovery.
Two friends invested in the same index fund. One sold during a downturn, crystallizing losses. The other held steady, reinvested dividends, and years later had doubled her wealth. The difference was not intelligence, it was patience.
Practical Insight: Wealth is built not by timing the market, but by time in the market. Adopt a long-term horizon and resist emotional decisions.

Lesson 6: Adaptability Is Wealth Resilience Over Prediction
The past few years have shown that shocks pandemics, geopolitical conflicts, and inflation spikes are inevitable. The lesson is not to predict perfectly, but to remain adaptable.
A consultant who diversified income streams combining employment, freelance work, and investments was able to pivot when one stream dried up. Her adaptability became her true wealth.
Practical Insight: Build resilience in your financial life. Diversify income, maintain liquidity, and cultivate skills that allow you to pivot when circumstances shift.

Lesson 7: Strategic Saving and Cost Management
Inflation and high living costs in 2024 reminded households that saving is not just about accumulation, it's about strategy. Businesses, too, learned that cost management can be as critical as revenue.
A family who automated savings into diversified accounts weathered rising costs better than those who relied on traditional low-interest savings. Their strategy preserved purchasing power.
Practical Insight: Don't just save save strategically. Use high-yield accounts, diversified investments, and automation to protect against erosion.

Lesson 8: Property and Real Assets Not Always a Safe Haven
Property has long been seen as a cornerstone of wealth. But in 2024, affordability crises and shifting markets showed that property is not immune to volatility.
A young couple stretched to buy in London, only to see stagnant growth. Meanwhile, investors who diversified into rental markets outside major cities saw stronger returns.
Practical Insight: Property can be powerful, but it is not infallible. Treat it as part of a diversified portfolio, not the whole.

Lesson 9: The Human Factor People as Assets
Financial growth is not just about numbers, it's about people. Teams, mentors, and networks are assets that compound over time. As Forbes experts noted, valuing people as key assets is central to sustained success.
A business leader who invested in employee development saw loyalty, innovation, and profitability rise. His competitors, who cut staff to save costs, struggled with turnover and stagnation.
Practical Insight: Invest in people yourself, your team, your community. Human capital is the foundation of all other forms of capital.

17.13 Reflection: The Wealth of a Learning Life

Financial growth is often measured in numbers net worth, investment returns, income streams. But the deeper truth is that the most enduring wealth is not stored in bank accounts or portfolios. It is stored in the mind, the heart, and the habits of a lifelong learner. Education, mentorship, and curiosity are the compounding assets that never depreciate. They are the wealth that sustains us through every season of life.

Throughout this chapter, we've seen how education opens doors, whether through formal degrees, vocational training, online learning, or self-study. Each pathway is a reminder that knowledge is not a privilege of the few, but a resource available to anyone willing to pursue it. The benefits extend beyond financial gain: education builds confidence, resilience, and the ability to adapt when the world shifts beneath our feet.

We've also explored the transformative power of mentorship. A mentor compresses decades of experience into moments of wisdom, offering shortcuts through mistakes and insights that no textbook can provide. Mentorship is not just about guidance it is about relationships. It is about someone believing in you enough to challenge you, stretch you, and remind you of what you are capable of. And when you, in turn, become a mentor, you continue the cycle of growth, passing on wisdom to the next generation.

And then there is curiosity the quiet force that keeps learning alive long after formal education ends. Curiosity is what drives us to ask questions, to explore new technologies, to read widely, to listen deeply. It is what keeps us from stagnation. In a world where industries transform overnight, curiosity is not a luxury it is survival. It ensures that we remain agile, relevant, and open to possibility.

The highlighted lessons of ongoing growth awareness of inflation, the importance of liquidity, the power of diversification, the role of technology, the necessity of patience, and the value of adaptability are all anchored in this deeper truth: learning is the thread that ties them together. Without learning, we repeat mistakes. With learning, we refine wisdom. Without learning, we cling to outdated strategies. With learning, we evolve.

So as you close this chapter, consider this: your greatest investment is not in stocks, bonds, or property. It is in yourself. It is in your willingness to keep learning, to seek mentors, to stay curious, and to apply lessons with humility and courage.

Because in the end, the richest people are not those who stop learning once they've "made it." They are the ones who remain students of life open, adaptable, and generous with what they know. They are the ones who understand that financial growth is not just about accumulation, but about transformation.

Let your life be a testament to this truth: that the wealth of a learning life is the wealth that never stops growing.

Chapter 18: Adapting to Change

18.1 Introduction: The Constant of Change

Change is life's only guarantee. It arrives uninvited, often at the most inconvenient times, and rarely in the form we expect. Sometimes it comes as a sudden disruption, a job loss, a health crisis, a global pandemic. Other times it creeps in quietly, through shifting markets, evolving technologies, or the slow passage of time. Whether abrupt or gradual, change demands a response. And in that response lies the difference between stagnation and growth, despair and resilience, collapse and reinvention.

For many, change feels like loss. It strips away the familiar and forces us into uncertainty. Yet for others, change becomes a catalyst, a doorway to new opportunities, fresh perspectives, and unexpected strength. The difference is not in the change itself, but in how we meet it. Resilience is the bridge between disruption and renewal. It is the ability to bend without breaking, to adapt without losing one's core, and to see possibility where others see only endings.

Consider the story of a mid-career professional who was suddenly laid off after two decades in the same company. At first, the shock was paralyzing. But instead of clinging to the past, she chose to see the layoff as an invitation to reinvent herself. She enrolled in a digital skills program, built a new network, and within a year launched a consultancy that gave her more freedom and fulfilment than her old job ever had. The change she once feared became the turning point of her life.

This is the paradox of change: what feels like an ending is often the beginning of something new. The challenge is not to avoid change that is impossible but to cultivate resilience to navigate it with clarity, courage, and creativity.

Resilience is not about being unshakable or immune to hardship. It is about flexibility, perspective, and recovery. Psychologists describe resilience as a set of skills that can be learned and strengthened: emotional awareness, problem-solving, adaptability, and social connection. In financial and personal life alike, resilience is the difference between being derailed by change and being propelled by it.

When economies shift, resilient individuals adjust their strategies. When relationships evolve, they adapt with empathy. When personal setbacks occur, they draw on inner and outer resources to rebuild. Resilience does not eliminate pain or difficulty it transforms them into growth.

The Purpose of this Chapter

This chapter will explore three dimensions of adapting to change:

1. Managing Change and Building Resilience – practical principles for navigating uncertainty with strength.
2. Personal Stories About Embracing the Unexpected – real-life examples of individuals who turned disruption into opportunity.
3. Tables of Resilience Strategies – structured, actionable tools to help readers apply resilience in their own lives.

Together, these sections will show that resilience is not abstract, it is practical, learnable, and deeply human. Change is not the enemy. It is the raw material of growth. Every disruption carries within it the seed of reinvention. The question is not whether change will come it will. The question is how we will meet it. With fear, or with resilience? With resistance, or with openness? With despair, or with hope?

This chapter invites you to see change not as a threat, but as a teacher. To embrace resilience not as a trait you either have or don't, but as a skill you can cultivate. And remember that the richest lives are not those without change, but those that adapt, evolve, and thrive because of it.

18.2 Managing Change and Building Resilience

Change is inevitable. It arrives in many forms career transitions, economic downturns, health challenges, technological disruption, or personal loss. While we cannot control when or how change comes, we can control how we respond. The ability to adapt with strength and clarity is what we call resilience.

Resilience is not about avoiding difficulty or pretending everything is fine. It is about navigating through uncertainty with perspective, flexibility, and courage. According to resilience research, it is a skill set that can be cultivated, not a fixed trait. This means anyone can learn to become more resilient, regardless of personality or background.

The Nature of Resilience

At its core, resilience is about bouncing forward not just bouncing back. It's not about returning to who you were before change, but about becoming stronger, wiser, and more adaptable because of it. Resilience is not a return to the familiar it's a redefinition of what's possible.

Many people imagine resilience as sheer toughness, a kind of emotional Armor. But true resilience is more like elasticity. It's the ability to bend without breaking, to absorb impact and still remain whole. Like a tree in a storm, the resilient person doesn't resist the wind they move with it, rooted but flexible.

Flexibility: Adapting to What Is

Resilience begins with flexibility, the ability to adjust plans and expectations when circumstances shift. Life rarely unfolds exactly as we imagine. Jobs change. Relationships evolve. Health fluctuates. The resilient person doesn't cling rigidly to one outcome. They adapt. They pivot. They find new ways to move forward.

Author Insight: I once spent months preparing for a business launch that fell apart days before going live. At first, I was devastated. But instead of scrapping the idea entirely, I reworked the concept, scaled it down, and launched a smaller version. That version became the foundation for something even better. Flexibility didn't just save the project it reshaped it into something more sustainable.

Perspective: Reframing the Setback

Resilience also requires perspective the ability to see setbacks as temporary and surmountable, not permanent or defining. When we're in the middle of a challenge, it can feel like the end. But resilient people zoom out. They remember that this moment is one chapter, not the whole story.

Perspective allows us to ask, what is this teaching me? instead of Why is this happening to me? It transforms pain into purpose and struggle into strength.

Resourcefulness: Creating New Paths

When the usual routes are blocked, resilience calls on resourcefulness. It's the ability to use creativity and problem-solving to find new paths forward. It's making the most of what you have, even when it's not ideal.

Real-Life Example: During the pandemic, a London-based theatre actor named Marcus lost all his stage work. Rather than wait for theatres to reopen, he began offering virtual storytelling sessions for children. His videos went viral, and he eventually launched a digital platform for creative education. What began as a crisis became a calling because he was willing to innovate.

Connection: Drawing Strength from Others

Resilience is not a solo act. It's sustained by connection. Supportive relationships between friends, family, mentors, and communities act as emotional scaffolding. They remind us of we're not alone. They offer perspective, encouragement, and sometimes, a lifeline.

Whether it's a conversation, a shared meal, or a simple check-in, connection fuels resilience. It turns isolation into solidarity and struggle into shared strength.

18.3 Principles of Managing Change

1. Acceptance Over Resistance

Change often triggers resistance. We cling to the family, even when it no longer serves us. Acceptance does not mean passivity, it means acknowledging reality so we can respond effectively.
Practical Step: Write down what has changed in your life. Circle what you can control, underline what you cannot. This simple exercise shifts focus from resistance to action.

2. Sphere of Control

The Sphere of Control model reminds us that stress multiplies when we focus on what's beyond our influence. Instead, resilience grows when we concentrate on what we can control our actions, mindset, and communication.
Practical Step: Create three columns: Control, Influence, Cannot Control. Fill them in. Then commit to spending 80% of your energy on the first two.

3. Mindset Shift

Psychologists call this cognitive reframing: viewing challenges as opportunities for growth. Instead of asking, "Why is this happening to me?" ask, "What can I learn from this?"
Storytelling Example: A manager facing redundancy reframed the event as a chance to pursue entrepreneurship. What began as loss became liberation.

4. Self-Care as Strategy

Resilience is not built in crisis it is built in daily habits. Sleep, exercise, nutrition, and mindfulness are not luxuries; they are lifelines.
Practical Step: Schedule resilience into your calendar. Protect time for rest, movement, and reflection as fiercely as you protect work deadlines.

5. Social Support

Strong relationships are buffers against stress. Sharing experiences reduces isolation and builds perspective.
Practical Step: Identify three people you can call in times of change. Reach out before you need them. Resilience is relational.

18.4 Frameworks for Building Resilience

The Change Curve

Based on Elisabeth Kübler-Ross's model, the Change Curve describes the emotional journey through disruption:

1. Shock/Denial – "This can't be happening."
2. Anger/Frustration – "Why me?"
3. Confusion/Low Mood – "I don't know what to do."
4. Acceptance – "This is real. I can adapt."
5. Growth – "I am stronger because of this."

Practical Application: Identify where you are on the curve. Naming your stage normalizes the experience and helps you choose the right strategy.

The Five Pillars of Resilience

1. Self-Awareness – Recognizing emotions and strengths.
2. Mindfulness – Staying present amid uncertainty.
3. Self-Care – Protecting physical and mental health.

4. Positive Relationships – Building supportive networks.
5. Purpose – Anchoring in values and meaning.
Practical Application: Rate yourself 1–5 on each pillar. Focus on strengthening the lowest score.

18.5 Resilience in Practice: Stories

• Corporate Reinvention: A team facing organizational restructuring used the Sphere of Control model to focus on what could influence team culture, communication, and skill-building. Instead of collapsing under uncertainty, they emerged stronger and more united.
• Personal Renewal: A single parent navigating divorce leaned on social support and mindfulness practices. Over time, she reframed her story from "broken family" to "new beginning." Her resilience became a model for her children.
• Health Challenge: A man diagnosed with chronic illness shifted from despair to purpose by mentoring others with the same condition. His resilience transformed personal pain into collective healing.

Exercises

1. Resilience Journal: Each evening, write:
a. One challenge you faced today.
b. How you responded.
c. What you learned.
Over time, this builds awareness of your growth.

2. Resilience Rituals
Create small daily practices morning gratitude, evening reflection, weekly check-ins with a friend. Rituals anchor you when everything else feels uncertain.

3. Resilience Rehearsal
Imagine a future disruption (job loss, relocation, health scare). Write down how you would respond using the five pillars. This mental rehearsal strengthens preparedness.
Managing change and building resilience is not about eliminating uncertainty, it's about cultivating the inner and outer resources to face it with courage. Resilience is built in small, daily choices: choosing perspective over panic, connection over isolation, and growth over fear.
Because in the end, resilience is not about bouncing back to who you were it's about bouncing forward to who you are becoming.

18.6 Personal Stories About Embracing the Unexpected

1.The unexpected will always comes.

Jobs will shift, health will falter, economies will fluctuate, and relationships will evolve. But within every disruption lies a choice: to resist or to embrace, to collapse or to create.
The stories in this section remind us that resilience is not about avoiding change, it's about transforming through it. It's about finding the courage to say, "This is not the end of my story. It is the beginning of a new chapter."

2. Personal Stories About Embracing the Unexpected

Change often arrives uninvited. It rarely asks for permission, and it almost never comes at a convenient time. Yet, in the lives of countless individuals, what first appeared as a setback became the seed of reinvention.

These stories remind us that resilience is not abstract as it is lived. It is the quiet courage to face the unexpected and the creativity to turn endings into beginnings.

Karen's Story: Reinvention Through Caregiving

At 46, Karen Whitehead's life was upended when her mother fell ill. She left her corporate job to become a full-time caregiver. For many, this would have been the end of a career trajectory. But Karen chose to see it differently.

While caring for her mother, she enrolled in a master's program in counselling. The flexibility of study allowed her to balance caregiving with learning. What began as a detour became a new path. Today, Karen runs a thriving practice supporting families in transition.

Lesson: Change often strips away the illusion of control, but it can also reveal hidden callings. Karen's story shows that resilience is not about clinging to the old but about embracing the new with courage.

Leslie's Story: From Burnout to Business

Leslie Scott had what many would call success: a six-figure salary, a prestigious role, and a busy lifestyle. But beneath the surface, she was burning out. The stress became unbearable, and she made a radical choice she quit.

She rented a cabin in the woods, seeking space to heal. In that quiet, she rediscovered creativity. She began making natural bath products as a form of therapy. What started as self-care grew into Walton Wood Farm, a multi-million-dollar company.

Lesson: Sometimes, the unexpected change is the one we choose. Leslie's story reminds us that walking away from what no longer serves us can open the door to what truly fulfils us.

Brad's Story: A Café Called Resilience

At 53, Brad Gold was laid off from his corporate job. For months, he wrestled with fear and self-doubt. But he also carried a lifelong dream: to open a café. With his severance package, he took the leap.

Eighteen years later, his café is still thriving. It's not just a business, it's a community hub, a place where people gather, connect, and feel at home.

Lesson: Change can push us toward dreams we've long postponed. Brad's story shows that resilience is not just about survival, it's about daring to pursue what matters most.

Craig's Story: Health as a Catalyst

Craig Shapiro's life changed when he was downsized from his newspaper job. At first, the loss felt devastating. But instead of spiraling, he turned inward. He focused on his health, adopting a vegan lifestyle and committing to fitness.

This personal transformation became a platform for advocacy. Craig began writing about wellness, building a new career as a health coach and speaker. What began as loss became a mission.

Lesson: Change often redirects us toward neglected areas of life. Craig's story shows that resilience is not just about adapting externally but about transforming internally.

18.7 Global Perspective: Collective Resilience

Change is not only personal it is collective. While individuals adapt to life's challenges, entire communities, industries, and nations are often called to evolve together. In these moments, resilience becomes more than a private virtue it becomes a shared force. And when people unite in response to disruption, something extraordinary happens, innovation accelerates, bonds deepen, and new possibilities emerge.

Post-Pandemic Reinvention

The COVID-19 pandemic was a global shockwave that tested every system—healthcare, education, business, and beyond. But amid the uncertainty, communities around the world responded with creativity and courage.

Restaurants that once thrived on foot traffic transformed into delivery hubs overnight. Chefs began offering meal kits and virtual cooking classes. Fitness studios launched Zoom workouts and on-demand wellness platforms. Artisans who relied on local markets pivoted to Etsy, Instagram, and Shopify, reaching global audiences from their living rooms.

These weren't just survival tactics they were acts of reinvention. They demonstrated that resilience isn't about returning to what it was, but about reimagining what it could be.

Real-Life Example: In Lagos, Nigeria, a small tailoring business called Threads by Tayo faced closure when lockdowns halted in-person sales. Rather than fold, Tayo began livestreaming sewing tutorials on Instagram. Her audience grew rapidly, and she launched an online course for beginners. Within a year, she had students from over 20 countries, and a new revenue stream that far exceeded her pre-pandemic earnings. Her pivot didn't just save her business, it expanded it.

Migration and Renewal

Another powerful example of collective resilience is found in the stories of migrants and refugees. Families displaced by war, climate change, or political instability often arrive in new countries with little more than hope. Yet time and again, they rebuild not just their lives, but their communities.

They open restaurants that introduce new cuisines. They start businesses that create jobs. They bring cultural traditions that enrich the social fabric. Their resilience lies not only in survival, but in contribution.

In Germany, for instance, the influx of Syrian refugees in 2015 sparked both challenges and opportunities. One standout story is that of Karam, a Syrian engineer who fled Aleppo and resettled in Berlin. After learning German and navigating the local bureaucracy, he co-founded a tech startup that helps other refugees match their skills with job opportunities. His company is now partners with NGOs and government agencies across Europe, turning his personal journey into a platform for collective uplift.

The Shared Lesson

Resilience is magnified when shared. When people come together whether in crisis or transition, they create networks of support, innovation, and renewal. Collective adaptation shows that change, while disruptive, can also be a catalyst for solidarity.

Whether it's a neighborhood rebuilding after a natural disaster, a diaspora community preserving culture abroad, or a global workforce redefining how we work resilience thrives in connection.

So as you navigate your own transformation, remember you're not alone. Your strength is part of something bigger. And when we rise together, we don't just recover, we evolve.

18.8 Themes Emerging from These Stories

Across the diverse experiences shared in this journey from personal reinvention to financial transformation certain themes rise to the surface. These aren't just patterns, their principles. They reveal how people navigate disruption, reclaim agency, and build lives of meaning and momentum. Let's explore five of the most powerful themes that emerge:

1. Loss as a Beginning

What feels like an ending often becomes the start of something new. Whether it's the loss of a job, a relationship, or a long-held identity, many of the individuals in these stories found that their lowest moments became turning points. Loss stripped away what was familiar but in doing so, it cleared space for reinvention. One woman, after being made redundant during a corporate downsizing, finally pursued her dream of becoming a therapist. What began as grief became growth. Her story reminds us that endings are not failures, they're invitations to begin again, often with more clarity and courage than before.

2. Creativity in Crisis

Change has a way of unlocking hidden talents and passions. When routines are disrupted, we're forced to think

differently, act boldly, and tap into parts of ourselves we may have ignored. Crisis becomes crucible for creativity.
A young man in Manchester, once a bartender, began painting during lockdown to cope with anxiety. His art gained traction online, and within a year, he was selling prints and hosting virtual exhibitions. What started as therapy became a thriving side business. His creativity didn't just help him survive it helped him thrive.

3. Courage to Pivot
Resilience requires bravery to step into the unknown. Many of the people featured didn't have a perfect plan they had a willingness to try. They pivoted careers, launched businesses, or returned to school. They embraced uncertainty not because it was easy, but because staying stuck was harder.
One father of three left a 15-year career in retail to train as a software developer. It was scary. It was humbling. But it was also liberating. His pivot wasn't just professional, it was personal. It proved that reinvention is always possible, no matter what your age or stage.

4. Health and Well-being
Disruption often prompts a return to what matters most. Many used their turning points to prioritize physical and emotional wellness. They began walking, journaling, meditating, or simply resting. They realized that wealth without health is hollow and that well-being is a form of wealth in itself.
One woman recovering from burnout began each day with a 10-minute walk and a gratitude list. It didn't fix everything overnight, but it grounded her. It gave her the strength to rebuild from the inside out.

5. Community as Anchor
Support networks amplify resilience and reduce isolation. Whether through family, friends, faith groups, or online communities, connection was a lifeline. It offered encouragement, accountability, and a sense of belonging.
A group of friends in London formed a "resilience circle," meeting monthly to share goals, setbacks, and wins. Over time, they became each other's safety net—and springboard. Their collective strength made each individual stronger.

18.9 Practical Takeaways for Readers

The unexpected will always come. Jobs will shift, health will falter, economies will fluctuate, and relationships will evolve. But within every disruption lies a choice: to resist or to embrace, to collapse or to create. The stories in this section remind us that resilience is not about avoiding change, it's about transforming through it. It's about finding the courage to say, "This is not the end of my story. It is the beginning of a new chapter."
Here are five practical takeaways to help you navigate that chapter with clarity and strength:

Reframe the Narrative
When life throws you off course, it's easy to ask, "Why me?" But that question often leads to blame, shame, or paralysis. A more empowering question is, "What now?" This shift moves you from victimhood to agency. It invites you to take the next step, however small, and to see disruption as a doorway not a dead end.
Author Insight: After a failed business venture in my early twenties, I spent months stuck in self-doubt. But the moment I asked, "What now?" everything changed. I enrolled in a course, rebuilt my confidence, and eventually launched a new project that succeeded. The failure didn't define me—but my response did.

Small Experiment
You don't need to overhaul your life overnight. Start with small, low-risk experiments. Test ideas. Explore curiosities. Build confidence through action.

Real-Life Example: Leslie, a single mother in Bristol, began making natural bath products in her kitchen as a form of stress relief. She gave them to friends, who encouraged her to sell them online. She started with a small Etsy shop, reinvested her profits, and eventually launched a full-fledged skincare brand. What began as a hobby became a thriving business because she dared to start small.

Learning Support

You don't have to do this alone. Share your journey with trusted friends, mentors, or communities. Let others hold space for your fears, reflect your strengths, and remind you of your progress. Support doesn't make you weak, it makes you human.

Whether it's a financial accountability partner, a therapist, or a local entrepreneur group, connection accelerates healing and growth.

Prioritize Health

Change can be exhausting. Use it as a cue to reset not just financially, but physically and emotionally. Revisit your sleep, nutrition, movement, and mental health habits. A strong body and calm mind are your greatest assets in times of transition. Even a daily walk, a journal entry, or a digital detox can restore clarity and energy.

Stay Open

The path forward may not look like the past and that's the point. Let go of rigid expectations. Stay curious. Be willing to evolve. Sometimes the life you're meant to live is waiting just beyond the life you thought you wanted.

18.10 Tables of Resilience Strategies

Resilience is not a vague quality reserved for the exceptionally strong, it is a set of skills and practices that anyone can develop. The challenge is that in times of change, our minds often default to fear, resistance, or paralysis. Structured strategies help us move from reaction to response, from overwhelm to agency.

This section presents resilience strategies in table form, making them easy to reference, compare, and apply. Each table highlights a different dimension of resilience: core skills, everyday practices, and responses to the stages of change.

Table 1: Core Resilience Skills

These are the foundational abilities that allow individuals to adapt to change. They are not innate traits but learnable skills that can be strengthened through practice.

Skill	Description	Practical Actions
Emotional Awareness	Recognizing and managing emotions effectively	Journaling, mindfulness, naming feelings instead of suppressing them
Problem-Solving	Tackling challenges methodically	Break problems into steps, weigh pros/cons, brainstorm alternatives
Social Connections	Building supportive networks	Join groups, nurture friendships, seek mentors
Adaptability	Flexibility in thinking and behavior	Reframe setbacks, experiment with new approaches
Positive Outlook	Maintaining hope and perspective	Gratitude journaling, affirmations, reframing challenges

Deep Insight: Research shows that resilience is not about avoiding stress but about how quickly and effectively we recover from it. These core skills are the building blocks of that recovery.

18.11 Table 2: Everyday Resilience Practices

Resilience is not built in crisis it is built in daily habits. These practices strengthen our capacity to handle disruption when it comes.

Category	Strategies	Examples
Self-Care	Protect physical and mental health	Sleep 7–9 hrs, exercise, balanced diet
Mindset	Reframe challenges	Replace "I can't handle this" with "I'll grow through this"
Control Focus	Direct energy where it matters	List what's in your control vs. not
Support Systems	Lean on relationships	Weekly check-ins with friends/family
Growth Orientation	Learn from change	Journal lessons, take new courses, embrace curiosity

Storytelling Example: A manager navigating organizational restructuring used the "control focus" strategy. Instead of obsessing over leadership decisions, she focused on her own team's morale and communication. Her team not only survived the transition but thrived, becoming a model for others.

18.12 Table 3: The Change Curve and Resilience Responses

The Change Curve (adapted from Elisabeth Kübler-Ross's model) describes the emotional journey through disruption. Recognizing where you are on the curve helps you choose the right resilience strategy.

Stage of Change	Typical Feelings	Resilience Strategy
Shock/Denial	Disbelief, avoidance	Pause, breathe, gather facts
Anger/Frustration	Resistance, stress	Channel energy into exercise, journaling
Confusion/Low Mood	Fatigue, doubt	Seek support, practicing self-compassion
Acceptance	Openness, clarity	Focus on controllables, set small goals
Growth	Confidence, renewal	Build new routines, mentor others

Deep Insight: People move back and forth along the curve. Resilience is not about skipping stages but about moving through them with awareness and support.

18.13 Table 4: Organizational Resilience Strategies

Change often affects not just individuals but entire teams or organizations. Leaders can foster resilience by embedding it into culture.

Focus Area	Resilience Strategy	Practical Example
Communication	Transparent, frequent updates	Weekly team briefings during change

Flexibility	Encourage adaptive roles	Crosstrain employees for multiple functions
Support Systems	Provide resources for well-being	Employee assistance programs, coaching
Learning Culture	Promote continuous growth	Training budgets, innovation labs
Recognition	Celebrate adaptability	Acknowledge individuals who model resilience

Storytelling Example: A tech company undergoing digital transformation created "resilience champions" within each department employees trained to support peers emotionally and practically. This peer-to-peer model reduced stress and built collective strength.

18.14 Table 5: Personal Resilience Toolkit

This table offers a quick reference for individuals to build their own resilience toolkit.

Tool	Purpose	How to Use It
Resilience Journal	Track growth and lessons	Write 3 reflections daily: challenge, response, learning
Breathing Exercises	Calm nervous system	Practice 4-7-8 breathing during stress
Gratitude Practice	Shift mindset	List 3 things you're grateful for each morning
Support List	Build connection	Identify 3 people you can call in crisis
Learning Habit	Stay adaptable	Dedicate 30 mins weekly to new skills

Resilience is not a single act, it is a system of habits, mindsets, and support. The tables in this section are not meant to be read once and forgotten; they are designed as living tools, to be revisited whenever change arrives.

The key is to remember that resilience is not about avoiding difficulty but about navigating it with strength and clarity. By cultivating core skills, embedding daily practices, recognizing the stages of change, and building both personal and organizational toolkits, we prepare ourselves not just to survive disruption but to grow through it.

Because in the end, resilience is not about bouncing back to who we were it's about bouncing forward to who we are becoming.

Conclusion: Your Journey of Wealth, Meaning, and Legacy

Every journey has a destination, but the journey of wealth is different. It is not about reaching a single point where you can finally say, "I've made it." Instead, it is about walking a path that continually evolves one that integrates money, meaning, resilience, and legacy into a life of purpose.
This book has explored wealth in its many dimensions: financial growth, philanthropy, resilience, education, and legacy. Now, as we close, it is time to gather the threads, reflect on the key lessons, and chart a way forward.

Key Takeaways Summarised

1. Wealth is Holistic
Wealth is not just about money. It is about the integration of financial capital with emotional, intellectual, and social capital. True prosperity is measured not only in what you accumulate, but in how you live, how you give, and how you grow.

2. Education is the Ultimate Investment
Knowledge compounds faster than money. Lifelong learning, mentorship, and curiosity are assets that never depreciate. They keep you adaptable in a world where industries shift, technologies disrupt, and opportunities emerge unexpectedly.

3. Resilience is Essential
Change is inevitable. The ability to adapt, recover, and reinvent yourself is the foundation of lasting success. Resilience is not about avoiding hardship but about transforming through it.

4. Philanthropy Creates Legacy
Giving is not just about generosity it is about impact. Whether through money, time, or creativity, philanthropy ensures that your wealth becomes a force for good that outlives you.

5. Mindset Shapes Outcomes
Scarcity thinking limits; abundance thinking expands. The way you see money influences the way you use it. A mindset of growth, gratitude, and possibility opens doors that fear, and scarcity keep closed.

6. Legacy is Lived, Not Just Left
Legacy is not only about what you pass on at the end of life it is about how you live now. Every decision, every act of generosity, every lesson you teach your family is already shaping the story that will be told about you.

Encouragement to Embark on Your Wealth Journey

The journey of wealth is not a privilege reserved for the few, it is an invitation extended to all. Too often, people hesitate to begin because they believe they lack resources, knowledge, or the perfect timing. They wait for the "right moment," the "right income," or the "right opportunity." But the truth is this: the right moment is always now. Wealth is not built in a single leap; it is cultivated step by step, decision by decision, habit by habit by habit.
This section is called action. It is encouragement to begin where you are, with what you have, and to trust that the journey itself will shape you into the person capable of stewarding greater resources, deeper meaning, and lasting legacy.

Wealth as a Journey, not a Destination

One of the most common misconceptions about wealth is that it is a finish line. People imagine that once they reach a certain number in their bank account, they will finally feel secure, fulfilled, and free. But wealth is not a static destination, it is a dynamic journey.

• Wealth is growth. It evolves as you evolve. What wealth means to you at 25 may look very different at 55.
• Wealth is alignment. It is about bringing your financial decisions into harmony with your values and vision.
• Wealth is stewardship. It is not just about accumulation, but about how you use what you have to create impact.

When you see wealth as a journey, you release the pressure of perfection. You no longer need to have it all figured out before you begin. You simply need to take the next step.

Starting Where You Are

Many people delay their wealth journey because they feel unprepared. They think, “I’ll start saving when I earn more,” or “I’ll invest once I understand everything.” But waiting only delays growth.

• If you have £10, you can begin by saving £1.
• If you have one free hour a week, you can begin by learning something new.
• If you have a single skill, you can begin by sharing it with others.

The point is not how much you start with it is that you start. Small beginnings compound into significant outcomes. Just as a seed grows into a tree, small financial habits grow into wealth over time.

A young woman in Manchester began her wealth journey by saving just £20 a month. At first, it felt insignificant. But over time, she increased her contributions, invested in index funds, and built a habit of consistency. Ten years later, she had not only financial stability but also the confidence to start her own business. Her journey began not with abundance, but with intention.

Facing the Fear of Change

Embarking on a wealthy journey often stirs fear. Fear of failure. Fear of making mistakes. Fear of losing what little you have. These fears are natural, but they should not be final.

Resilience teaches us that mistakes are not the end they are the curriculum. Every misstep is a lesson, every setback a teacher. The only true failure is refusing to begin.

Encouragement Insight: Think of your wealth journey as a series of experiments. Some will succeed, some will fail, but all will teach you something valuable. The courage to begin outweighs the risk of imperfection.

Wealth Beyond Money

Another barrier to beginning is the belief that wealth is only about money. This narrow view keeps many people stuck waiting for a windfall, a raise, or a “better time” to start building. But as we’ve explored, wealth is multidimensional. It’s not just about what you earn or own—it’s about who you become and how you live.

True wealth includes:

• Emotional Wealth: Peace of mind, resilience, and confidence. It’s the ability to sleep well at night, to bounce back from setbacks, and to trust yourself in uncertain times.
• Intellectual Wealth: Knowledge, skills, and curiosity. It’s the mindset of a lifelong learner who invests in understanding, not just outcomes.
• Social Wealth: Relationships, networks, and community. It’s the strength of your support system, the quality of your connections, and the generosity you extend to others.
• Spiritual Wealth: Purpose, meaning, and alignment with values. It’s knowing why you do what you do and feeling that your life is guided by something deeper than profit.

When you embark on your wealthy journey, you are not just building financial capital, you are cultivating a richer, fuller life. Money is a tool, not a destination. It amplifies who you are, but it cannot replace what truly matters.

Real-Life Example: In Lagos, a man named Chinedu began his wealth journey not with money, but with learning. He didn't have a high-paying job or a business to scale. But he had time, hunger, and a library card. He is committed to reading one book a month on finance, mindset, and personal growth. Titles like Rich Dad Poor Dad, The Richest Man in Babylon, and Think and Grow Rich became his mentors.

At first, nothing changed outside. But internally, his mindset shifted. He began to see opportunities where he once saw obstacles. He started budgeting, saving, and networking with like-minded people. Eventually, he launched a small side hustle offering financial literacy workshops in his community. That led to partnerships, speaking engagements, and eventually, investment opportunities.

Chinedu's intellectual wealth became the foundation of his financial wealth. But more than that, he gained confidence, purpose, and a sense of contribution. His journey wasn't just about building a bank account it was about becoming someone who could steward wealth with wisdom.

This is the essence of wealth beyond money. It's the understanding that your greatest assets are often invisible. Your mindset. Your habits. Your relationships. Your values. These are the roots that support lasting prosperity.

So if you're waiting to "have more" before you begin don't. Begin with what you already have. Read. Reflect. Connect. Serve. Grow. Every step you take toward emotional, intellectual, social, or spiritual wealth strengthens your foundation for financial success.

Because in the end, the richest life is not the one with the most zeros, it's the one with the most meaning. And that kind of wealth is available to everyone, starting now.

The Power of Community

Wealth is not built in isolation. While personal discipline and vision are essential, the most successful journeys are those shared with other mentors, peers, family, and communities. The path to financial freedom becomes clearer, stronger, and more sustainable when we walk together.

Community offers what no spreadsheet can: wisdom, accountability, encouragement, and emotional resilience. It transforms wealth-building from a solitary pursuit into a shared experience one where ideas are exchanged, setbacks are softened, and victories are celebrated.

Mentors: Wisdom in Compressed Time

Mentors are living libraries. They compress decades of experience into moments of insight. A single conversation with someone who's walked the path before you can save years of trial and error. Whether it's a seasoned investor, a business owner, or a financially savvy elder, mentors offer perspective that can't be Googled. They help you avoid common pitfalls, challenge your blind spots, and stretch your thinking.

Peers: Accountability and Encouragement

Peers are your mirror and your momentum. They reflect your progress, hold you accountable, and remind you that you're not alone. A peer group can be a sounding board for ideas, a safe space for vulnerability, and a source of motivation when your energy dips. When you surround yourself with people who are also committed to growth, your standards rise—and so do your consistency.

Family: Motivation and Legacy

Family is often the "why" behind the wealth journey. Whether it's providing for children, supporting aging parents, or breaking cycles of financial struggle, family gives your goals emotional weight. But family is also part of the legacy. The habits you model, the conversations you initiate, and the values you pass down shape how future generations relate to money. Wealth becomes not just a resource—but a responsibility.

Real-Life Example: The London Wealth Circle

In London, a group of five friends formed a "wealth circle." They meet monthly in each other's homes or local cafés to share financial goals, discuss books like The Psychology of Money and Your Money or Your Life, and support each other's progress. Each member came from a different background, one was a teacher, another a freelance designer, another a civil servant but they shared a common desire: to grow financially and personally.
Over time, the circle became more than a meeting it became a movement. Members paid off debt, started side businesses, invested in index funds, and even co-hosted workshops for their wider community. But the most profound change wasn't just in their bank accounts it was in their confidence, clarity, and sense of agency. Their collective journey amplified their individual success.

Resilience Along the Way

Your wealth journey will not be linear. There will be setbacks, unexpected expenses, market downturns, personal challenges. There will be moments when your progress stalls, your confidence dips, and your plans unravel. But resilience is what transforms these obstacles into opportunities. It's the quiet strength that keeps you moving forward, even when the road is rough.
Resilience isn't about perfection, it's about persistence. It's the ability to adapt, recalibrate, and continue with intention. It's what turns a financial dip into a lesson in patience, a career disruption into a pivot point, and a failed plan into a refined vision.

When Markets Dip: Learn Patience
Market downturn is inevitable. Whether it's a global crisis or a sector-specific slump, prices will fall. But resilient investors don't panic, they pause. They zoom out and remember that every major crash in history has eventually given way to recovery. The dotcom bust, the 2008 financial crisis, the COVID-19 dip all was followed by growth.
Author Insight: During the 2008 crash, I watched my retirement account lose nearly 35% of its value. I was tempted to pull out, but I remembered my long-term goals and stayed invested. Within five years, not only had the account recovered it had grown beyond its original value. That experience taught me that resilience isn't just about holding on, it's about holding firm.

When Income Fluctuates: Build Adaptability
Life doesn't always pay on schedule. Freelancers face dry spells. Entrepreneurs weather slow seasons. Even salaried workers can face layoffs or unexpected expenses. These moments test your flexibility.
Resilient individuals respond by adjusting not abandoning their plans. They revisit budgets, explore new income streams, and lean into creativity. They understand that adaptability isn't weakness, it's wisdom.
Real-Life Example: In London, a graphic designer named Amina lost half her client base during the pandemic. Instead of giving up, she pivoted to offering online design workshops and digital templates. Within a year, she had built a new income stream that was more scalable and less dependent on client cycles. Her setback became her breakthrough.

When Plans Fail: Refine Your Vision
Not every strategy will succeed. Not every investment will grow. Not every goal will unfold as expected. But failure doesn't mean you're off track, it means you're learning.
Resilience invites you to ask: What is this teaching me? Maybe your timeline was too ambitious. Maybe your assumptions need revisiting. Maybe your goals have evolved. That's okay. Growth is rarely a straight line.

Encouragement to Begin Today

The most important step is the first one. Not tomorrow. Not next year. Today.

Too often, we delay our wealth journey because we believe we're not ready. We tell ourselves we need more money, more time, more knowledge. But the truth is, readiness is not a prerequisite, it's a result of action. Clarity comes from movement. Confidence grows through momentum. And every small step you take today is a declaration: "I am on my wealth journey."

You don't need to overhaul your life overnight. You just need to begin. Here are five simple, powerful ways to start:

- Open a savings account. Even if you can only deposit £10, you've created a container for your future. That account becomes a symbol of your intention.
- Read a chapter of a financial book. One idea can shift your mindset. One story can spark a breakthrough.
- Write down your wealth vision. What does financial freedom look like to you? What kind of life are you building? Putting it on paper makes it real.
- Have a conversation with your family about values. Wealth isn't just about money, it's about meaning. Talk about what matters most.
- Give something time, money, or skill to someone in need. Generosity activates abundance. It reminds you that you already have something to offer.

Real-Life Experience: The Power of One Step

In Birmingham, a man named David had spent years living paycheck to paycheck. He felt overwhelmed by debt and unsure where to begin. One evening, after reading a blog post on financial freedom, he decided to take one small step: he opened a separate savings account and transferred £25 into it.

That single act changed everything.

It wasn't the amount it was the mindset. That account became his "freedom fund." Each week, he added a little more. He started reading books like The Richest Man in Babylon and Your Money or Your Life. He created a simple budget. He joined a local financial literacy group. Within two years, David had paid off his credit cards, built a three-month emergency fund, and started investing in a low-cost index fund.

But more than the numbers, he gained something deeper: belief. He no longer saw himself as someone who was "bad with money." He saw himself as a builder. And it all started with one small step.

Author Insight: The Day I Began

I still remember the day I wrote down my first wealthy vision. It wasn't fancy, just a few lines in a notebook. But it was honest. I wanted freedom. I wanted to give generously. I wanted to live without fear. That vision became my compass. And every decision from every book I read, every account I opened, every conversation I had was shaped by that moment of clarity.

Your wealthy journey is not about chasing more it is about becoming more. More intentional. More resilient. More generous. More aligned with the life you want to live and the legacy you want to leave.

The journey ahead will not be without challenges. But every challenge is an invitation to grow. Every step, no matter how small, is progress. And every act of courage whether saving, learning, giving, or adapting compounds into a life of meaning and abundance.

So begin today. Begin with what you have. Begin with who you are. Because the greatest wealth you can build is not just in what you accumulate, but in who you become along the way.

Reflection and Actionable Next Steps

As you close this book, pause to reflect:

- What does wealth mean to me beyond money?
- What values do I want my financial decisions to reflect?
- How can I begin today to align my resources with my purpose?

Actionable Next Steps

1. Define Your Wealth Vision

Write a one-page statement of what wealth means to you—financially, emotionally, and socially. This becomes your compass for decision-making.

2. Start a Learning Habit

Dedicate 30 minutes each week to financial education—whether through books, podcasts, or courses. Over time, this habit compounds into wisdom.

3. Build Resilience Routines

Create daily practices that strengthen adaptability: journaling, exercise, gratitude, or mindfulness. These habits prepare you for change before it arrives.

4. Engage in Giving

Choose one small way to give time, money, or skills and make it a regular practice. Giving aligns wealth with meaning and builds legacy.

5. Plan Your Legacy

Begin conversations with family about values, not just assets. Legacy is built in dialogue as much as in documents.

6. Create a Wealth Roadmap

Break your goals into short-term (1–3 years), medium-term (3–7 years), and long-term (10+ years). Review and adjust annually.

7. Surround Yourself with Mentors and Peers

Build a circle of people who challenge, inspire, and support you. Wealth is not built in isolation—it is cultivated in community.

Reflection: The Wealth Journey A Story of Becoming

Wealth is not about chasing more it is about becoming more. More intentional. More resilient. More generous. More aligned with the life you want to live and the legacy you want to leave.

True wealth isn't measured solely by numbers in a bank account. It's reflected in the clarity of your decisions, the peace in your relationships, the purpose behind your work, and the impact you leave behind. It's about living with direction, not just accumulation. It's about becoming the kind of person who stewards resources with wisdom, not fear who builds not just for themselves, but for others.

The journey ahead will not be linear. There will be moments when progress feels slow, when setbacks shake your confidence, when the path forward seems unclear. But every step whether forward, sideways, or even backward part of your growth can be if you approach it with curiosity and courage. Every challenge is a teacher. Every delay is a chance to deepen your roots. Every win is a reminder of what's possible.

So step forward with confidence. Begin today. Because the greatest wealth you can build is not just in what you accumulate, but in who you become along the way.

The Wealth Journey: A Story of Becoming

Imagine standing at the edge of a path that stretches into the horizon. The air is alive with possibility, though the road ahead is shrouded in mist. You cannot see every turn, but you sense that each step will shape not only your finances but your character, your relationships, and your legacy.

This is not just a journey of money it is a journey of meaning. It is the Wealth Journey.
Along this path, you will learn to set goals not just for what you want to have, but for who you want to be.
You'll learn to say no to distractions and yes to discipline. You'll learn to invest not only in stocks and funds, but in your health, your mindset, your family, and your community.
You'll discover that generosity multiplies wealth, not diminishes it. That clarity is more powerful than hustle.
That peace of mind is a form of prosperity. And that the most valuable asset you'll ever manage is your own growth.
There will be seasons of planting and seasons of harvest. Times of pruning and times of flourishing. But through it all, you'll be building something far greater than a portfolio you'll be building a life of purpose.
So take the first step. Or the next one. Wherever you are, begin again. The Wealth Journey is not about perfection it's about progress. It's about becoming the kind of person who doesn't just chase success but defines it on their own terms.
Because in the end, wealth is not a destination. It's a way of walking. A way of living. A way of becoming.

And your journey has already begun.

Milestone 1: Foundation – Defining Your Wealth Vision

The first step is not about numbers. It is about clarity. You pause at a quiet clearing, journal in hand, and ask yourself: What does wealth mean to me?

For some, wealth is freedom, the ability to choose how to spend time. For others, it is security the peace of knowing their family is safe. For still others, it is impacting the joy of giving and leaving a legacy.

You write your own definition. It includes money, yes, but also health, relationships, learning, and purpose.

This vision becomes your compass. From now on, every decision whether about saving, spending, or giving will be measured against this deeper definition of wealth.

Lesson: Wealth without vision is directionless. Vision without action is powerless. Together, they form the foundation.

Milestone 2: Learning – Investing in Knowledge

The path leads you to a library built into the landscape. Its shelves are filled with books, podcasts, and courses. You step inside and begin to learn not only about money, but about mindset, resilience, and growth.

You discover that financial literacy is not a privilege, but a skill anyone can cultivate. You learn about budgeting, investing, and the psychology of money. You also meet mentors along the way people who compress decades of experience into moments of wisdom.

At first, the information feels overwhelming. But slowly, patterns emerge. You realize that knowledge compounds faster than money. Each lesson equips you to make better decisions, avoid costly mistakes, and seize opportunities.

Lesson: The best investment you will ever make is in yourself.

Milestone 3: Habits – Building Daily Practices

Further along the path, you reach a village where people live by rhythm and routine. Here, you learn the power of habits.

You set up automatic savings, track your expenses, and practice gratitude each morning. You begin journaling about challenges and lessons learned. At first, these actions feel small, almost insignificant. But as days turn into weeks, you notice change.

Your confidence grows. Your resilience strengthens. You understand now that wealth is not built in grand gestures, but in consistent, daily choices.

Storytelling Example: A villager tells you how she began by saving just £10 a week. Over time, her savings grew into investments, and her investments grew into freedom. Her story reminds you that small steps compound into big results.

Lesson: Habits are the scaffolding of resilience and the engine of growth.

Milestone 4: Growth – Expanding Financial Capacity

The road widens into a bustling marketplace. Here, opportunities abound investments, side hustles, new technologies. At first, you feel overwhelmed. But then you remember your vision and your learning.

You diversify your portfolio, explore new income streams, and embrace digital tools that make your money work harder for you. You learn that growth is not about chasing everything, it's about adapting wisely, balancing risk with resilience.

Storytelling Example: You meet a craftsman who once relied solely on local sales. When the market shifted, he embraced online platforms. His income doubled, but more importantly, his confidence soared. His adaptability became his true wealth.

Lesson: Growth comes not from comfort zones, but from courage zones.

Milestone 5: Giving – Creating Impact

Beyond the marketplace lies a community square filled with laughter and connection. Here, you discover the joy of giving.

At first, you give modestly an hour of your time, a small donation, a skill shared freely. But soon, you see the ripple effect. Your giving inspires others. Your generosity multiplies meaning.

You involve your family, teaching them that wealth is not only about what you keep, but about what you release into the world. You realize that giving is not subtraction, it is multiplication.

Storytelling Example: A young boy in the square tells you how a scholarship changed his life. He says, "Someone I'll never meet believed in me." You realize that your giving can create legacies you may never see.

Lesson: Wealth finds its highest purpose in generosity.

Milestone 6: Resilience – Adapting to Change

The path takes a sudden turn into stormy weather. Winds howl, and the road becomes uncertain. This is the season of change.

At first, fear rises. But then you remember the resilience skills you've built. You focus on what you can control, lean on your support systems, and reframe challenges as opportunities.

The storm does not break down you; it strengthens you. You emerge from it wiser, more adaptable, and more grounded in your vision.

Storytelling Example: Along the way, you meet a woman who lost her job during an economic downturn. Instead of collapsing, she retrained, pivoted careers, and built a new life. Her story reminds you that resilience is not about avoiding storms, it's about learning to dance in the rain.

Lesson: Change is not the enemy. It is the teacher.

Milestone 7: Legacy – Living and Leaving Your Story

Finally, the path leads to a mountaintop. From here, you can see the road behind you and the horizon ahead. You gather your family and share your story not just the numbers in your accounts, but the values that guided your journey.

You begin shaping your legacy, not as something distant, but as something lived daily. Every choice, every act of generosity, every lesson passed on is already part of the inheritance you are leaving behind.

Storytelling Example: A grandfather tells his grandchildren, "My wealth is not just in what I leave you, but in what I've taught you." His words echo in your heart. You realize that legacy is not only about assets it is about wisdom, character, and love.

Lesson: Legacy is not left at the end it is lived every day.

The Journey Continues

As you stand on the mountaintop, you realize there is no final destination. The Wealth Journey is ongoing. Each milestone is not an end, but a beginning. You will revisit them again and again refining your vision, learning anew, strengthening habits, adapting to change, giving generously, and shaping legacy.

The path is yours to walk, but you are never alone. Others walk beside you—mentors, peers, family, and future generations. Together, you are building not just wealth but meaning. Not just prosperity, but purpose.

Appendix: The Wealth Journey Workbook

This workbook is designed to transform inspiration into action. Each milestone of the Wealth Journey includes reflection questions, journaling prompts, and practical exercises. Readers can revisit these sections regularly, as the journey is ongoing and cyclical.

Milestone 1: Foundation – Defining Your Wealth Vision

Reflection Questions
• What does wealth mean to me beyond money?
• Which values do I want my financial decisions to reflect?
• How do I currently define success, and does it align with my deeper vision?

Journaling Prompts
• "When I imagine a wealthy life, it looks like..."
• "The values I want to guide my financial journey are..."

Practical Exercise
• Write a one-page Wealth Vision Statement. Include financial goals, lifestyle aspirations, and values. Keep it visible as your compass.

Milestone 2: Learning – Investing in Knowledge

Reflection Questions
• What financial topics do I feel least confident about?
• Who could I learn from (mentors, books, podcasts, courses)?
• How has learning shaped my financial decisions in the past?

Journaling Prompts
• "The financial skill I most want to master is..."
• "A mentor who could guide me is..."

Practical Exercise
• Create a Learning Plan: choose one book, one podcast, and one course to complete in the next 3 months.

Milestone 3: Habits – Building Daily Practices

Reflection Questions
• What are my current money habits? Which serve me, and which hold me back?
• How consistent am I with saving, budgeting, or tracking expenses?
• What daily practices could strengthen my resilience?

Journaling Prompts
• "One small habit I can start today is..."
• "When I think of consistency, I feel..."

Practical Exercise
• Automate savings (even a small amount).
• Track expenses for 30 days.
• Begin a Resilience Journal: each day, write one challenge, your response, and what you learned.

Milestone 4: Growth – Expanding Financial Capacity

Reflection Questions
- How diversified are my income streams and investments?
- What opportunities for growth am I currently overlooking?
- How comfortable am I with risk and adaptability?

Journaling Prompts
- "Growth for me looks like..."
- "The opportunity I've been hesitant to pursue is..."

Practical Exercise
- Review your financial portfolio. Identify one area to diversify.
- Brainstorm 3 potential side hustles or new income streams.
- Explore one new financial tool or platform this month.

Milestone 5: Giving – Creating Impact

Reflection Questions
- What role does generosity play in my life right now?
- How do I want my giving to reflect my values?
- Who or what causes matter most to me?

Journaling Prompts
- "The impact I want my giving to have is..."
- "When I give, I feel..."

Practical Exercise
- Choose one way to give regularly (time, money, or skills).
- Involve family or friends in a giving activity.
- Write a Giving Mission Statement a short paragraph about why and how you give.

Milestone 6: Resilience – Adapting to Change

Reflection Questions
- How do I typically respond to unexpected change?
- What support systems do I have in place?
- What past challenges have made me stronger?

Journaling Prompts
- "A time I adapted successfully was..."
- "When I face change, I want to remember..."

Practical Exercise
- Create a Sphere of Control List: write down what you can control, influence, and cannot control.
- Identify 3 people you can call in times of change.
- Practice one resilience daily (breathing, mindfulness, reframing)

Milestone 7: Legacy – Living and Leaving Your Story

Reflection Questions

- What do I want my family, friends, or community to remember about me?
- How am I already living my legacy today?
- What values do I want to pass on to the next generation?

Journaling Prompts
- "The story I want my life to tell is…"
- "The values I want to leave behind are…"

Practical Exercise
- Write a Legacy Letter to your family, sharing your values and vision.
- Begin a family conversation about money and meaning.
- Draft a simple legacy plan (financial and non-financial).

How to Use This Workbook

- Revisit often. Your answers will evolve as your journey unfolds.
- Be honest. These exercises are for you there are no right or wrong answers.
- Take small steps. Don't try to do everything at once. Choose one exercise per milestone to begin.
- Celebrate progress. Every reflection, every habit, every act of giving is part of your legacy.

How to Use This Guide

- Pick one theme at a time. Don't try to read everything, choose what resonates with your current stage.
- Pair classics with modern voices. For example, read Think and Grow Rich alongside The Psychology of Money to see how perspectives have evolved.
- Reflect as you read. Ask: How does this apply to my own wealth journey?
- Share with others. Discuss these books with family, friends, or peers to multiply their impact.

Appendix: Recommended Authors & Sources

Your journey doesn't end with this book. The voices below have shaped the way we think about wealth, resilience, and legacy. They offer timeless wisdom, practical strategies, and fresh perspectives to deepen your understanding.

Wealth & Financial Growth

• Benjamin Graham – The Intelligent Investor
• Robert Kiyosaki – Rich Dad Poor Dad
• Thomas J. Stanley & William D. Danko – The Millionaire Next Door
• Morgan Housel – The Psychology of Money
• Tony Robbins – Money: Master the Game
• Vicki Robin & Joe Dominguez – Your Money or Your Life
• Mary Buffett & David Clark – Buffettology
• Hoxton Wealth (2024) – Insights on inflation, liquidity, and diversification
• First Wealth (2025) – Guidance on resilience in financial planning
• Forbes Finance Council (2024) – Expert commentary on valuing people as assets

Resilience, Change & Adaptability

• Sheryl Sandberg & Adam Grant – Option B
• Brené Brown – Rising Strong; Daring Greatly
• Angela Duckworth – Grit
• Carol Dweck – Mindset
• Elizabeth Kübler-Ross & David Kessler – On Grief and Grieving
• Ryan Holiday – The Obstacle Is the Way
• Mind UK – Practical guides on stress management and resilience
• Cambridge Network – Maintaining resilience in times of change
• Cooper Magazine – Essential skills for managing change and stress
• Ignite HCM – Building resilience and adaptability in uncertainty
• Reality Pathing – 10 Evidence-Based Strategies to Enhance Resilience

Legacy, Meaning & Generational Wealth

• Stephen R. Covey – The 7 Habits of Highly Effective People
• James E. Hughes Jr. – Family Wealth: Keeping It in the Family
• Clayton Christensen – How Will You Measure Your Life?
• David Brooks – The Second Mountain
• Mary L. Trump – Too Much and Never Enough
• Ibram X. Kendi – Black Fortunes
• BookAuthority (2025) – 20 Wealthy Families Biography Books That Define Legacy and Power

Biographies & Case Studies

- Inspirationalife – Stories of personal reinvention and resilience
- Reader's Digest – Profiles of individuals embracing unexpected change
- SmartAsset (2024) – 10 Books That Can Help You Build Wealth
- Flibos (2025) – Impactful Literature on Money and Wealth Building

Resources & Further Reading

For those ready to go deeper.

Books

- The Intelligent Investor by Benjamin Graham

A timeless classic on value investing and long-term strategy.

- One Up on Wall Street by Peter Lynch

Accessible insights from one of the most successful fund managers in history.

- Common Stocks and Uncommon Profits by Philip Fisher

A foundational guide to evaluating growth companies.

- The Psychology of Money by Morgan Housel

A modern, mindset-focused take on how we think about wealth and investing.

- Principles by Ray Dalio

A blend of investing philosophy and life lessons from a hedge fund titan.

Websites & Tools

- Investopedia

Definitions, tutorials, and articles for beginners and advanced investors.

- Morningstar

Independent research and analysis on stocks, ETFs, and mutual funds.

- Yahoo Finance

Real-time market data, news, and portfolio tracking.

- Seeking Alpha

Community-driven insights, analysis, and commentary on market trends.

- Google Finance

Quick access to stock charts, news, and company profiles.

Apps for Beginners

- Freetrade (UK) — Commission-free investing with a clean interface.
- eToro — Social investing platform with copy-trading features.
- Trading 212 — Easy-to-use app with fractional shares and educational tools.
- Shares.io — UK-based app focused on community and simplicity.

Podcasts & Videos

- We Study Billionaires (The Investor's Podcast Network)
- The Compound & Friends by Ritholtz Wealth
- BiggerPockets Money Podcast
- MoneyWeek (YouTube UK)
- The Plain Bagel (YouTube — investing education)

Author Biography

Obinna Okeke is a wealth strategist, writer, and passionate advocate for financial empowerment. With a gift for translating complex financial and psychological concepts into clear, actionable steps, he equips readers to build wealth that is practical, sustainable, deeply meaningful sense of humor and a background in Law, Political Science

Driven by a passion for transformation, Obinna blends timeless wisdom with modern strategies to help individuals and families create financial security, resilience, and generational legacy. His work is rooted in authenticity and clarity, inspiring readers to start from zero and rise with confidence.

Beyond writing, Obinna shares his insights through mentoring, podcasting, and speaking, where he continues to champion the belief that true wealth is not only measured in money, but also in impact, purpose, and the lives we touch.

Disclaimer

The information provided in this book is for educational and informational purposes only. It reflects personal insights, research, and practical strategies that have helped individuals build financial awareness and long-term wealth. However, I am not a licensed financial advisor, investment professional, or certified expert.

Readers are encouraged to consult with qualified financial advisors, tax professionals, or legal experts before making any investment decisions. The examples and strategies shared here do not guarantee financial success and may not be suitable for every individual or circumstance.

Investing involves risk, including the potential loss of principal. Past performance is not indicative of future results. Always do your own due diligence and make decisions based on your unique goals, risk tolerance, and financial situation.

This book is intended to inspire informed action—not to serve as personalized financial advice.

www.ingramcontent.com/pod-product-compliance
Lightning Source LLC
LaVergne TN
LVHW071343210926
848486LV00003B/221
9781918657074